BRIEF VIEW

OF THE

CASTE SYSTEM

OF THE

NORTH-WESTERN PROVINCES AND OUDH

BRIEF VIEW

OF THE

CASTE SYSTEM

OF THE

NORTH-WESTERN PROVINCES AND OUDH:

TOGETHER WITH AN

EXAMINATION OF THE NAMES

AND

FIGURES SHOWN IN THE CENSUS REPORT, 1882:

Being an Attempt to Classify on a Functional Basis all the Main Castes of the United Provinces, and to Explain their Gradations of Rank and the Process of their Formation

JOHN C. NESFIELD

GYAN

Published by

Gyan Publishing House
5, Ansari Road
Daryaganj, New Delhi-110002
Phone: 011-47034999, 9811692060
E-mail: books@gyanbooks.com

Distribution Network
gyanbooks.com
India, USA, Canada, UK, Australia

ISBN: 978-93-6780-356-1 (HB)

First Published, 1885

2nd Impression 2024

Printed at: Gyan Press, Delhi.

BRIEF VIEW OF THE CASTE SYSTEM OF THE NORTH-WESTERN PROVINCES AND OUDH

Author: JOHN C. NESFIELD

BRIEF VIEW

OF THE

CASTE SYSTEM

OF THE

NORTH-WESTERN PROVINCES AND OUDH,

TOGETHER WITH AN

EXAMINATION OF THE NAMES

AND

FIGURES SHOWN IN THE CENSUS REPORT, 1882,

Being an attempt to Classify on a Functional Basis all the Main Castes of the United Provinces, and to Explain their Gradations of Rank and the Process of their Formation.

28TH FEBRUARY, 1885.

BY JOHN C. NESFIELD, M.A., OXON,
Inspector of Schools, Oudh.

ALLAHABAD:
NORTH-WESTERN PROVINCES AND OUDH GOVERNMENT PRESS.
1885.

ERRATA.

Page 2, line 1.—*For* "the paper" *read* "this paper."
" 12 " 56.—*For* "section 120" *read* "sloka 120."
" 15 " 41.—*For* "caste—gradation" *read* "caste gradation."
" 24 " 44.—*For* "father supplies the new jars" *read* "potter supplies the new jars."
" 30 " 41.—*For* "stages of arts" *read* "stages of art."
" 36 " 3.—*For* "coasidered" *read* "considered."
" 37 " 43.—*For* "demed" *read* "deemed."
" 62 " 11.—*For* "tasma" *read* "tasmád."
" 64 " 54.—*For* "though multiform" *read* "thou multiform."
" 72 " 38.—*For* "mystery of Brahmá" *read* "mystery of Brahma."
" 88 " 30.—*For* "statements appenned" *read* "statements appended."
" 98 " 15.—*For* "creation; of a" *read* "creation of a."
" 103 " 3.—*For* "not bora within" *read* "not born within."
" 114 " 52.—*For* "embodiments of these" *read* "embodiments of those."

TABLE OF CONTENTS.

JAINS.

MUHAMMADANS.

BRIEF VIEW

OF THE

CASTE SYSTEM

OF THE

NORTH-WESTERN PROVINCES AND OUDH,

TOGETHER WITH AN

EXAMINATION OF THE NAMES AND FIGURES SHOWN IN THE CENSUS REPORT, 1882.

On the 17th February, 1881, a census was for the first time taken of the two provinces (Oudh and the North-West) combined. Prior to this there had been three censuses of the North-West and one of Oudh. In the report of the census taken in 1881 the results were published without any distinction of province; and as the inter-provincial landmarks were purely artificial, the statistics were set forth in a more compact form than they had ever been before. The tribes and castes of Oudh are identical with those of the North-West, by which they are on all sides surrounded. In fact, if the caste area could have been extended so as to include the Delhi districts of the Panjab and the Behar districts of Bengal, the range of view would have been still more complete. For this is the area of Hindustan proper, and the caste system within this area has a distinct character of its own, differing in some respects both from that of the Indus valley to the west of it and from that of the Gangetic delta to the east known as Bengal proper.

2. The dissertation which follows makes no pretensions to going beyond the area of the North-Western Provinces and Oudh, and it takes as its basis the names and figures collected in the census of 1881 and published in 1882 in the report compiled by Mr. Edmund White, C.S. It represents an attempt, which I was deputed to undertake nine months ago, in addition to my ordinary duties, to carry out the suggestion contained in the Home Department Circular No. $\frac{4}{119\text{-}128}$, dated 21st September, 1882, to the address of the Local Government, *viz*, "to collect statistics of castes and occupations and thus utilize the information brought together at the last census," and also to make some proposal as to the shape in which the several castes might be arranged, with a view "to the statistics being eventually published in a uniform manner for each province." As it was presumed that the report compiled by Mr. White embodied all the information which the district officers had collected at the time of taking the census, I thought it better to examine the subject from a purely independent standpoint—that is, in the light of such information as I happened to possess already respecting Indian castes or have been able to procure since from private sources of various kinds. With the help of M. Ambika Prasad, Deputy Inspector of Schools, Lucknow, who was appointed to aid me in this work, and whose assistance has throughout been most valuable, enquiries have been addressed to various quarters, wherever there seemed to be any likelihood of useful information being procured. My aim has been to show to what extent, if any, the number of castes enumerated in the census report can be reduced and simplified, and what castes, if any, have been omitted; to describe in general terms the occupation, both past and present, for which each tribe and caste is distinguished—a point about which nothing is said in Section XXIII on "castes" in the preliminary dissertation of the report; and to devise some plan for arranging and classifying the several tribes and castes, which in form VIII of the census report are given merely in alphabetical order.

3. A minute description of the industries, customs, and traditions of every single tribe or caste would, of course, be a work of many years. Nothing more, therefore,

than a general account of each group has been attempted in the paper. But as a specimen of the enquiries which are being made respecting individual tribes or castes, and of the nature of the results which might be elicited if these enquiries are continued, I attach herewith an account of the Thárus and Bogshas, containing as minute a description as I could compile out of the information collected by myself since June, 1884, when this work was first commenced.

4. In form I of the twenty-one census forms prescribed by the Census Commissioner for India, the total population of the North-Western Provinces and Oudh, including persons of all creeds and nationalities, is shown as 44,107,869. In form III the total population, classified according to religions, is shown as follows :—

1.	Hindus	38,053,394	
2.	Muhammadans	5,922,886	
3.	Jains	79,957	
			44,056,237
4.	Sikhs	3,644	
5.	Christians	47,664	
6.	Buddhists	103	
7.	Brahmos	6	
8.	Jews	101	
9.	Parsis	114	
			51,632
	Total		44,107,869

If we exclude Nos. 4-9, which have nothing to do with the subject of Indian caste, and attend only to Hindus, Jains, and Muhammadans, the remainder is 44,056,237.

HINDUS.

5. To take the Hindus first. The total just shown (38,053,394) tallies with the total given at the bottom of form VIII, and this form professes to give "details of Hindu castes for the province" (*vide* table of contents). It is clear, therefore, that none but Hindu castes are intended to be included in this form. But the intention does not appear to have been consistently acted out. For some of the castes included in the statement are not Hindu at all, but Muhammadan. This is true, for example of the Juláha or Muhammadan weaver caste, the Ghosi or Muhammadan milkman caste, and of the Charkata or Muhammadan caste of elephant-keeper. It is also to a large extent true of fakirs or the Muhammadan mendicant classes, and of Kunjras or the caste of green-grocers, Kamángars or the caste of bowmaker and painter, Páwarias or the caste of musicians, and many more.

6. The detailed list of Hindu castes given in form VIIIB consists of three different parts : (*a*) a list of one hundred and eighty *castes* given in alphabetical order, (*b*) a list of eleven "*races* not returned by caste" and given, like the preceding, in alphabetical order; (*c*) an aggregate of 16,121 persons under the single heading of "unspecified."

7. About the "unspecified" there is of course nothing further to be said. As to the list of "races not returned by caste," it appears that the principle has not been strictly carried out ; for in the preceding list of 180 castes some names are entered which refer to races or tribes and not to castes, as, for example, Gurkhas, Tharus, Saharias, and others. Perhaps the list was intended for *foreign* races or tribes—that is, persons or communities not indigenous to the province, but immigrants from other provinces or territories who have become domiciled within its area, but have not amalgamated with the native population, so as to form a real part of it ; such persons, for example, as Bengalis, Gujaratis, Kashmiris, &c. But if this was the principle intended (and such appears to have been the case), three tribes should have been omitted—namely, Bhil, Gond, and Kol, all of whom are to be found in the districts south of the Ganges and Jumna and are strictly indigenous to the soil ; and one more should have been added, *viz.*, Gurkha, which is placed in the census report among the indigenous castes, though it is really a tribe of Nepal.

8. As the caste-names shown in the census report have been given in merely alphabetical order, the first thing to be done was to attempt to lay down some principle on which castes could be classified. The scheme which I have prepared is shown in detail in the thirteen tabular statements hereto appended. A brief summary of their contents may, however, be shown in this place in the following form:—

Serial No. of groups.	Name of group.	Number of tribes and castes.	Number of persons shown in census.
I.	Casteless tribes	19	427,629
II.	Castes connected with land—		
	A. Allied to hunting state	11	1,870,010
	B. Allied to fishing state	9	1,978,136
	C. Allied to pastoral state	7	5,657,187
	D. Agricultural.	11	6,004,067
	E. Landlords and warriors	1	3,127,207
	Total	39	19,064,236
III.	Artizan castes—		
	A. Preceding metallurgy	10	8,510,925
	B. Coeval with metallurgy	15	1,506,864
	Total	25	10,017,789
IV.	Trading castes	20	1,671,390
V.	Serving castes	10	2,236,150
VI.	Priestly castes	6	4,690,850
VII.	Religious orders	2	344,430
	Total of the provincial tribes and castes ...	121	38,024,845
	Foreign races not returned by caste	...	12,428
	Unspecified	...	16,121
	GRAND TOTAL	121	38,053,394

9. It will be seen that I have divided the native Hindu population of the province, as distinct from the foreign and the unspecified, into seven main groups or classes. The first consists of those backward and semi-savage tribes which have not yet been absorbed into caste, and which I have, therefore, designated by the name of the casteless tribes. The other six groups consists of the great divisions of caste into which the people of Hindustan have become gradually distributed and absorbed in the course of thousands of years, each group being distinguished from every other by some speciality of function which marks its general character. The two largest of these six groups (the group of landed castes and that of artisan castes) are further sub-divided into smaller groups, each representing some phase of industry peculiar to itself, the rank of which in the scale of human progress has determined the rank held by the castes corresponding to it in the Hindu social scale. The plan, therefore, on which the castes have been classified in this paper is intended to be something more than a merely symmetrical arrangement. It is intended to explain the order in which the several castes came into existence, and thus to account for the degree of social importance and respectability in which they stand to the general community. If, for example, the stage of culture is a low one, it will be invariably found that the caste corresponding to this stage and practising one or more of the industries peculiar to it stands low in the eyes of the Hindu community generally, and so on through all variations of caste and all stages of industry up to the highest.

10. It must be here remarked in passing that such a theory as the above is not compatible with the modern doctrine which divides the population of India into Aryan and Aboriginal. It presupposes an unbroken continuity in the national life from one stage of culture to another, analogous to what has taken place in every other country in the world whose inhabitants have emerged from the savage state. It assumes, therefore, as its necessary basis, *the unity of the Indian race.* While it does not deny that a race of "white-complexioned foreigners," who called themselves by the name of Arya, invaded the Indus valley *viâ* Kabul and Kashmir some four thousand years ago and imposed their language and religion on the indigenous races by whom they found

themselves surrounded, it nevertheless maintains that the blood imported by this foreign race became gradually absorbed into the indigenous, the less yielding to the greater, so that almost all traces of the conquering race eventually disappeared, just as the Lombard became absorbed into the Italian, the Frank into the Gaul, the Roman (of Roumania) into the Slav, the Greek (of Alexandria) into the Egyptian, the Norman into the Frenchman, the Moor (of Spain) into the Spaniard ; and as the Norwegians, Germans, &c., are at this day becoming absorbed into Englishmen in North America, or as the Portuguese (of India) have already become absorbed into Indians. I hold that for the last three thousand years at least no real difference of blood between Aryan and aboriginal (except perhaps in a few isolated tracts, such as Rajputana, where special causes may have occurred to prevent the complete amalgamation of race) has existed ; and the physiological resemblance observable between the various classes of the population, from the highest to the lowest, is an irrefragable proof that no clearly-defined racial distinction has survived—a kind of evidence which ought to carry much greater weight than that of language, on which so many fanciful theories of ethnology have been lately founded. Language is no test of race ; and the question of caste is not one of race at all, but of culture. Nothing has tended to complicate the subject of caste so much as this intrusion of a philological theory, which within its own province is one of the most interesting discoveries of modern times, into a field of enquiry with which it has no connection. The "Aryan brother" is indeed a much more mythical being than Râma, or Krishna, or any other of the popular heroes of Hindu tradition whom writers of the Aryan school have vainly striven to attenuate into solar myths. The amalgamation of the two races (the Aryan and the Indian) had been completed in the Panjab (as we may gather from the Institutes of Manu) before the Hindu, who is the result of this amalgamation, began to extend his influence into the Ganges valley, where by slow and sure degrees he disseminated among the indigenous races those social and religious maxims which have been spreading wider and wider ever since throughout the continent of India, absorbing one after another, and to some extent civilizing, every indigenous race with whom they are brought into contact, raising the choice spirits of the various tribes into the rank of Brahman or Chhatri, and leaving the rest to rise or fall in the social scale according to their capacities and opportunities.

11. Equally incompatible with the theory advanced in this paper is that of the old semi-mythical division of caste into Brahman, Kshatriya, Vaisya, and Sudra. This classification has done almost as much to prevent men from studying and describing Indian castes as they are as the modern fiction which divides them into Aryan, aboriginal and mixed. But of the two, the older doctrine comes much nearer to the truth, for it makes the differences of caste depend upon differences of functions, the only basis on which Indian castes have been formed ; while the other, ignoring function or consigning it only to the second place, attempts to make caste a question of blood and appeals to the futile evidence of language in support of this. It has been proved (conclusively as I think) by modern scholars that the old fourfold division was not even of Indian origin, and was never actually in force in India except as a current tradition, the only reality which attaches to it to this day. Professor Kern and the late Dr. Haug, of the Educational Department, Bombay, have independently shown that the same division of classes existed among the common ancestors of the Perso-Aryans and the Indo-Aryans, before the latter had separated themselves from their kinsfolk and established settlements in the Indus valley. In the *Yâsna* (XIX., 46) these four classes are mentioned under the names of Athrava, Rathaesthao, Vastriya-fshuyant, and Huiti. The first Atharva is merely the Perso-Aryan original or equivalent of the Indian Atharvan or fire-priest, one of the numerous names for professional priest which, in common with "Brahman," are to be found in the Vedic hymns and liturgies. One of the Vedas, as is well known, is called the Atharva, and this was pre-eminently the manual of the "Brahman" or superintendent priest. The second name, Rathaesthao merely signifies "one who rides in a chariot," and is therefore a correct equivalent to

the Sanskrit "Ratheshtha," "Rajanya," and "Kshatriya," the names by which knights and high-class warriors are called in the Vedic hymns. The third, Vastriya, comes very near in sound to the Indian "Vaisya;" and such resemblance is not at all irreconcileable with the fact that Indian grammarians have derived the word "Vaisya" from the root *vish*, "to inhabit." The fourth class, Huiti, answers both in name and function to the Indian "Sudra;" for in the ancient society of Persia the Huitis were "workmen, servants, and petty traders," and there is no known Sanskrit root to which "Sudra" can be traced. Professor Kern also quotes the following verse from *Yasna*, XIX, 44 :—"This command, which the creative spirit has spoken, embraces the four classes (*pishtra*)," that is, is intended to apply to the entire population, and he contends that *pishtra* is the equivalent of the Sanskrit *varna.* Nothing could be more natural than that the Aryan tribes, who migrated into India, should have preserved the tradition of the four classes into which their own population was roughly divided, and that the names themselves should have gradually acquired new applications and uses under the altered circumstances of society and country. After a *modus vivendi* had been established between the invading foreigner and the conquered indigenes, and the two races had begun to be fused, as they eventually were, into a single whole, the titles "Brahman" and "Kshattriya" were reserved to the priests and nobles of whatever blood, who in course of time became stereotyped into distinct castes ; while the name "Sudra" was applied to the lowest or menial classes of the people, and "Vaisya" to the intermediate ones. But there is nothing to show that the last two ever became castes as the first two did, and the written evidence that we possess is entirely against the supposition. These classes (Vaisya and Sudra) are very rarely, if ever, alluded to in the great national epics, the Rámáyan and Mahábhárata, the best authority that we possess for the state of society in ancient India ; whereas we are constantly reminded of the existence of Brahmans and Kshatriyas, and of lower classes of men, like barbers, carpenters, fishermen, potters, and the like. Again in the Mánava Code the vagueness that hangs about the names of Vaisya and Sudra is in such striking contrast with the clear and precise account given by the author respecting the Brahman and Kshatriya castes and the various industrial classes existing in his own time, that we are driven to suppose that such castes as Vaisya and Sudra did not really exist, but that these words merely expressed a rough classification of the people outside the radius of Brahmans and Kshatriyas. There seems, then, to be no reason for supposing that the old fourfold division of caste was indigenous to Indian soil, or that it ever really represented the caste system of the Indian people. In any case the caste system of the present day is something entirely different, and the attempts that have been made to adapt existing castes to the classifying framework of Vaisya and Sudra have resulted in nothing but confusion and failure.

12. *The casteless tribes.*—The list of tribes whom I have put together under the general designation of "the casteless tribes" will be seen in tabular statement, group I. These tribes are the last remains and sole surviving representatives of the aboriginal Indian savage, who was once the only inhabitant of the Indian continent, and from whose stock the entire caste system, from the sweeper to the priest, was fashioned by the slow growth of centuries. They enable us to form some faint idea of what the ancient tribes of Hindustan were like, say some six thousand years ago, before cattle-grazers, husbandmen, artisans, traders, and the priestly and royal clans had been differentiated into distinct social and industrial types. Their manners and notions will be found to correspond in many respects with those of the most backward races in various parts of the world, and it is only by looking at them from this comparative standpoint that their manners are worth studying. In religion these tribes cannot be called either Hindu or Muhammadan, though they have picked up some of the tag ends of both creeds through the inevitable operation of many centuries of contact. If the tools and weapons which they use are better than what could be found among the savages of the Pacific or in the continent of Africa, this is not because they themselves have advanced beyond the Stone age of the world, but only

because they can readily supply themselves with iron implements and weapons manufactured by their more advanced kinsfolk in the Indian towns and villages among which they wander. The distinctive characteristic of almost all these tribes is that they lead a wandering life, are incapable of sustained toil, and subsist to a large extent on the animals, roots, and fruits spontaneously provided by nature. There is no space in a paper like this, which aims at giving a rough description and analysis of the entire system of Indian castes, to furnish a detailed account of any one of these primitive tribes. The essay on Tharus and Bogshas, referred to already in para. 3 and published in the January number of the *Calcutta Review*, may serve as a specimen of what can be done in this direction, if minute inquiries are made and leisure can be found for putting the results into shape.

13. If the reader will refer to the list of names given in group I as shown in the annexed table, he will see that they have been arranged as far as possible in geographical order. The Thárus and Bogshas, who head the list, inhabit the sub-Himálayan forest which forms the northern boundary of Hindustan. The four tribes who are placed at the bottom of the list (see serial Nos. 15-19) dwell in the forests to the south of the Ganges and Jumna. The Bhils, Gonds, and Saharias, all of whom are to be found in the Jhánsi Division, belong to the Central Indian plateau rather than to the plains of Hindustan. The Kols however, whose name is mentioned last of all, belong strictly to the Ganges valley and are to be found in considerable numbers in the forests of Mirzapur, Allahabad, and Bánda. A peculiar interest attaches to this tribe, as being the savage ancestors of the great weaver caste called Koli or Kori, and of the great agricultural caste called Kori or Kachhi. The Thárus in the north and the Kols in the south have retained many of the simple virtues of the untutored savage, and to such people the forest is the natural home. The remaining tribes (omitting the Bhils, Gonds, and Saharias) dwell in the intervening deforested plain, and lead a precarious life as thieves, gang-robbers, jackal-hunters, trappers, fowlers, jugglers, acrobats, and hereditary prostitutes—savages whom the surrounding civilization has demoralized rather than improved, because it has failed to assimilate, and whom Manu described as "sinful and abominable wretches," never to be permitted to reside within the haunts of men.

14. Before leaving the subject of the casteless tribes I must describe briefly how the names and figures shown in my tabular statement, group I, have been obtained, and in what respect they differ from those given in the census report, form VIII B :—

(*a*) *Dom.*—Under this name no distinction has been made in the census report between Dom the savage and Dom the musician. The former is a filthy, degraded being, who apes the Hindu and is regarded with universal loathing. The latter is a Muhammadan, holding rather a respectable place in native society, and is by no means devoid of culture. It would not be difficult to show how Dom the musician has sprung up out of Dom the savage. But the two classes are now so entirely distinct, and have been so for so many centuries, that they must not be confounded. The distinctive name of the Muhammadan Dom is Mirási.

(*b*) *Bandi.*—Only 40 persons have been recorded against this name. Bandi is not a tribe, but an occupation—the occupation of catching live birds for sale. Such men generally belong to the tribe called Banmánush, and in this tribe, therefore, I have included them.

(*c*) *Bahrupiya, Bajgi, Nat, Karnatak, Natak, Bhantu, Sampera.*—These seven names do not really represent seven different tribes, as the insignificant number recorded against many of them clearly shows. They may all be considered to belong to the tribe generically known as Nat. In my own table, therefore, I have included them all under this name. They are the jugglers, mimics, actors, acrobats, snake-exhibitors, &c., who wander among the villages of Hindustan and receive fees or gifts in exchange for the amusement which they afford.

(*d*) *Brijbasi, Gandharp, Kanchan, Tawaif, Nayak, and Negpatar.*—These six names may all be summed up under the common name of Kanchan or Paturiya. In my own statement, therefore, I have added up all the figures recorded against these names and entered the sum against the name Kanchan. Kanchans are the hereditary prostitutes of Hindustan—an extraordinary function, which can only be explained by tracing it to the savage age.

(*e*) I have included in my own list two tribes which are not mentioned in form VIIIB. of the census report, *viz.*, Aheri and Musarha. The first (Aheri) has been avowedly mixed up with Bahelia, and the second (Musarha) with Banmánush (see appendix 12 of census report). I think, however, that both of these identifications are incorrect. The Aheri is a savage tribe, while the Bahelia is a peaceful caste. The Musarha is decidedly less savage than the Banmánush and claims to be considered as distinct.

15. *Castes allied to the hunting state.*—Turning to group IIA, "castes allied to the hunting state," we find that the manners and notions of the people included in this list come nearest to those of the savage and casteless tribes named in the preceding table. Their status in the caste system is so low that it is almost doubtful whether they should be called castes or tribes. My chief reason for putting them in the list of castes as distinct from that of tribes is that they have ceased to hunt the jackal, like Kanjars, &c., have abandoned the wandering life, and have made a more distinct approach, though still a very distant one, towards Hinduism. They live in the outskirts of villages and have long been a recognized element in the constitution of the Hindu township, where they are employed as watchmen, village messengers, &c. All the castes named in this list are addicted to drunkenness, to the prostitution of their daughters, and to the eating of swine's flesh; all of which practices are forbidden by Hinduism. Not one of them is allowed to enter a Hindu temple, and no respectable person would touch water drawn by their hands. No Brahman, except those who are set aside as inferiors by their brethren, will enter their houses, or discharge for them, even outside of the house, any of those functions for which Brahmans are usually employed. All this tends to show that, as compared with other Hindu castes, they hold the lowest rank in the scale of respectability. And this tallies with the fact that the stage of culture to which they are most nearly allied, namely, the hunting, is the lowest and earliest stage in the development of human industry.

16. The names shown in the appended table (group IIA) have been placed as far as possible in the order of rank, the lowest and meanest of the castes or tribes being placed first, and so on. The Bauriyas are certainly the lowest class of people named in the list. From the local inquiries which I have made, and from the testimony of a writer in the journal of the Asiatic Society of Bengal, who lived less than a century ago, it is clear that their reclamation from a wandering life, in Hindustan at least, is a thing of very recent date. Within the memory of living men they were jackal-hunters and wanderers, as the Kanjars, Haburas, and others still are, whom I have classed among the casteless tribes. The very names of some of the other castes included in group IIA disclose the stage of culture, out of which they arose and to which they are still more closely allied than to any other. Thus Bahelia, the fowler caste, is derived from *bahali* or *bahari*, a falcon; Dhánuk is derived from *dhánu*, a bow; and Pási from *pás*, a snare. The name Khangár appears to be only a variant of the name *Kanjar*. In character and manners the Khangár is simply an improved Kanjar, just as the Khangár Chattri is an improved form of his ancestor, the Khangár hunter. Perhaps the most respectable of the castes or tribes named in this list is the Khatík, who from a wandering fowler has developed into a domiciled poulterer, from a boar-hunter into a pig-rearer, and from a hunter and slayer of wild animals generally into the caste of butcher to the Hindu community. Of all these castes it must be said that, as hunting and trapping are becoming less and less profitable pursuits, owing to the increasing destruction of forest and the constantly increasing pressure of population on the means of subsistence, they are rapidly giving up their original callings.

and taking to agriculture. In almost all parts of Hindustan they are now largely employed as field-labourers and sometimes as tenants-at-will on small plots of land.

17. One thing more must be noted in reference to these castes: it is they (together with some of the casteless tribes which preceded them) who furnish the bulk of the criminal classes by whom the peace of the country is disturbed. Not being able, as savage tribes in a purely savage land would be, to make war upon each other, they wage a secret war against the community which despises them and to which they are still imperfectly assimilated. Under a Government less strong than the British, they would at once rise in rebellion against society and revert to their ancestral savagery. Let us hear what Colonel Sleeman wrote of the Pasis of Oudh only thirty-four years ago, before the Native or Nawabi Government was abolished :—"They are employed as village watchmen, but with few exceptions are thieves and robbers by hereditary profession. Many of them adopt poisoning as a trade; and the numbers who did so were rapidly increasing, when Captain Hollings, the Superintendent of the Oudh Frontier Police, proceeded against them as thugs under Act III of 1848. * * * * These Pásis of Oudh generally form the worst part of the gangs of refractory taluqdars in their indiscriminate plunder. They use the bow and arrow expertly, and are said to be able to send an arrow through a man at the distance of one hundred yards. There is no species of theft or robbery in which they are not experienced and skilful, and they increase and prosper in proportion as the disorders in the country grow worse. They serve any refractory landowner or enterprising gang-robber without wages for the sake of the booty to be acquired." (*Vide Tour Through Oudh*, Vol. I, pages 333—4). What the Pásis were in Oudh only thirty-four years ago, the Arakhs, Bhars, Khangárs, Dhánuks, &c., were in Upper India generally during the anarchy which preceded the establishment of British rule.

18. I must now explain how the names and figures collected in my own table, group IIA, have been obtained, and in what respect they differ from those given in the census report:—

(*a*) Báwaria and Boria are entered in the census as if they were different castes, whereas they are but one caste with the name differently spelt. I believe that the correct spelling is Bauriya.

(*b*) Bhar and Raj-Bhar might, for the sake of simplicity, be amalgamated into one, as Raj-Bhar is only a clan of Bhar; I have therefore included both under the name of Bhar in preparing my own statement.

(*c*) Pasi and Pasia, which are separately mentioned in the census, are really one. There is a clan of these called Raj-Pási, corresponding to the Raj-Bhar, but the author of the census report has, rightly as I think, made no separate mention of them.

(*d*) Tarikash, Kotwar, Pahari, Pahri, and Buláhar are not castes, but names of occupations. Tarikash means toddy-drawer; Kotwar means guardian; Pahari or Pahri (the same name differently spelt) means one who keeps periodical watch; Buláhar means village messenger. Men employed for such purposes are almost always taken from the castes mentioned in this list, and that is my reason for having included them in group IIA.

(*e*) Khairwar, Karár, and Khairna, against whom respectively only 56, 436, and 81 persons have been recorded, cannot, from the smallness of the numbers, be regarded as three distinct tribes. They appear to be merely various names of one tribe, which is generally known as Khairwar, and whose *habitat* is in or near the southern forests of Hindustan. I have accordingly included them all under the name of Khairwar.

(*f*) I have not been able to discover any definite clue regarding the Dhingars and Dangis, who are said to consist of 1,694 and 3,220 persons respectively. As the Dhingar caste or tribe is to be found in Mirzapur, I am led to think that they are the same as the Dhangars, who are numerous in the neighbouring districts of Behar (see Bengal Census Report, 1872, page 158, where they are classed among the

" aboriginal or semi-aboriginal tribes"). Not knowing what else to do with Dangis, I have put them among Dhingars or Dhangars.

(*g*) No mention has been made in the census report of the caste or tribe called Dusadh ; yet the caste certainly exists in the eastern districts of the province. In character and habits they are about on the same level with Pasis, Bhars, Arakhs, &c. It is said that Dusadhs formed a large part of the native levies whom Clive took into drill, and through whom he laid the foundation of the British Empire in India. The military capacities of the Dusadhs are quite in keeping with what Colonel Sleeman described of the Pasis of Oudh only thirty-four years ago.

19. *Castes allied to the fishing state.*—This brings us now to the series of castes " allied to the fishing state," all of whom are included in tabular statement, group IIB. In point of culture the fishing state is little, if at all, higher than the hunting, and in many countries the two industries have not unfrequently co-existed within the same tribe. In India, however, they seem to have kept generally apart, as was the case among the native races of North America. The castes of fishermen have acquired a higher degree of respectability in this country than those of hunters, partly because water in the Hindu creed is a much more sacred element than land, partly because there is less apparent cruelty in the capturing of fish than in the slaughtering of animals, and partly because even the highest and purest castes (including Brahmans) have been compelled to recognize certain classes of men as pure enough to draw water for their use rather than accept the necessity of always drawing it for themselves. Thus, considerations of convenience as well as of religion have combined to place the Kahar or water-caste on a higher social level than the Pási or trapper. The consequence is that many members of the water-castes have left their original calling of fisherman and boatman and have become domestic servants, being called *Kahars* in Hindu houses and *Bhistis* in Muhammadan and European ones. The trust placed in them by their masters has refined their manners and given them a taste for honesty, which is exemplified in the fact that a man convicted of directly stealing his master's money is fined by his fellow-castemen on pain of dismissal from the fraternity ; and this is another reason why they have acquired a higher status in society. The fishing castes are not debarred the privilege of entering a Hindu temple, as are the hunting castes.

20. In the list of fishing castes, as in that of the hunting, I have mentioned the lowest and meanest one first. This is the Meo, whose status and history are exceptional. His inveterate propensity to robbery and crime of all kinds recalls the savage state from which he has sprung. Disowned by the other castes who practise the craft of fishing, disliked and reprobated by Hindus of every class or grade, he is turning more and more Muhammadan, and as such he has assumed the name of Mewáti. Further west, in Rajputana and elsewhere, he has taken the name of Mina, which is only a variant of Meo, and which, like Meo, signifies " fish." But outside of Hindustan he is mostly known as a robber, and has almost, if not entirely, abandoned his original craft. In Hindustan, too, his propensity to violent crime is well known, and during the mutiny he gave us more trouble than almost any other native tribe. Like the Pásis of Oudh during the time of the Nawábi Government, " they formed the worst part of the gangs of sepoys in their indiscriminate plunder." But he is still known in Hindustan as a daring boatman and fisherman, and especially as the catcher of river tortoises. I believe myself that the clan of Chattris, called Kachhwáhá or Kachhapagháta (tortoise-killer), were originally Meos, and there is no doubt whatever that a Meo clan of Chattris exists at the present day.

21. As regards the other castes named in this list, there is not much to be added to what has been said already in para. 19. The names by which some of them are called disclose the stage of culture out of which they sprung and to which they are still allied. Thus *Kahar* means a water-carrier, *Mallah* means boatman, *Kewat* (a corruption of the Sanskrit *Kaivarta*) means " one whose occupation is in water,"

and *Dhimar* (anciently spelt as Dhivara) is an old name for fisherman. *Bind*, *Chain*, and *Gaud* are tribal, as distinct from functional, names. A special interest attaches to the *Gaud* tribe, as this tribe has, on my theory of caste, formed the nucleus of the Gaur Brahmans and the Gaur Chattris, whose name is properly spelt as "*Gaud*" and not "Gaur." The caste called Dhuriya, Turha or Turi was originally an offshoot from the savage Dom, but has now become an entirely distinct class. To each of these castes there are sub-castes or clans, whose status in point of culture and respectability is not always equal. Thus there are some who keep pigs, like the hunting castes named in the previous list, and all such are on the same social level with Pasis, Arakhs, Bhars, &c. These would not be able, if they wished, to enter into domestic service. All the fisherman castes without exception are from their childhood addicted to drunkenness—a practice entirely opposed to orthodox Hinduism.

22. It remains for me to show how the names and figures given in my own table (group IIB) have been obtained, and to what extent they differ from those given in the census report:—

(*a*) Gorcha and Gharuk (see names in census, form VIIIB), are subdivisions of Chains; I have therefore included them with Chain.

(*b*) Kadhars and Tatwas are nearly, if not quite, identical with Mallahs; I have therefore made no separate mention of them in my list, but included them amongst Mallahs.

(*c*) Turha is the same caste as Dhuriya or Turi and has been included with it.

(*d*) Singhar is not a caste, but a name which could be applied to any one who cultivates the singhár or water-nut, as all the castes named in this list are in the habit of doing.

(*e*) Kahar. This is an ambiguous word. Generically, it is applied to all the castes named in this list (except the Meo), because individual members of these castes can and sometimes do enter into domestic service as Kahar or "water-carrier." Specifically, the name is given to that caste which has entirely and for many generations continuously withdrawn from the occupation of fishing, boating, &c., and which now exclusively devotes itself to domestic service. *Kahar* in the former sense is not the name of any one caste, and should therefore not appear as such in the list. *Kahar* in the latter sense comes under a totally different category and belongs to the list of serving castes for whom a separate tabular statement (group V) has been provided; I have therefore omitted the name *Kahar* altogether in the statement called group IIB.

(*f*) There are four well-known castes, of whom no separate mention has been made in the census report: these are Kewat, Gaud, Gaudia, and Dhimar. The author has pointed out in a note to page 136 of his Preliminary Dissertation that Gaud, which he incorrectly spells as *Gond*, has been included among Kahárs, because the "Gond" of the Gangetic valley must not be confounded with the "aboriginal Gond" of Central India, as was done in the previous census. The names, however, are not the same. One is *Gaud* and is pronounced in English as *Gaur*. The other is *Gond* and is pronounced as *Gond*. The tribes are certainly very distinct, but as long as each appears in its proper place and with its appropriate spelling, *Gaud* in group IIB and Gond in group I., no confusion can arise.

23. *Castes allied to the pastoral state.*—Ascending a few steps higher in the social ladder, we come to those castes which are "allied to the pastoral state." The occupation of cattle-grazing, as I need scarcely add, represents a higher grade of culture than that of hunting or fishing: and hence the pastoral castes stand on a higher social level in the Hindu community than the castes which preceded them. The change from the hunter to the nomad, and from the wandering cattle-grazer to the stationary one, must of course have been gradual: and the first nomads were almost as much addicted to robbery and bloodshed as men who lived by hunting and fighting only. This is true at the present day, for example, of the Bedouin tribes of Arabia and Egypt,

and some of the Tartar tribes of Central Asia. Every phase of nomadism is represented at the present day in India, as I shall presently show, by some corresponding caste ; and in the tabular statement annexed (group IIC) I have given the names of these castes, as far as possible, in the order of that phase of culture to which they are most nearly allied, the lower being mentioned first and the higher last.

24. If the reader will refer to the tabular list (group IIC), in which these castes have been collected, he will observe that the names by which they are called, indicate very clearly the stage of culture, out of which they originally rose and to which as castes they still approximately correspond. Thus Goshi is derived from *Gosha*, a cattle-pen. Gadaria, the shepherd caste, is derived from *Gadar*, an old Hindi word for sheep. Ahar and Ahir are variants of the Sanskrit *Abhir*, which means nomad, "one who wanders about." This caste or tribe was known to Pliny under the name of Abhiri. Gujar is simply a variant of *Gochar*, which means "cattle-grazer." The Ját caste has retained its tribal, instead of taking a functional, name, on account of the fame of the great popular hero, Krishna, who was born in its ranks.

25. As was stated above, there are various gradations of rank, corresponding to the various grades of nomadism, among the pastoral castes of India. Thus the Gaddi or Goshi, who has been placed first, that is, lowest, in my tabular list, is not merely a cattle-grazer but a cattle-lifter, and he recalls in other respects the predatory or earliest phase of nomadism. If he can find space, as he still does, on the sides of the Vindhya hills, he prefers to this day the purely migratory to the settled life. The Hindu caste is generally called Gaddi, and Ghosi is the Muhammadan counterpart. Amongst Muhammadans the Ghosi ranks quite as low as the Gaddi amongst Hindus and for the same reason. The very name "Gaddi" appears to be merely a variant of Gadiya, Gidiya, or Gandila—a tribe of savages and cutthroats, of whom only a few are now to be found in Hindustan, though they are said to be still numerous in the Panjáb as a clan of the predatory Sánsis. Thus Gaddi the cowherd is merely an improved form of Gadia the savage, just as Khangár is an improved form of Kanjar, Dhuriya of Dom, Ahír of Banmánush, &c. A man of the Gaddi caste cannot enter a Hindu temple, which proves that his status in society is as low or almost as low as that of the hunting tribes or castes. The castes standing next to the Ghosi or Gaddi in order of respectability are the Ahar and the Gujar. The former is by *name* merely a variant of Ahír, but in character he is less civilized. He therefore constitutes a distinct caste and is recognized as such by all Hindus. The Gujars, especially those in the Meerut Division, are notorious for their predatory habits. In the Moghal times they were largely employed as watchmen, a clear proof of their thievish and lawless propensities ; and in the time of the sepoy mutiny they gave as much trouble as the Meos, plundering friend and enemy indiscriminately. The Ahír is very different. He is as a rule orderly and peaceable wherever he lives ; and from a wandering cattle-grazer or nomad, which (as his name implies) he originally was, he has for several generations past been settling down as a stationary husbandman, and this not so much from choice as from the constantly increasing scarcity of fields or forests suited to his ancestral calling. The Gadaria resembles the Ahír in character and pursuits, except that he grazes sheep and goats instead of cows and buffaloes. He is largely occupied in wool-shearing and wool-weaving, and he adheres to this calling as long as he can in preference to agriculture. The Rewári or camel-breeder is a respectable caste, belonging to Rajputana rather than to Hindustan. The Ját stands higher in the social scale than any of the other castes belonging to this group. The name Ját or Jád is simply the modern Hindi pronunciation of the Sanskrit Yádu or Jádu, the tribe in which the great popular hero, Krishna, was born. In the Prem Ságar and elsewhere the Yádu tribe is described as simply pastoral, and the flirtations of Krishna with the milkmaids would lose all force and significance on any other hypothesis. Krishna, then, was a great nomad king, who achieved renown as a victorious warrior no less than as an amorous swain ; and the tribe in which he was born became, owing to the fame of his greatness, the highest and most powerful

of the pastoral tribes of Upper India, as it has remained to this day. His modern worshippers and admirers, not satisfied with thinking of him as a cowherd, have raised him to a Rajput; and hence in the western districts of the Pánjáb no clear distinction between Játs and Rájputs can now be made out. In Hindustan, however, the Játs are still many degrees below Chattris or Rájputs. Nor have they entirely thrown off the nomad and predatory instinct: for, as Mr. Beames remarks, "not long ago they were notorious cattle-lifters, nearly as bad as their neighbours, the Gujars" (Elliot's *Supplemental Glossary*, Vol. I, page 136). As a caste they still retain many of the customs and traditions peculiar to the pastoral state; but their present occupation is chiefly agricultural, and in the Meerut Division they are said to raise finer crops of sugar than any of the agricultural castes proper.

26. A brief allusion must be made in passing to the theory repeated by almost all writers on Indian ethnology, that the pastoral castes, especially the Ját, the Gujar, and the Ahír, are of Scythian origin, that is (I presume) of neither Aryan nor indigenous blood. Several reasons have been alleged in support of this view. Speaking of the Játs, Mr. Williams remarks that "the custom of the *karáo*, the marriage of a widow with the brother of a deceased husband, clearly indicates a Scythian origin" (*Oudh Census Report*, 1869, Vol. I, page 93). Again, the same writer speaking of the Ahírs (see page 100) gives some countenance to the notion that the word Ahír is derived from *ahi*, a snake, and considers that the regard for snakes shown by this caste "must be a relic of the old serpent-worship, and seems to confirm the supposition of a Scythian origin for this caste." In using the argument drawn from the remarriage of widows Mr. Williams was only following Sir Henry Elliot, who remarks that "Ahirs conform to the customs of Gújars and Játs in respect to the marriage of the elder brother's widow" (see *Supplemental Glossary*, Vol. I, page 5); and in several of the Gazetteers of the North-Western Provinces lately published allusion is made to the community of this custom as a mark of community of origin. The ethnology of the Gújars is learnedly discussed by General Cunningham, who identifies them with the Tochari, *alias* Yuchi, *alias* Kushan, *alias* Kaspiroi, *alias* Thagarii, *alias* Kuei-shwang, *alias* Korson, Korsea, Khuransu, or Koruno; and in this way they are lodged at last in the city of Khorasan and traced to a Scythian origin (see *Archæological Report*, Part IV, pages 25-29). Independently of this, Sir Henry Elliot had already identified the Játs with the Getœ or Massa-Getœ of ancient Scythia, and these again with the Yuechi, Yuchi or Yuti, whom General Cunningham has identified with the Gujars (*Supplemental Glossary*, Vol. I, page 133). Finally, the Scythian origin of the Játs has been accepted as an historical fact by Dr. W. W. Hunter, who includes the Nága tribes also in the same category; for *Nága*, as he shows, means snake, and "serpent-worship formed a typical characteristic of the Indo-Scythic races" (*Indian Empire*, Chapter VII, page 173, edit. 1882). In his "Brief History of the Indian People," which is the text-book for the entrance examination to the Calcutta University, several thousands of youths throughout the presidency of Bengal are now being taught that the Indian population is made up of three distinct racial elements—the Aboriginal, the Aryan, and the Scythian. In Chapter VIII of this volume he remarks:—"The third race, the Scythian, held a position between the other two. The Scythian hordes who poured into India from 126 B. C. to 400 A. D. were neither hunters like the Indian non-Aryan tribes, nor cultivators like the Aryans. They were shepherds or herdsmen who roamed across the plains of Central Asia with their cattle and whose one talent was for war."

The grounds, then, on which the Scythian origin of the pastoral castes has been maintained are three in number: (1) the custom of the *karáo*; (2) the worship of snakes; (3) the identification of proper names. The first argument is worth nothing, because the marriage of the elder brother's widow was a Hindu custom legalized by Manu's Code (see extract in margin), and though it has since been

"Should a younger brother have begotten a son on the wife of his deceased elder brother, the division (of property) must then be made equally between that son, who represents the deceased, and his natural father: thus is the law settled."—*Chapter IX, section* 120.

prohibited to the higher castes by the code of Parásara, it is still practised by all the lower castes, and is not, nor ever has been, confined to the Gújars, Ahírs, and Játs. The second argument is likewise worth nothing, because snakes are worshipped all over India by all castes alike, and have at different times been worshipped all over the world, wherever snakes are to be found. The third argument (the identification of proper names) is ingenious, but not convincing. The reader is already aware that Ját is simply the modern Hindi pronunciation of Yádu or Jádu, that Ahír can be easily traced to the Sanskrit Abhír, and that Gujar is merely a variant of Gochar or cattle-grazer.

Even if it could be proved that these castes were of Scythian blood, the result would only strand us in deeper ignorance than before; for the best authorities are not agreed as to who the Scythians were, some contending that they were Aryans and others Mongols. Considering that these so-called Scythian tribes of India are in physical characteristics precisely similar to the rest of the Indian population, it is vain to expect one to believe that they are of an alien ethnical stock. Moreover, the the pastoral castes are the necessary intermediate link between the hunting and the agricultural; and this fact alone, unless we are to discredit the analogies of history and the conclusions of science, is sufficient to prove that they are not of foreign but of indigenous blood.

27. The differences between the names given in the census report and those shown in my own table (group IIB) are in this instance very slight :—

(*a*) Gaddi has been entered as an equivalent name to Goshi, as the former is the name of the Hindu caste and the latter that of the Muhammadan counterpart. Even Ahírs and Gújars who have become Muhammadan frequently call themselves by the name of Goshi.

(*b*) Baona, against which only 143 persons have been recorded in the census, is (so far as I can learn) a sub-class of Gaddi, amongst whom, therefore, I have included them.

(*c*) Dhandhor, against which only eight persons are recorded, signifies etymologically "one whose wealth lies in cattle," being derived from *dhan*, wealth, and *dhor*, cattle. It is not the name of a caste. Such a name might be applied to any one who lives by cattle. But I learn that it is not unfrequently used as an euphemism for cattle-lifter; I have therefore included them amongst Gaddis.

28. *Agricultural castes.*—We come now to the agricultural castes proper—those whose sole or chief industry from several centuries past has been the cultivation of the soil. Agriculture represents, as is well known, a higher phase of industry than either hunting or nomadism, nor is it difficult to see how this industry arose out of the two which preceded it. So long as man subsists by hunting game, catching fish, gathering wild fruits or seeds, and digging bulbs and roots out of the earth, he feeds himself much in the same way as the birds and beasts. But natural intelligence must soon suggest to him that if seeds or roots are put into the earth by his own hands, they will grow there quite as readily as if they were sown or planted by nature. The same instrument which he uses as a spear for hunting game serves equally well for dibbling seeds into the soil. Again, to plant a root is much the same kind of process as to dig one up; and here, too, the same instrument which he uses as a pick or hatchet serves also as a hoe. Such is the form of agriculture coeval with the hunting and fishing states. A higher stage begins to be reached when men by inverting the hoe and giving it a handle change it into a plough. Having learnt to tame and rear cattle for use, instead of hunting them for game, it is not long before they find out how to attach them to the plough, instead of dragging the plough through the earth by their own labour. Agriculture at this secondary stage is chiefly nomadic; that is to say, men seldom cultivate the same piece of land for a second year; they are owners of the crop raised on it, but not of the soil itself. It is only when men remain permanently on the same patch of land and have acquired the right of permanent occupation and of transmission to their children, that the agricultural state proper has been reached. It is then that villages and towns are formed; new

arts and industries spring up ; trade finds for itself new channels ; and new ideas of duty, public as well as domestic, are suggested to the mind. The agricultural state, then, ranks decidedly higher in the scale of human progress than either the hunting or the merely pastoral states. By the same law the agricultural castes in India, which *ipso facto* represent the agricultural state, stand higher in the Hindu social scale than the castes preceding them.

29. The names by which most of the agricultural castes are called (*vide* group IID) tell their own tale. Lodhá signifies "clod-breaker," being derived from *lod*, a clod of earth, and *há*, breaker. Kándu is derived from *kánd*, a river-bank. Similarly Kachhi is derived from *kachh*, the alluvial soil on the banks of rivers, which, on account of its lightness and the superior facilities for irrigation, must have come under the plough at an earlier date than the dryer and harder soil of the uplands which were once covered with forest. Kurmi is derived from *Kurma*, the tortoise incarnation of Vishnu, which is specially worshipped by agricultural castes, as the fish that supports the earth. Tamboli is derived from *tambol*, the pan creeper, and the name is well suited to the caste specially employed in rearing this delicate herb. Máli is derived from *málá*, a wreath of flowers—an appropriate name for the caste which has made flower-gardening its peculiar function. Bhuinhár is derived from *bhú* or *bhúmi* (the earth) and *hár* (taker or possessor), and is very properly applied to a caste the members of which pride themselves upon being owners or landlords, and not merely tenants of the soil they cultivate. Thus, if other evidence were wanting, the names by which the agricultural castes are called show clearly enough to what stage of industry they belong. The generic name of most of these castes is Kishán or plougher, as Gwála or milkman is the generic name of the pastoral castes, and Kahár or waterman of the fishing castes, and Chirimar or fowler of the hunting castes.

30. As in the case of the pastoral castes already described, so among the agricultural castes proper, there is a graduated scale of dignity which is recognised by the general Hindu community, and which we must now endeavour to account for. Omitting the Bhot and the Kamboh—both of foreign origin and neither of much importance—the castes enumerated under this heading stand as follows in the order of dignity, the lowest being mentioned first and the highest last :—

I.	... Lodhá. Bayár.	III.	... Tamboli. Mali.
II.	... Kándu. Káchhi. Kurmi.	IV.	... Tagá. Bhuinhár.

31. The Lodhá and Bayár not only stand lowest in the list of agricultural castes, but they are socially inferior to the best of the pastoral, just as the Gaddi and Goshi, the lowest of the pastoral castes, rank below the best of the fishing or waterman classes. Nor is this at all inconsistent with our general theory of gradation. For the course of human progress is spiral rather than rectilinear, because humanity advances only by a series of reactions against the point of vantage last gained. The traditions and sympathies of the Lodhá connect him very clearly with the semi-savage Musarhá, whom I have placed among the "castelsse tribes"—from which it might be inferred that his adoption of the agricultural status is comparatively recent as compared with that of others. And this inference coincides with the fact ; for it is well known to those who have lived in Oudh that there are some families of Lodhs or Lodhás, who to this day prefer the rougher task of felling trees and making the first clearance of land to the tamer and more monotonous industry of tilling the open plain. The Bayár holds about the same rank as the Lodhá. His name is identical with that of an old tribe of freebooters, who are celebrated in local traditions as builders of mud forts and founders of petty kingdoms. Both of these castes are still occasionally addicted to turbulence—a mark of their more recent reclamation from savagery.

32. The three next castes—the Kándu, the Kurmi, and the Káchhi—are peaceable and industrious, wherever they are to be found. Their status is about on a par with

that of the best of the pastoral castes (the Ját and the Ahír), but decidedly above that of the rest. The Kándu is an offshoot from certain fishing tribes, and like them cultivates the *singhára* or water-nut. He also raises crops of grain, especially of rice; and from a rice-grower he has developed in some places into a rice-parcher, for the sale of which he sometimes keeps a shop. The Kurmi (called also Kunbi) is the greatest grain-growing caste in India, and he has been deservedly called "the backbone of the country." The women and children take almost as active a part in the labour of the fields as the men. The British Government has generally recognized his superior skill as a cultivator by fixing a higher assessment on his lands than would be demanded from a Brahman or Chattri occupant. The Káchhi sometimes grows grain like the Kurmi, but is chiefly known as a market-gardener. Some of the most prosperous members of this caste hold large plots of land in the vicinity of towns and cities, where they raise crops of poppy, potato, tobacco, sugar, &c. The name "Kachhi," as we have shown, is functional and not tribal. But another name, Koeri, by which he is sometimes called, shows that the wandering and semi-savage Kol, who is still to be found in the districts south of the Ganges, was his remote ancestor, though every tradition of such descent appears now to have been forgotten. Another synonym, Muráo, appears to point to some other ancient, but now forgotten, tribe as the joint ancestor of this useful and industrious caste.

33. The five castes whom we have named thus far still indulge in the flesh of field-rats, a habit which tends to lower them in the eyes of their fellow-countrymen, and connects them remotely with the Ugras, Pukkasas, and other savages who are denounced in Manu's Code as "hunters of animals that dwell in holes." But the four castes remaining to be described abstain entirely from such unclean diet, and this is one of the reasons why they hold a higher rank than the preceding. The Tamboli and the Mali stand next above the Kurmi and Kachhi. The first is the well-known and respected caste of pán-grower. In the rearing of this plant they enjoy an exclusive monopoly, which must have taken its rise from the fact that only the son of a pán-grower himself can acquire the secret of rearing such a delicate herb. It is the custom of this caste not merely to grow the plant, but to prepare it for sale, and to keep a shop for this purpose. If the trade prospers, the Tamboli takes to money-lending and usury, the trade proper of the Oswáls, Agarwáls, Khatris and others: and I feel no doubt that these wealthy and distinguished castes have at various times been recruited from pán-growing families. The Mali is the well-known caste of flower-gardener. His art, like that of the Tamboli, indicates a degree of refinement above that of the mere grain-grower and vegetable-gardener. But a refined art leads to a corresponding refinement in manners, feelings, and mode of life generally, and any caste which practises such art or arts rises to a proportionate height in the social scale. Such has been the case with the Máli, and such is the theory of caste—gradation assumed in this paper. Another fact which has raised the Mali above his fellows is one connected with religion. To Hindus of all ranks, including even the Bráhman, he acts as a priest of Mahádev in places where no Goshayen is to be found, and lays the flower-offering on the lingam by which the deity is symbolized. As the Mali is believed to have some influence with the god to whose temple he is attached, no one objects to his appropriating the fee which is nominally presented to the god himself. In the worship of those village godlings whom the Brahman disdains to recognize, and whom the Goshayen is not permitted to honor, the Mali is sometimes employed to present the offering. He is thus the recognized hereditary priest of the lower and more ignorant classes of the population. It is not at all improbable that certain Mali families have at times gained admission into the ranks of Brahmanhood.

34. This brings us lastly to the two highest of the agricultural castes, the Tagá and the Bhuinhar. There are two great facts which place them above all the preceding castes. Firstly, they do not allow the remarriage of widows, whereas every

caste hitherto named in this paper permits the practice. This shows that they have been for a much longer period under Bráhmanical influence, and they have acquired an increased dignity in consequence. Secondly, they are generally owners, and not merely tenants, like the castes previously named, of the land on which they raise their crops. In this respect they make a much nearer approach to the status of the Chattri or landlord caste, which ranks immediately above them. Almost all cultivators except the Tagá and Bhuinhar found it necessary to place themselves under the protection of some Chattri landlord, who, being of the warrior caste, protected them from aggression from without, on condition of receiving rent in return : whereas the Tagá and Bhuinhar have been their own landlords and protectors from the beginning. The one fact which places these two castes in a rank below that of Chattri and Bráhman landowners is that they till the soil with their own hands, whereas the Chattri and Brahman are compelled to employ hired labour for the purpose; the former thinking it beneath his dignity, and the latter against his religion, to handle the plough. The Tagá hunts the wild-boar and drinks spirituous liquors, just as the Chattri does. The Bhuinhar leans rather to the Brahman than to the Chattri type. In places where the Brahman element predominates he abstains from boar-hunting and wine, wears the Brahmanical thread, attends Brahmanical festivals, and adopts the same marriage ceremonies as Brahmans. To this day no Hindu can tell you distinctly whether a Bhuinhar is a Brahman or not: and there is no reason to doubt that many of the modern Brahmans are sprung from certain clans of Bhuinhars, who at some earlier age renounced affinity with their own brotherhood and entered into the ranks of the priesthood.

The gradually ascending scale of rank which we have now traced among the several agricultural castes, beginning with the Lodh who was lately a savage of the woods, and rising by degrees to the Bhuinhar, who is almost a Brahman, illustrates on a smaller scale the process by which the entire system of castes throughout the Indian continent was brought into existence, and exemplifies the principle by which their several ranks in the social scale have been determined.

35. It remains to state briefly in what respects the names of the agricultural castes shown in my own table (group IID) differ from the names given in the census report :—

(*a*) Kachhar and Kachhwa, against which only 290 and 1,587 persons have been recorded respectively, are not names of separates castes, but merely variants of the name Kachhi ; I have therefore included them in the same total.

(*b*) Gamela, Khagi and Setwar, against which 1,754, 38,007, and 26,498 persons have been recorded respectively, are names not of separate castes, but of sub-castes of Kurmis ; I have therefore included them all under the name of Kurmi.

(*c*) Bot, against which only 3,191 persons have been recorded, is not a separate caste, but merely another way of spelling or pronouncing Bhotiya, against which 9,205 persons have been entered. Originally immigrants from the northern hills, they have for several centuries past been domiciled in the plains, but still retain the features of hill men.

(*d*) Mal, against which only 3,218 persons have been recorded, is the same as Mali or Gardener.

(*e*) Pattiar is the only agricultural caste named in the census report which I have not been able to identify. Perhaps it was written for *pattidar*, or co-sharer of a landed property. If this was the case, the 547 persons recorded against the name (all of whom, too, are said to belong to a single district, Fyzabad) cannot be called a caste.

36. *The landlord and warrior caste.*—We come now to the fifth and last of the series of "castes connected with the land." This is the landlord or warrior caste, whose name is variously known as Rájput, Chattri, or Thakur. The function of this

caste, if we look to its original status, is to protect and rule all other castes, receiving rent and taxes in return. The Chattri proper is the landlord, warrior, and ruler. Such a caste cannot but take precedence, in point of dignity, of all castes and classes of men subject to its authority; and hence the Mánava Code has assigned to it a rank second only to that held by priests or Brahmans, who by the same code are the advisers, secular as well as spiritual, of the kings and rulers of the earth.

37. In every part of the world, wherever agricultural settlements have superseded nomad hordes, the landlords or landed aristocracy have led and organized the armies of the State and have constituted pre-eminently the military class or caste. India has been no exception to the rule. The very name Chattri (or Kshatriya as it was originally spelt) implies this. For though the name "Kshatriya" has been universally used to designate a warrior, its primary meaning is "landlord," being derived from *Kshatra*, which signifies the possession of a territorial domain. One of the other titles, "Rájput," signifies "a man of royal blood"—a further indication of the original identity of the landowning and militant functions. This double meaning of warrior and landlord within a single word finds its analogue in the language of the Greeks, amongst whom the landed aristocracy were called the *aristoi*, the root of which is identical with that of *Ares*, the god of war. The term "baron," which in most countries of Europe was given to the owners of large landed estates, is derived from a root signifying manliness and valour; and it is needless to add that these territorial magnates were distinguished throughout the middle ages, like the Indian Rájput, for their love of fighting and high sense of honour. The king himself was only a baron on a larger scale, just as the Indian rája was merely a magnified Chattri.

38. The fact of the names of this caste being purely functional, and not tribal, gives no countenance to the theory so commonly expressed by writers of established reputation, that Chattris are the direct descendants of the Aryan tribes who came from Central Asia, while the castes below them are of aboriginal or mixed blood. And if space permitted, it would not be difficult to show that this theory is opposed both to the testimony of the Hindus themselves and to the teachings of history. "In the savage state," says Mr. Herbert Spencer, "there are no owners of the tract occupied, save the warriors who use it in common for hunting. During the pastoral life good regions for cattle-feeding are held jointly against intruders by force of arms. And where the agricultural state has been reached, communal possession, family possession, and individual possession have from time to time to be defended by the sword. Hence in the early stages the bearing of arms and the holding of land habitually go together." Now when we reflect that each of the three stages alluded to in this passage have existed in India for some thousands of years, and are represented even to this day (as I believe I have proved in this paper) by corresponding castes, it might be assumed on *à priori* grounds that each stage of industry has contributed its quota of victorious chieftains, and that the caste of Chattris is simply a congeries of men, of any tribe whatever, who were able at various times to seize lands and keep them, and who by intermarriages and alliances with others of their own status built up by degrees a separate class or caste distinct from and above the rest of the community. This is exactly what we find to have been the case in reading the histories and names of many of the Chattri families given in the published Gazetteers of these provinces. Among the names of these families or clans we find Barwár, Khangár, Gaharwár (a variant of Khairwar), Gadariya, Gujar or Bhat-Gujar, Yadu or Yadon, Meo, *Gaud* (*Anglice* Gaur), Chamar-Gaur, Jaiswár, Bandel, Domwar, Khági, Nág or Nágbansi, Baheliya or Bheriya, Gadiya, &c. The reader, who has attended to the names of the hunting and pastoral castes already described, will perceive at once the identity between these names and those of the Chattri clans just quoted; and such identity shows clearly enough what the origin of many of the modern Chattris really was. Any clan, which had gained possession of estates and was able to

bequeath them to their posterity, came as a matter of course under the patronage of Brahmans, and its leading men were thus gradually educated into kinship with the older members of the aristocratic caste, who had received a similar education before them. A caste which lives only for territorial dominion and military renown cannot afford to be exclusive. It thrives only by expansion—that is, by incorporating within its ranks men, of whatever tribe, who have proved their fitness by force of arms and whose alliance would add to the power and wealth of the fraternity. If men of the modern Chattri caste were the pure-blooded descendants of the ancient Arya, it is a singular circumstance that so many of these Aryan knights, who are supposed to have come from some country west of the Indus, should have assumed the tribal names of the indigenous Indian savage, and that out of the 99 clan names collected by Mr. Sherring there should be only one (Bhrigu-bansi) which can be traced to the Vedic age. Once educated and civilized after the Brahmanical model, the territorial chieftain, whatever his ancestry may have been, becomes a Chattri nobleman, and with the help of some Bhát or bard or other mendacious parasite acquires a genealogy, which raises him to a position in his own country similar to that held by the Spartiatæ in Lacedæmon, the Aristoi in Athens, the patricians in Rome, or the barons in Europe. In Upper India the manufacturing of Chattris is a process still going on before our eyes, and what is happening now has been in operation for the last two thousand years at least. For example, the Janwárs of Oudh held till lately a very obscure status as Rajputs, and on account of the doubtfulness of their origin they were compelled to be content with local alliances. But now they have begun to marry their daughters to the Rathors and Kachhwáhás of Rajputana (Oudh Gazetteer, Vol. II., 219). A writer in the North-Western Provinces Gazetteer (Vol. VIII., page 73), speaking of the Rájputs of the Muttra district, remarks that "about six-sevenths of them are of impure blood, and are not admitted by the higher clans to an equality with themselves. The crucial test," he adds, "of purity of blood is the rejection of the custom of *karao* (remarriage of widows)." But such a test, far from proving or disproving purity of blood, merely shows whether the clan has or has not become perfectly Hinduized according to *modern* notions; and three or four generations are quite enough to turn an Indian savage into an orthodox Hindu, if the opportunity comes in his way. Moreover, I have proved already in para. 26 that in the time of Manu's Code the remarriage of widows was under certain conditions prescribed as a duty by Brahmanical law.

There is strong reason to believe that most of the Oudh Chattris are of Bhar blood, but it would be too lengthy to quote the evidence in this place. "There are two Bhar landlords," writes Mr. Sherring, "in the Mirzapur district. But these men, disloyal to their tribe, though wise in their generation, feeling the grievous burden of their social position, affect a Rajput title, notwithstanding that it is well known that they are descended directly from the Bhars" There is nothing to prevent such men, two or three generations hence, from buying husbands for their daughters from some scion of the royal tribes, if they have sufficient wealth. It is a mark of honor in all castes, and especially among Chattris, that a man must seek to marry his daughter into some clan higher than his own: and this custom, which has been in force for the last two thousand or three thousand years, has been one of the causes at work by which families of the lowest origin have been slowly but surely raised into the ranks of the landed aristocracy, until at last all distinctions of race and blood have become obliterated. The Chattri himself is merely a Tagá who disdains to hold the plough. The Tagá is merely a more cultivated form of Kurmi. The Kurmi is only an improved form of Lodh. The Lodh is not many degrees above a savage forester.

39. In speaking of the Chattri or Rajput as the ruling and warrior caste, I was of course referring to its original function rather than to its present status. Between the ideal Chattri of the old Hindu period and the Chattri of the present day a wide difference exists. Its function as the *ruling* caste received a shock from the

Muhammadan conquest, from which it never recovered : and many Chattris of high rank have at various times embraced the creed of Islam in order to retain their estates. What survived of this function was annihilated by the establishment of British rule. The other function, that of fighting, still to a certain extent remains ; for the native regiments, through whom the Mahrattas were defeated and the provinces of Upper India added to the empire, were largely recruited from the ranks of the warrior caste. But the Pax Britannica is rendering even this function almost a thing of the past. The Chattris in fact have seen their best days, and for several centuries past have been a down-going race. They have not had sufficient intellectual keenness to compete with Brahmans and Kayasths under the new order of things, and a large number of their estates have passed into the hands of successful pleaders and merchants. Many of those who have managed to keep their lands will before long be compelled to hold the plough for themselves.

40. In the census report two entries are made on account of this caste—Chauhan and Rajput. Chauhan, however, is only one of the numerous clans of Chattris or Rajputs, and if one clan is to be separately mentioned, the same should be done with all. I think, however, that in a census of castes, where simplicity is so much to be aimed at, the generic caste name is sufficient. Detailed information respecting the clans is given in the Gazetteers of the different districts.

41. This completes the long series of "castes connected with the land," of which a brief description has been given under the five subordinate headings of hunting, fishing, cattle-grazing, agriculturist, and landlord. It is not surprising to find that this large group contains 19,064,236 persons, or nearly one half of the entire population of the province. As we have already more than once implied, the original distinctions between hunter, fisherman, cattle-grazer, and agriculturist are becoming more and more effaced as time goes on ; and all industries connected with the land are becoming more and more merged into that of agriculture. Such names, then, as hunter, fisher, &c., denote the origin and explain the social status of the castes corresponding rather than describe the functions or industries which they chiefly practise at the present day. It is curious to note, however, how the original functions peculiar to these several castes have survived in tradition. Thus, for example, at the present day, certain hunting and pastoral castes, such as the Musarha and the Gaddi, are in the habit of parcelling out wide tracts of country among themselves as if they were still owners of the soil, for purposes of root-digging, hunting, fruit-gathering and cattle-grazing ; and when an appropriation of this kind is given as a daughter's dowry, the monopoly so conferred is respected by the rest of the fraternity. Again, there is no such thing in India as a farm, in which glebe and pasture lands are maintained side by side as parts of a single holding ; and the same man, whatever his caste may be, never combines ploughing and cattle-rearing as parts of a common industry. It appears, then, that the tradition of the original diversity between the pastoral and the agricultural states and between the castes corresponding has been strong enough to keep the two industries apart up to the present day ; whereas in every other country, where agriculture has reached the same stage of advance that it has done in India, they have become completely amalgamated, the one being considered incomplete without the other.

42. *The artisan castes.*—We now come to a series of castes whose functions are altogether distinct from those of the preceding. These are the artisan castes. The generic name by which they are known in Upper India is that of Karigar. Here an entirely new law comes into play. It is now a thoroughly established fact that no nation or people can make any material advance in civilisation until they have discovered, or at least learnt to imitate, the art of metallurgy, and the ignorance of this art is the invariable mark of backward races all over the world. The hunting, fishing, and cattle-grazing industries can be and are carried to a high degree of efficiency without the use of metals. But agriculture cannot be practised, in any but the lowest and most rudimentary form, without the help of iron tools and implements ; and until

such appliances have been provided, hunting, fishing, or cattle-grazing will continue to be the predominant industry. Hence, roughly speaking, we may lay down the law that the agricultural state proper co-exists with, and cannot precede, the age of metallurgy, while the hunting, fishing and nomad states precede the age of metallurgy and are coeval with the inferior stages of art.

43. The same law has determined the rank or social status of the several artisan castes of India. It will be invariably found, if we look into the status of each of them individually, that those castes or trade-unions, which represent the inferior stages of art, stand lower in the social scale—that is, receive a less degree of respect from the Hindu community generally—than those which represent or are coeval with the metallurgic stage; and that all such castes are about equal in rank, as members of the Hindu community, to those castes which are allied to the hunting, fishing, and pastoral states. It will also be found that those artisan castes, which represent or are coeval with the metallurgic age, hold almost the same rank as the agricultural castes proper. Such a coincidence cannot have been fortuitous; and the theory enunciated in this paper, that the social status of a caste is determined by the stage of culture to which it is most nearly allied, shows how it came to pass.

44. The artisan castes, then, have been classified in this paper under two main headings—A, those which preceded the age of metallurgy; B, those that represent this age or are coeval with it. Details of the castes belonging to each class are shown in the accompanying tables, called respectively group III A and group III B. Any and every kind of commodity produced by human contrivance or human skill, as distinct from the raw materials furnished by the soil or from the animals which live thereon, is considered to be a product of art and comes within the functions of the artisan castes. This is the sense in which the term "artisan" is meant to be understood in this paper. This, too, is what the natives of India mean by the term *karigar*, "artificer or skilled workman."

45. *A—Preceding the age of metallurgy.*—Among the artisan castes of the lower or pre-metallurgic age there is a graduated scale of dignity or rank similar to what has been shown to exist in the case of the hunting, fishing, pastoral, and agricultural castes already described. In the following list, as in those given above, an attempt has been made to group them approximately in the order of dignity, the lower being placed first and the higher last:—

I. { Bansphor—Basket-maker, &c.
Bari—Leaf-plate-maker.

II. { Chamár—Hide-skinner and tanner.
Mochi—Cobbler.

III. { Dhuna—Cotton-carder.
Kori—Weaver.

IV. { Teli—Oil-presser.
Kalwar—Spirit-distiller.
Kumhar—Potter.
Lunia—Salt-maker.

All of the industries included in the above list are compatible with a low stage of culture, and their equivalents (as might be easily proved if space permitted) may be found at the present day among the arts practised by savage and barbarous races in various parts of the world. If the people of whom such castes are composed could be eliminated from the rest of the Indian population and transported to some distant land or island of their own, any traveller visiting them and recording their customs and notions would not hesitate to class them with such races as may be found at the present time in Polynesia or in Central Africa, or in parts of the American continents.

46. The names by which the above castes are distinguished from the rest of the community show clearly enough that it was some speciality of function, and not community of blood or community of religion, which brought the several castes into existence. Thus the name Bansphor, the caste of basket-makers, &c., is derived from *bans*, "a bamboo," and *phur* or *sphur*, "to split." Another and a better-known name

for this caste is Dharkár, which signifies rope-maker, being derived from *dhar*, "rope," and *kár*, "maker." Bári, the name of the leaf-plate-making caste, is derived from *bári*, a plantation or orchard : another name for this caste is Bargi, derived from *barg*, a Persian word for leaf. Chamár, the name of the tanner caste, is derived from *chamra*, "hide." Mochi, the name of the cobbler caste, is derived from *moohna*, "tweezers or pincers," one of the instruments used in working leather: another name of this caste, "Dabgar," is derived from *dab*, the pressing or flattening of the hide. Dhuna, the name of the cotton-carding caste, is derived from *dhun*, "to beat out, comb, or card." Bunkar and Joria, synonyms of Kori, the weaver caste, are derived respectively from *bun*, to weave, and *jor* to join, that is, to put the threads together in alternate pairs as warp and woof. Teli, the name of the oil-man caste, is derived from *til*, the sesame plant, from which oil is very largely extracted. Kalwar is probably a variant of Khairwar, a tribe noted for the extraction of an intoxicating juice from the khair tree. Kumhár, the name of the potter caste, is an abbreviation of *kumbakár*, and is derived from *kumba*, an earthen pot, and *kár*, maker : the Persian name of this caste is Kashgar, which is derived from *kásah*, "a cup," and *gar*, "maker." Lunia, the name of the salt-making caste, is derived from *laun* or *naun*, "salt," and hence another name for the caste is "Nunera." Thus there is not a single caste in this list which is not designated by a functional as distinct from a tribal name.

47. The Dharkar or Bansphor is the lowest caste in the list. And this tallies with the fact (which could be easily proved from the known characteristics of modern savages elsewhere) that the special industry represented by this caste, *viz.*, that of making baskets, reed-mats, grass-ropes, &c , is the lowest of human arts. The traditions of the Dharkar connect him very distinctly with the savage Dom or Chandál, of which tribe he has sometimes, but erroneously, been called a clan. The Dharkar is simply a reformed Dom ; that is, he has left off eating dogs, burning corpses, executing criminals, and sweeping away filth for hire ; but he has retained the ancestral art or industry of making chairs, mats, baskets, &c., out of reeds and cane. The differences between them have now become so marked, that the offshoot constitutes a stationary or settled caste, while the ancestor remains to this day a wandering savage. If the theory with which we started is correct—that the casteless and savage tribes supplied the raw materials out of which the entire caste system was gradually fashioned—it is quite natural that the lowest of the artisan castes should trace its origin to one of the lowest of the indigenous tribes. It is well known that basket-making in Europe is the special industry of gypsies.

48. The Bari stands many degrees higher in the social scale than the Dharkar, although the industry which he represents, *viz.*, that of making cups and plates of leaves skewered or stitched together with leaf fibres, is almost or quite as low as that of the other. This apparent exception to the general theory enunciated in this paper is easily explained. If leaf plates and cups were used only by low-caste people, the Bari would stand no higher than the Dharkar. But they are used by the highest castes as much as by the lowest ; and hence considerations of practical convenience have compelled the former to recognize the Bari as pure and respectable enough to make plates for them. The same considerations, as we have already shown, raised the Kahar or water-carrying castes above the hunting. The result has been that Baris, like Kahars, have taken largely to domestic service, in which they are chiefly employed as table-servants, waiters, &c. When the master goes out in his palanquin at night, the servant accompanies him as torch-bearer, and hence torch-making has become one of the special industries of the Bari caste. The strictest Brahmans—those at least who aspire to imitate the self-denying life of the ancient Indian hermit—never eat off any plates other than those made of leaves, and it is very probable that, through long attendance on such masters, some Baris have imperceptibly learnt the Brahman's craft and raised themselves into the ranks of Brahmanhood. Notwithstanding the comparative respect in which the Bari is thus held, he is merely an offshoot from the

semi-savage tribes known as Banmánush and Musarhá. He still associates with them at times; and if the demand for plates and cups (owing to some temporary cause, such as a local fair or an unusual multitude of marriages) happens to become larger than he can at once supply, he gets them secretly made by his ruder kinsfolk, and retails them at a higher rate, passing them off as his own production.

49. Descending once more into a social level almost as low as that of the Dharkar, we come to the caste of Chamár, the speciality of whose function is that of hide-skinning and the conversion of the hide into leather. The Chamár is a very numerous caste, and may have sprung out of several different tribes, like the Dom, Kanjar, Habura, Cheru, &c, the last remains of whom are still outside the pale of Hindu society. Originally he appears to have been an impressed labourer or *begar*, who was made to hold the plough for his master, and received in return space for building his mud-hovel near the village, a fixed allowance of grain for every working day, the free use of wood and grass on the village lands, and the skins and bodies of all the animals that died. This is very much the status of the Chamár at the present day. He is still the field-slave, the grass-cutter, the remover of dead animals, the hide-skinner, and the carrion-eater of the Indian village. The *rápi* or tanner's knife is worshipped by this caste at the annual festivalof Diwáli. The women are the midwives of the Hindu community. The position of Chamárs has improved in some cases under British rule. Some have learnt the English language, attended dispensaries, and become native doctors—a profession well-suited to their traditions, as they do not share in the objections felt by some of the higher castes to the use of the dissecting knife. There are a few Muhammadan converts from the Chamár caste, who are called Kharkatá or Charkatá.

50. The caste of Mochi or cobbler is an offshoot from that of Chámar, but yet as castes they have become quite distinct; for they do not eat together nor intermarry. The industry of tanning is preparatory to and lower than that of cobblery; and hence, by the general law announced throughout this paper, the caste of Chamár ranks decidedly below that of Mochi. The ordinary Hindu does not consider the touch of a Mochi so impure as that of a Chamár, and there is a Hindu proverb to the effect that "dried or prepared hide is the same thing as cloth;" whereas the touch of the raw hide, before it has been tanned by the Chamár, is considered a pollution. The Mochi does not eat carrion like the Chamár, nor does he eat swine's flesh; nor does his wife ever practise the much-loathed art of midwifery. He makes the shoes, leather aprons, leather buckets, harness, portmanteaux, &c., used by the people of India. As a rule, he is much better off than the Chamár, and this circumstance has helped amongst others to raise him in the social scale. A considerable proportion of the Mochi caste has become Muhammadan.

51. The two next castes are those whose special industry is connected with cotton. The first, the Dhuna, called also Behna, is the cotton-carder and thread-twister. The second, the Kori, Joria, or Bunkar, is the weaver or cloth-maker. As the former industry is preparatory to and lower than the latter, so the caste of Dhuna ranks below that of Kori.

The material used by the Dhuna is furnished by the Salmali or cotton-bearing tree, which is, no doubt, identical with what Herodotus called "the wool-bearing trees of Ethiopia." The Dhuna gathers the cotton-pod as it falls, beats out its contents into fine particles with an instrument resembling a bow, and twists them into threads. The industry is closely akin to that of making ropes out of the fibres of grass, reeds, and roots, in which the Dharkar excels. But in consequence of its being more refined, the cast of Dhuna stands higher than that of Dharkar.

52. The material used by the Kori is the thread supplied by the Dhuna; and thus the weaver caste has risen imperceptibly out of that of the cotton-carder, in the same way as the cobbler caste has risen out of the tanner. The art of weaving or plaiting threads is very much the same process as that of plaiting osiers, reeds,

and grass, and converting them into baskets and mats. This circumstance explains the puzzle why the weaver caste in India stands at such a low social level. In countries like England, which have gone beyond the agricultural stage and entered fully into the scientific and commercial, weaving (by machinery) has become a very respectable form of industry. But India has never gone beyond the agricultural stage; and hence weaving has remained, what it originally was, the occupation of an ignorant and inferior class of people. The Kori ranks, however, several degrees above the Chamár or tanner; for amongst Hindus herbs and their products (cotton being of course included) are invariably considered pure, while the hides of dead animals are regarded as a pollution. Owing to the large importation of machine-made stuffs from Europe, the business of the Kori, whose weaving is all done by hand, has become very much depressed, and many of the rising generation are growing up totally ignorant of the ancestral craft. They are now taking to grass-cutting, ploughing, &c., like Chamárs. The weaving caste has two functional names (Joria and Bunkar, the meaning of which has been already explained), and one tribal name, Kori. The last shows that the Kol (or Kor) tribe contributed largely to the personnel of the caste; and this fact is quite in keeping with our theory, that weaving represents a low stage of art, and that the first weavers in India sprang from a wandering and semi-savage tribe, such as the Kols still are. Muhammadan converts from the weaver caste are called Juláhá.

53. The four castes remaining to be described in this list stand at rather a higher level than any of those previously named, except the Bári, whose case is peculiar. These four are allowed, but not encouraged, to enter a Hindu temple, whereas all the preceding castes, except the Bári, are absolutely excluded.

The Teli is perhaps the lowest of the four. He presses oil from the *til* or sesame plant, and such oil is largely used by all classes of the Indian community for cooking food, anointing the body, softening leather, and healing sores. He also extracts oil from the seed of the nim tree, of the castor plant, the mustard plant, and the thorny shrub called Bharbhánd, which grows wild in the jungles. The art of the oilman has been greatly improved by that of the agriculturist, who has supplied him with many kinds of oil-yielding plants which the jungle does not afford. Nevertheless, the art itself in its earlier and less refined forms preceded the age of agriculture, and must be counted among the lower types of industry. This is why the caste has always ranked low. The Teli never extracts oil from the bodies of animals, as Kanjars and others of the lowest tribes of Hindustan are accustomed to do. Probably, however, he learnt the first rudiments of his art from such tribes, and is himself an offshoot from them.

54. The Kalwár ranks a little higher than the Teli, because there is more skill and less dirt in the practice of his art. His trade as a private occupation has been destroyed by the British Government, which has taken the distilling and sale of liquors entirely into its own hands. The Kalwár still finds some opportunity, however, of following his old pursuit by working in the Government distilleries and taking out licenses for the sale of spirits. But the majority have taken to other kinds of trade or to agriculture, the common goal to which all the decayed industries of India are tending. The art of the Kalwár, like that of the Teli, has been known to almost all the backward races of the world, and cannot by any means be counted among the higher types of industry. Hence the status of the Kalwár has always been low. The name, as I stated above, is probably a variant of *Khairwár*, or "catechu-maker," a process which is very similar to that of drawing juice from the palm-tree and fermenting it into a spirit. The name of Kalwár then, if this identification is correct, implies that the caste has sprung up out of such tribes as Chain, Khairwár, Musarha, &c., all of whom are skilled in making the intoxicating juice called catechu.

55. The Kumhar or potter represents a form of industry about equal in rank to that of the Teli or Kalwár, and hence his status in the social scale is much the

same as theirs. It is now a well-established fact that pottery was known in the Stone age of the world; and the art was found to be in full vogue among the Fijian savages of the Pacific and among the native races of North America, when they were first visited by voyagers from Europe. The potter's wheel is an application of the mill-stone, but the lowest stage of the art can probably be traced to basket-making. Men discovered without much difficulty that their baskets could be made water-tight by smearing them over with clay. Afterwards by putting such baskets on the fire, it was found that while the reeds and osiers were consumed, the clay not only remained, but was strengthened and hardened by the fire. Eventually clay vessels were made without the help of the basket framework, and hence pottery was developed into a distinct art. All the casteless tribes of India are skilled in making baskets; and hence we may infer that the potter caste sprung out of one or more of these tribes, and that the Dharkár may have been the intermediate caste.

56. The Lunia or salt-making caste closes this list. His industry has been even more destroyed than that of the Kalwár, and by the same cause. Now he has taken to road-making, well-digging, mud-masonry, &c., and his industry corresponds very nearly with that of the English navvy. In the days of his prosperity he manufactured salt and saltpetre out of the *usar* or alkaline soils, in which Upper India abounds. He still does so occasionally at night time and in secret. As a digger and delver in the earth he not unfrequently stumbles upon field-rats, and these form part of his diet, when he can get them. His status in the social scale is about equal to that of the Lodh or Lodha, the lowest of the agricultural castes.

57. In connection with the above castes, some reference must be made in this place to the position which some of them hold in the constitution of the Hindu township or village commune—a kind of municipal and self-sufficing body, which characterized the civilization of the Hindus from very early times, and which is not by any means extinct. Allusion has already been made in para. 15 to the village watchman—a post assigned from the oldest times to some man of the hunting or predatory tribes (such as Pási, Khangár, Arakh, Bhar, &c.) who abstained from robbing, and prevented others from robbing, the residents of the village, on condition that he received his stipulated reward and was allowed to build a hut for himself and family on the outskirts of the hamlet. Among the artisan castes which we have just described there are two—the Chamár and Kumhár—who are essential factors in the constitution of the township. The Chamár removes the carcasses of cows and buffaloes, takes off their hides, tans them into leather, makes the leather buckets used for drawing water from the wells into the fields, and makes shoes for some of the residents. Were it not for the leather buckets made by Chamárs, no water could be drawn from wells for the irrigation of crops during the long dry mouths of the year, and the labour of the husbandman would be lost. The function of Kumhár or potter is useful at all times, but comes more markedly into use at times of child-birth, marriage, and funerals. On the twelfth day after a child has been born, when the final bath is given to the mother on leaving her sick chamber, all the earthen pots of the household are discarded and replaced by new ones. At the time of the celebration of a marriage the father supplies the new jars, in which Ganges water, barley, and lighted oil are placed in honor of Ganesha, the god of luck, and without which the marriage ceremony could not be performed. On the tenth or thirteenth day after a death, all the earthen vessels of the house are destroyed and replaced by new ones, as on the twelfth day after a birth. Of each of the three functionaries whom we have named—the watchman, the hide-tanner, and the potter—it may be said that on special occasions, or for services of exceptional merit, they receive some special remuneration in cash or kind; and that for ordinary services they receive a stipulated portion of the produce of each of the two annual harvests. Additional presents are made to them in the great anniversaries of Diwáli, Holi, and Dashara.

58. It remains for me to describe in what respect the names and figures shown in group IIIA. differ from those given in the census report:—

(*a*) ***Basket-makers.***—Kharot, Gogh, and Charu, against whom 3,610, 369, and 514 persons have been recorded respectively in the census report, have been included in my own table amongst Dharkars or Bansphors, to whom they really belong. For the name Bansphor given in the census I have substituted Dharkar, as the former name is sometimes applied to men of any tribe or low caste (such as that of sweeper for example) which follows the occupation of basket-making, &c., as an accessory to other callings.

(*b*) *Leaf-plate-makers.*—Bargi, Bargahi, and Sijwari, against whom 1,189, 3,777, and 376 persons have been recorded respectively in the census report, are not separate castes, but merely synomyms of Bari, and have therefore been included in this caste in my own table.

(*c*) *Leather-workers.*—No mention is made in the census report of the Mochi or cobbler caste, the members of which have evidently been mixed up with Chamárs. I am unable, therefore, to separate the figures, but I have added the name Mochi to the list of castes belonging to this table.

(*d*) Kharkatas are Chamárs who have become Muhammadan; they have, therefore, been included by me amongst Chamárs.

(*e*) Dabgar, Karal, and Jaiswar, against which 1,231, 333, and 832 persons have been recorded respectively in the census report, are not separate castes, but sub-classes or synomyms of Mochi, and under this name I have included them in preparing my own table.

(*f*) ***Thread-twisters.***—Katwa, against which 122 names have been recorded in the census report, is not a caste, but a sub-class or synonym of Dhuna, under which name I have included them.

(*g*) ***Weaver.***—Joria, Bunkar, and Balai, against whom 10,923, 6,635, and 189 persons have been respectively recorded, are not separate castes, but synonyms of Kori, under which name I have included them.

(*h*) ***Oil-makers.***—Badiphul, against which 429 persons have been recorded, is included by me amongst Telis.

(*i*) ***Potters.***—Balahi, against which 121 persons have been recorded, is included by me amongst Kumhars.

(*j*) Raj and Kathyara, against which 9,683 and 295 persons have been recorded, are not names of castes, but of the occupation of brick-layers. As such men are generally of the potter caste, I have included them amongst Kumhars.

(*k*) *Salt-makers.*—Parbia, Agaria, and Sunkar, against which 6,205, 1,384, and 1,084 persons have been recorded, are sub-classes or local titles of the caste of Lunia, under which name I have therefore included them.

59. *B.—Coeval with the age of metallurgy.*—The upper artisan castes (*vide* group IIIB.) are those which represent, or are coeval with, the age of metallurgy. They may be arranged as follows in point of rank or social respectability, the highest being mentioned last:—

I.	Sangtarash	Stone-cutter.
II.	Kamángar and Tirgar	Bow-maker and painter.
	Barhai	Carpenter.
	Gokai	Wood-carver.
III.	Lohar	Ironsmith.
	Kasera	Brass-moulder.
	Thathera	Brass-engraver.
	Sonar	Goldsmith.
IV.	Manihár	Bracelet-maker.
	Tarkihar	Earing-maker.
V.	Darzi	Tailor.
	Patwa	Braid-maker.
	Chipi	Cloth-stamper.
	Rangrez	Dyer.
VI.	Halwai	Confectioner.

60. The above castes, as was shown above, represent higher stages of art, and consequently stand higher in the social scale than those named in the preceding list. The marks of social superiority possessed by these castes are the following :—(1) Men of the highest Hindu castes or classes can sit down in their company without loss of dignity; (2) no Hindu, not even a Brahman, would refuse to drink water drawn by their hands; (3) they are more punctilious than the castes named in the previous list in the Hindu observances of bathing, praying, &c., at the appointed times and in the appointed methods ; (4) they are allowed the freeest access to the inside of a Hindu temple, whereas the previous castes are either discouraged from entering a temple or absolutely excluded ; (5) they decline to drink water drawn by any caste whose services as a water-carrier would be rejected by a Brahman ; (6) they invariably eat their food on the *chauka* or floor on which it has been cooked, and would reject as impure any cooked food that has been taken outside the chauka. On the other hand they rank decidedly below Brahmans from the fact that they allow the marriage of widows and indulge in the use of spirituous liquors ; and it is needless to add that the functions which they represent, being of a purely material or industrial order, are of much less social dignity than that of Brahman or priest. The average rank of the castes is about equal to that of Tambolis and Malis (see above para. 33), but below that of Tagás and Bhunihárs, since neither of the two last named allow the remarriage of widows.

61. As in most of the preceding lists, the names by which the several castes are called show very clearly the nature of the functions which distinguish them from the rest of the community, and by which they have been called into existence as separate castes or classes. Sangtarash means "stone-trimmer" or "stone-cutter," being derived from two Persian words, *sung* and *tarash*. Kamángar and Tirgar mean respectively "bow-maker" and "arrow-maker," being derived from *kamán* (bow) and *tir* (arrow), both of Persian origin. Barhai (carpenter) is an abridged pronunciation of *bardhai* and is derived from the Sanskrit root *bardh*, which signifies "to bore a hole." Gokain or Gokai (wood-carver or engraver) is derived from the Hindi *khonch*, which means to cut a hole or scoop out. Lohar is derived from *loha*, iron; Kasera from *kánsa*, bell-metal; Thathera from *thathi*, a brass platter ; and Sonar from *savarna* or *sona*, gold, all of Sanskrit origin. Manihar and Turkihar, the names of the ornament-making castes, are derived respectively from *mani*, a gem, and *turki*, an earring, both of Sanskrit origin. Darzi, the name of the tailor caste, is derived from Persian *darz*, sewing, or *darzan*, a needle, the Persian name having superseded the old Hindi name, "suji," which was derived from a Sanskrit root signifying "to sew," Patwa, the fringe-making caste, and Chhipi, the cloth-stamper, come respectively from *pat*, a piece of silk, and *chhapna*, to print, both of Sanskrit origin. Rangrez, the name of the dyer caste, is derived from two Persian words, *rang*, colour, and *rez*, sprinkling. Halwai, the name of the confectioner caste, is derived from *halwa*, a kind of sweetmeat in very common use among the middle and upper classes of the community. Thus every name in this list, without exception, is functional and not tribal.

62. The caste first named in the list is Sangtarash. But I feel much doubt as to whether "caste" is the right term to apply to men of this class. It is certainly the name of an hereditary occupation, that of stone-cutting ; and it is certain that many men, on being questioned what their *jat* or caste is, will answer "Sangtarash." But if they are pressed with further enquiries regarding their origin, &c., it will generally be found that there is some other caste with which they still own connection, and to whose limits they are still restricted in the matters of marriage and convivial intercourse. Until it can be proved that "Sangtarash" represents a certain class of the community which disowns connection with any other caste and can neither intermarry nor eat and drink with any but persons of their own fraternity, it cannot be said that any such caste as Sangtarash exists ; for this is what the word "caste" implies, The men who follow the occupation of stone-cutting are generally Khatiks, Lunias, Ahirs, Gokais, Goshâyens, and Brahmans. If there is a caste of Sangtarash in the true

sense of the word, it will probably be found that it is made up of men who have deserted the ranks of the lower of the castes just named, and have thus established a new caste or trade union of their own. Gosháyens and Brahmans may and do follow the occupation of stone-cutting, but they would never consent to leave their own castes in order to enter a lower one. The Persian etymology of the name *Sangtarash* implies that the caste, if it exists at all, is of modern origin and foreign to the old Hindu system. The caste so called seems to have been continually struggling into existence, but never to have quite come to the birth; and this state of incompleteness has been due partly to the incongruous character of the men who have taken to the calling, but chiefly to the scarcity of stone and the consequent fewness of men to whom such an occupation is open. In Upper India one of the chief centres of the stone-cutter's art is Muttra, but not (I am told) so important a centre as Benares or Mirzapur. The art has been developed chiefly in connection with the making of idols and the ornamentation of temples, and this is why it has been cultivated by Gosháyens and Brahmans. In the Benares and Mirzapur districts it is not uncommon to find the door-posts of private houses made of stone instead of wood, and such door-posts are engraved with figures of Ganesha, the god of luck, of Lakshmi, the goddess of wealth, and of a fish as the incarnation of Vishnu. The men who work the quarries of Mirzapur are generally Ahírs or cowherds, who from grazing their cattle in the same neighbourhood have learnt to cut stone out of the rock and carry it into the towns for sale. Such Ahírs are sometimes called Peshraj—that is, men who bring and prepare stones for the mason.

63. From the workers in stone we come to the workers in wood, and three castes can be included in this category. Of wood-workers generally as of those who work in stone it should be understood that the *germs* of their respective arts are coeval with the savage age and are among the very earliest contrivances of human industry. But it is only when iron tools have come into vogue that either of these arts can acquire that degree of refinement which they have reached in India, and hence it is correct to include them, as has been done in this place, among the arts coeval with the age of metallurgy. The castes which practise them are in point of social status about on the same level as those which practise metallurgy itself.

Kamángar and Tirgar, which literally means the makers of bows and arrows, are sub-classes or offshoots of a single tribe or caste which in early Hindu times was known as Dhánuk, and which manufactured the spears, clubs, bows and arrows used by the hunting and pastoral tribes. The material chiefly used then, as now, for such purposes was the bamboo. Some remains of this Dhánuk or bow-making caste are still to be found in the city of Benares, where they sell bows, &c., as children's toys. In ancient India the bow was esteemed the best and greatest of weapons; and many of the old Kshatriya warriors are described as making their own bows and addressing them by names as if they were animated beings, like the Sikh doing worship to his guns. At the present day, when bows and arrows are no longer used for serious purposes, they are made only for toys; but as the demand for such articles is small, Kamángars have taken to many other kinds of industry. The use of the lathe, in which they specially excel, has put them in the way of turning out much finer work than the old bow or spear of bamboo. With this instrument they make toys and ornaments of all kinds, and they have acquired the additional art of painting them with coloured lacquer. From colouring rounded surfaces, they have learnt to paint flat or uneven ones, such as doors, window-frames, palanquins, &c., and thus it has come to pass that painting, rather than bow-making, is now the speciality of the Kamángar caste. The beautiful painting which is laid on pottery ware is chiefly done by them. The old fowling and hunting tribe of Dhánuk is still numerous in Upper India, but the bow-making portion of this tribe has for the most part abandoned the name of Dhánuk, and assumed that of Kamángar and become Muhammadan. All the Kamángars and Tirgars that I have seen or heard of profess the creed of Islam, and would not allow themselves to be mentioned in the same breath with the despised caste of

Dhánuk. The tradition of their origin has survived, however, firstly, in the name Kamángar or bow-maker, which is now almost a misnomer; secondly, in the fact that Tirgar women are sometimes employed as midwives in Muhammadan households, just as Dhánuk women are employed in Hindu ones; and, thirdly, in the fact that Kamángars are sometimes employed as bone-setters by Muhammadans, as Dhánuks are by the lower castes of Hindus. In reference to this third link it should be explained that Dhánuks and Kamángars are both skilled in straightening bamboo poles which are crooked or in curving the handles to cane walking-sticks. The first process in curving the canes consists in steeping them in boiling oil. Similarly the first process towards setting a bone is by softening the limb with heated oil; and thus the two industries have become amalgamated.

64. The Barhai is the well-known and time-honoured carpenter of the old Hindu township. As such he is a kind of public servant, and no village would be complete which did not contain one or more of such functionaries within its circle. Regularly once a year, in the month of Asárh (which takes in the latter half of June and the first half of July), and on some auspicious day selected by the Brahman or village priest, the agriculturist takes his plough to the carpenter to be repaired for the year's work, and rewards him partly in cash and partly with a gift of sweetmeats. All future repairs, until the next Asárh comes round, are done gratis, except that at the close of each harvest the carpenter receives a stipulated proportion of the produce. He is accustomed, too (like the watchman, the hide-tanner, and the potter described in para. 57), to receive presents of grain at the three great festivals of the Dashara, the Diwáli, and the Holi. His status is about equal in rank to that of the Kurmi or peasant, with whom his own interests are so closely linked. Besides making the plough used by husbandmen, he constructs the wagons, boats, boxes, bedsteads, &c., used by the community at large. There is reason to believe that the caste of carpenter sprang out of the fishing rather than the hunting tribes. The single-logged canoe, which is to be found among the most backward races in various parts of the world, and was known to the ancient Britons prior to the Roman invasion, is still made in India by the Barhai caste; but the first men who made boats of this rough description must have been themselves fishermen.

65. The speciality of the Gokain as distinct from that of the Barhai consists in carving and engraving the materials which the Barhai has furnished. His art, then, is more refined than that of the Barhai, and hence his social status is somewhat higher. There can be little doubt that the Gokain caste has sprung out of the Barhai in the same way as the Barhai himself sprang out of the Kewat or fisherman. The carvings on boats, door-posts, bullock-carts, &c., are the work of this caste. When the demand for such labour is slack, he takes to using the lathe like the Kamángar, and paints with various coloured lacquer the toys and ornaments which he turns out for sale. The Gokain is also noted as a carver and engraver of stone, especially of the ornamental stone pillars used at the doorways of temples and private houses. In this kind of art he is the most skilful of those castes which sometimes allow themselves to be called by the generic title of Sangtarash.

66. From the workers in stone and wood we come to the important series of castes, whose special industry consists in the working of metals, and who are therefore the typical representatives of the metallurgic age. The order in which I will now describe them coincides approximately with that of their rank or status in point of social respectability.

The Lohár or iron smith holds a place in the constitution of the village commune exactly similar to that of the Barhai, and he is remunerated on the same principle. The work of the wood-cutter and ploughman could not be carried on without him, and to the general public he is the maker of all kinds of iron tools, the metal-polisher, edge-sharpener, farrier, knife-maker, &c. It is owing to the ubiquitous industry of the Lohár that the stone-knives, arrow-heads, and hatchets of the indigenous tribes of Upper India (even those of the Dom, Kanjar, &c., who in character and habits are still almost as savage as their ancestors were some six thousand years ago), have been so entirely superseded by iron ones. The memory of the Stone age has not survived even in tradition. In consequence of the evil associations which Hinduism has attached to the colour of black, the caste of Lohár has not been able to raise itself to the same social level as the three metallurgic castes which follow. A piece of iron is not unfrequently kept in Hindu houses, especially in the lying-in chamber, to avert the evil eye.

67. The three castes which follow have no place in the staff of the village community similar to that held by the Lohár and Barhai. But the two brazier castes, the Kasera and Thathera, are held in almost universal request. There are scarcely any articles of furniture which a Hindu prizes so highly as the brass *lota* with which he draws water from the well, the *batuá* or brass bowl in which he cooks his food, the *thálhi* or brass platter on which he eats it, and the *tám* or copper platter on which he places the offerings of ghí, rice, water, &c., intended for the propitiation of his patron deity or deities. It is a mark of the deepest social depression not to be the owner of such articles, and no expression conveys a stronger idea of poverty than to say of a man that "he does not possess even a lota." In times of famine, it is by pawning or selling his lota that a man makes his last attempt to save himself and family from starving. The Kasera's speciality lies in mixing the softer metals (zinc, copper, and tin) and moulding the alloy into various shapes, such as cups, bowls, plates, &c. The Thathera's art consists in polishing and engraving the utensils which the Kasera supplies. His work, then, is more delicate than that of the Kasera, and his status in society is raised accordingly. The Thathera is thus related to the Kasera in the same way as the Gokain is related to the Barhai, the Mochi to the Chamár, the Kori to the Dhuna, or the Dhuna to the Kanjar. The upper artisan castes have been formed out of those standing immediately below them, just as the lower artisan castes have sprung out of the savage tribes.

68. The Sonár's work lies in gold and silver. He stands a little higher than those castes who manipulate the inferior metals, because his art, being more delicate and costly than theirs, brings him more into contact with the higher and wealthier classes of the community. It is not every Sonár who can set up business with his own capital: hence it is very common for men of the Khattri or banking caste to take a staff of Sonárs into their employment and set up a jeweller's shop. Owing to the dishonesty of a few of its members, the Sonár caste has in some places acquired rather a bad reputation for receiving stolen jewellery and throwing it into the crucible, so as to render recognition impossible. It is said, too, that there is a secret language in which this kind of traffic is carried on between themselves and their accomplices. This is probably one of the offences alluded to in Manu's Criminal Code in the following words :—"The most pernicious of all deceivers is a gold-smith who commits frauds; the king shall order him to be cut piecemeal with razors" (IX, 292). In contrast with the evil significance attaching to the black metal, iron, the brightest associations have been fastened by Hindus upon the shining metals, gold and silver: and this fact has tended to raise the Sonár caste in proportion, notwithstanding their suspected dishonesty. It was the belief of ancient Hindus that gold and silver, the most perfect of metals, arose out of the combination of fire with water, the purest of elements (Manu, V, 113).

69. The two castes now to be named (Manihár and Turkihár) are those whose speciality lies in making and moulding glass—a product which could only have come into vogue after the rise of the art of metallurgy; for both processes involve the use of the same element—fire—for melting, mixing, and transmuting the materials furnished by nature. The two glass-making castes stand on about the same social level as the Sonár. One industry—the making of mirrors—is common to both. Glass windows appear to have been unknown in India until Europeans introduced them. But from allusions occurring in the early literature, it is certain

that the ancient Hindus were acquainted both with looking-glasses and with the glass lens by which fire is drawn from the sunbeams. At the present day both castes exist almost entirely for the convenience of women.

The Manihár is not a member of the staff of which the old Hindu township is composed to the same extent as the ironsmith or the carpenter. But if some villages here and there happen to have no Manihár living in their midst, there is certain to be one or more in some other village within easy reach. His special industry is the making of glass-bracelets or bangles. The domestic life of a Hindu woman would be almost impossible without this: for the glass bangle is not worn for personal ornament, but as the badge of the matrimonial state, like the wedding-ring worn by women in Europe. The girl puts on her glass bangle for the first time when she starts on her *barát*, the marriage procession which leads her away to the bridegroom's house. After child-birth the mother, on leaving the room in which she has been lying, breaks her bracelet and is immediately provided with a new one by the wife of the Manihár, who receives cash in exchange for the bracelet and a gift of sweetmeats or grain for the ceremony of putting it on. When the husband dies, the widow must, at the moment of his death, break the bracelet off her wrist in token of widowhood, and till the day of her death she must never wear another, unless she marries again. These observances and prohibitions are binding on all classes of Hindus, even the very lowest; and hence it is no wonder that the Manihár commands general respect and is very widely scattered among the community. The word current amongst Hindus for bracelet in general is *churi;* but such is the value attached to the glass bangle worn as the badge of matrimony that the caste by whom it is made has received the metaphorical title of "Manihár," which means literally "a maker of gems or jewels." Jewellery in our sense of the word is made only by Sonárs. Any articles other than the glass bangle may be taken off or put on at pleasure and are intended for ornament only, but the glass bangle must be worn day and night, so long as the husband is alive.

The Turkihár caste makes the glass beads with which earrings and necklaces are studded. The ground-work of these ornaments is generally a piece of palm-leaf variously shaped and coloured. The earring worn by Hindu women is not a curved ornament attached to the ear by a hook, but a straight one, the thinner end of which is inserted into the lobe of the ear, while the thicker end studded with beads of glass is made to stand out. It is not considered fit for a widow to wear such ornaments, but the rule is much less strictly observed than that connected with the glass bangle.

70. The four next castes are those whose special industry lies in the making of wearing apparel. The Darzi or tailor makes clothes of silk as well as cotton fabrics, and works chiefly for men. The Patwa or fringe-maker uses the same materials, but works chiefly for women. The Chhipi or stamper is employed on cotton stuffs only; the Rangrez or dyer on cotton, silk, and woollen stuffs alike. It is easy to see that these four castes belong to the more advanced stages of arts, and that such castes could never have come into existence, if they had not been preceded by certain lower castes, whose industries were preparatory to theirs. Thus the weaver and the thread-twister (Kori and Dhuna), whom we have already described, paved the way for the tailor, dyer, &c., and the weaver himself learnt the rudiments of his art from the savage who gathered reeds and osiers from the forest and plaited them into baskets and snares. It is certainly a fact that the rank which these several castes hold in the Hindu social scale coincides with the rank of the arts corresponding; and as the same coincidence has been shown to exist in the groups previously named, it must be the result of a general law and not of chance. The substitution of Persian names for the old Hindi names of tailor and dyer indicate, what is the fact, that these industries have been largely patronized by Muhammadans, and that many members of the castes have embraced the creed of Islam. Silk fabrics, till lately, were not made in India, but imported *viá* Cabul. Woollen stuffs were, and are still, manufac-

tured by the Gadaria or shepherd caste. The cotton fibre, as we have shown already, grows wild on the simal tree, is twisted into thread by the Dhuna, and woven into cloth by the Kori.

71. The last caste of artisan to be named in this list is the Halwai, whose special craft lies in making sweetmeats, and who is therefore sometimes called Mithiya. The materials used in Hindu confectionery are milk, butter, flour, and sugar. It is obvious, then, that the art of the Halwai presupposes the industry both of the milkman and of the agriculturist. In other respects, too, his art implies rather an advanced stage of culture, and hence his rank in the social scale is a high one. There is no caste in India which considers itself too pure to eat what a confectioner has made. In marriage banquets it is he who supplies a large part of the feast, and at all times and seasons the sweetmeat is a favourite viand to a Hindu requiring a temporary refreshment. There is a kind of bread called *puri*, which contains no sugary element; but yet it is specially prepared by men of the sweetmeat caste. It consists of wheaten dough fried in melted butter, and is taken as a substitute for the *chapati* or wheaten pancake by travellers and others who happen to be unable to have their bread cooked at their own fire. With the exception of Brahmans, there is no class of men in India which declines to eat a buttered pancake prepared by the Halwai; and considering the immense amount of fuss (involving even forfeiture of caste) which is attached to the domestic fire-place, this says much for the respect in which the Halwai is held. As in the case of the Bari, the caste which makes leaf-plates for all classes of the community, considerations of general convenience have no doubt contributed something to the social respectability of the confectioner caste. The Halwai is a strict Hindu, but he has not gone so far in the direction of Brahmanism as to disallow the re-marriage of widows within members of his fraternity.

72. The names given in the census report do not differ much from those collected and arranged in my own table (group IIIB.) The differences are as follows :—

(*a*) Kamángar and Tirgar, which are shown as separate castes in the census report, and against which 1,365 and 309 persons have been recorded, are rather different names of a single caste. I have therefore included them both under the name of Kamángar.

(*b*) In the census report *Nalband* or farrier, *Barhia* or edge-sharpener, *Saikalgar* or metal-polisher, and *Lon* or point-maker, are given as separate castes; and the number of persons recorded against them is 3,230, 410, 845, and 209 respectively. These, however, are not separate castes, but only different occupations within the same caste of Lohár or ironsmith; I have therefore included them all among Lohárs. There is a tendency in these specialities to become hereditary; but the men who practise them have not, so far as I can learn, detached themselves from the parent stem, so as to render inter-marriage or the right of eating together impossible.

(*c*) Niyaria, or washer of gold-dust, against which name 1,276 persons have been recorded in the census report, is scarcely a separate caste, but rather a sub-class of Sonár or gold-smith. In this caste, therefore, I have included them.

73. This brings us to the end of the wealth-producing castes. They consist, as we have shown, of two great series or groups; the first of which comprises all those castes whose function it is to call forth and utilize the productive energies of land and water, and who are sub-divided into hunting, fishing, pastoral, agricultural, and landlord; while the second comprises those castes who practise the various arts or handicrafts, without which the industries of man on land or water could not be carried on, and these, as we have shown, are sub-divided into upper and lower, according as they do or do not precede the metallurgic age. All of these castes are producers of wealth, with the exception of the Chattri or landlord, who merely protects it; and he, too, is now becoming a producer, because he is learning to handle the plough. Before leaving the subject of these castes a few words must be said in this place in reference to the modern and widely accepted theory which divides the population of India into two

great racial sections known as Aryan and non-Ayran. To take the landed industries first. There is no reason to doubt that the indigenous tribes of India, before the Aryan invader had arrived, were versed in the arts of hunting and fishing and the rearing and grazing of cattle, and that they knew how to raise, on the alluvial banks of their rivers, crops of rice, juar, bajra, and any other grains that are indigenous to the soil. It is very probable, too, that the fishing tribes know how to raise crops of the singhára or waternut in the swamps and marshes in which their country abounds. The indigenous tribes, then, had come well within the nomad state, but were acquainted with agriculture only in its most rudimentary form. What the Aryan tribes did, then, was to introduce more regular habits of industry, better kinds of tools, better methods of agriculture, and the grains of the temperate zone, such as wheat, barley, oats, gram, none of which are indigenous to the Indian soil, and which will only grow during the Indian winter, and thus gradually to establish the agricultural state proper, with all the settled industries that accompany it, in substitution for the wild and migratory life of the aboriginal hunter or nomad. Again, to take the case of the various arts or handicrafts. There is no reason to doubt that the lower kinds of art, such as basket-making, thread-twisting, weaving, oil-pressing, pottery, salt-making, the brewing of spirituous liquors, &c., were known to the indigenous tribes of India before the Aryan stranger had appeared ; for the like have been found to exist among modern savages, and the manners and notions of the Indian castes which practise these crafts are much on the same level as those of the backward races in other parts of the world. What the Aryans did, then, was to introduce the art of metallurgy, and with this the higher kinds of art, including that of agriculture itself, which invariably come with it or follow it. Now if we are to suppose that the Indian castes are distinguishable into Aryan and non-Aryan, the most rational application of such a theory would be to place the agricultural castes and the metal-working castes on the Aryan side, and all the castes which preceded these on the non-Aryan. But the theory has been made to run in a groove far less consistent with the fact. It accepts as true the old fourfold division of castes into Brahman, Kshatriya, Vaisya, and Sudra, and says that the first three are of Aryan blood, while it degrades the fourth, in which all the agricultural and metal-working castes are included, to the rank of non-Aryan. The only escape from these contradictions is to put the Aryan out of account altogether ; that is, to recognize once for all that whatever improvements or changes in industry, language, and religion he may have introduced some four thousand years ago into the land of his adoption, his blood has become absorbed into that of the indigenous population, and that he no longer exists in India as a distinct racial unit, much less as a basis for the explanation or classification of caste.

74. *Trading castes.*—The remaining castes, that is, those which are not connected with any industry either by land or water and are not engaged in any kind of art or handicraft, and which are, therefore, distributors and consumers, but not producers, of wealth, may be classified under three main headings as (1) trading, (2) serving or professional, (3) priestly. These three together make up only about one quarter of the entire population of the province ; and this is quite as large a proportion as could be expected in a country like India, which has not advanced from the agricultural stage into the scientific and commercial, and whose chief wealth has always consisted in the produce of the soil.

75. The trading castes are enumerated in the tabular statement annexed (group IV). A considerable number of the castes included in previous lists are engaged in trade, but not in trade only ; for they are themselves the producers of the commodities in which they trade. Thus among the castes allied to the hunting state, there are many who practise the trade of butcher, poulterer, egg-seller, game-catcher, &c., besides hunting and trapping on their own account. Among the castes allied to the fishing state there are many who catch fish and make nets for sale, &c., besides fishing for their own personal wants. Among the pastoral castes many, in fact all, trade in milk, butter, wool, &c. Similarly the agricultural castes retain for their own use

only a small portion of what they produce, and dispose of the rest to men of the Baniya or shop-keeping classes: and there are some agriculturists, like the Kándu and the Tamboli for example, who keep shops themselves for the sale of the goods raised by their own labour. The same remark applies to all the artisan castes, from the lowest basket-maker up to the jeweller, tailor, or confectioner; for many of these men keep regular shops, or can do so if they choose. What we mean, then, by the trading castes, as distinct from those already enumerated and described, is that their special function consists in the distribution and exchange of wealth and has nothing to do with its production. If some of them have lately commenced to work in the fields (and what caste in India has not done so?), this does not affect the question of their original status as members of the Hindu community.

76. Among the trading castes proper there is a gradation of rank from low to high—not so clearly marked as among the landed and the artisan castes, but not less certainly the result of natural laws. These gradations depend partly on the social status of the classes with whom they are chiefly brought into contact, partly upon the degree of importance or dignity attaching to the commodities in which they trade, and partly on the amount of capital or wealth necessary to the practice of the trade itself. The very same conditions, as the reader will have observed, have determined the rank or social status of the several trading and commercial classes in our own country. The business of a green-grocer, for example, is about as low in England as it is in India, while that of banker is quite as high. There is no mystery in either case, and the three conditions which have been assigned as determining their rank apply equally to both.

77. The trading castes may be arranged as follows in the order of social respectability :—

I.	Banjara	Forest-trader.
II.	Kunjra	Green-grocer.
III.	Bhunja	Grain-parcher.
IV.	Raunia	Pedlars and small retail dealers who seldom keep regular shops.
	Kuta	
	Bilwar	
	Bhurtia	
	Lohia	
V.	Kasondhan	Traders who keep regular shops and deal in larger quantities of grain, spices, perfumes, cloth, &c., &c.
	Kasarbani	
	Vishnoi	
	Rastogi	
	Unaya	
	Orh	
	Maheshwari	
VI.	Dhusar	Bankers, money-lenders, wholesale dealers, &c.
	Agrahari	
	Agarwála	
	Bohra	
	Khatri	

All of the above castes, excepting the three first named (Banjara, Kunjra, and Bhunja, who stand lower in the social scale than the rest) are known by the generic name of Baniya, which means shop-keeper or merchant. The last five, who as a rule stand higher than the rest and trade in money rather than in commodities, are not uncommonly known by the more dignified title of Mahájan or banker. All but the first three wear the *janeo* or sacred thread and disallow the remarriage of widows.

78. The above list, however, does not profess to be exhaustive. It gives only the main castes belonging to the general head of trader. There are many minor ones, whose names and characteristics it is difficult to discover, and I know of no branch of the subject of Indian castes which presents so many and such petty complications as that connected with trade. This has arisen from more causes than one. In the first place (with the exception of the green-grocer and the grain-parcher), there is no speciality in the kind of trade which any one caste is accustomed to practise, to the

exclusion of other kinds. In this respect the trading castes of India differ essentially from those which, under the name of trade-guilds, grew up in the great commercial centres in Europe during the middle ages. Any trading caste in this country may deal in any kind of commodity that it prefers, and hence within the same caste every variety of trade will be found to exist. Thus the element of speciality which in the case of all the Indian castes previously named has been the mainspring of their existence, and which in England gave rise to the system of guilds or commercial castes known as grocer, draper, fishmonger, silk-mercer, goldsmith, &c., is here entirely wanting. In the second place, no restriction has ever been imposed by the laws or customs of the Hindus through which a man belonging to any of the landed or artisan castes could be debarred from setting up as a trader, if it pleased him. The business of trader has always been open to all comers alike; and no charters were ever issued conferring certain monopolies of trade upon certain families or clans, as was formerly the case in Europe. Consequently there has been a continual influx of families from the various industrial castes, who have detached themselves from the ancestral caste and calling, but have not coalesced with each other, so as to form a compact trade-union of their own, united by the bond of common sentiments and traditions. Thus the Bhunja is an offshoot from the fisherman caste, the Lohia from the iron-smith, the Kasondhan from the brazier, the Pathel from the agriculturist (Kurmi), the Unaya from the writer (Kayasth), the Bohra from the Brahman, the Khattri from the warrior. But these offshoots have neither amalgamated with each other nor made common cause with trading castes already existing. The caste prejudice which they brought with them has survived the separation from the parent stem, and jealousy, rather than a desire for union, has been the feeling uppermost in their minds. Thirdly, trade is not a pursuit in which hereditary skill is necessary to success, whereas in the various arts and handicrafts described under the heading of artisan, and in many of the functions connected with hunting, fishing, cattle-grazing, and agriculture, a man has little chance of becoming a proficient, unless he commences to acquire from early boyhood, and under his father's tuition and guidance, that degree of manual dexterity and quickness which can seldom or never be acquired by an adult beginner. The consequence has been that while in the case of artisans, &c., there is a system of clearly-defined castes, each distinguished from the other by some hereditary peculiarity of craft, in the case of traders almost every distinction of caste that can be said to exist is a distinction without a difference.

79. Notwithstanding all this, the majority of the trading castes have adopted names which designate in some form or other the trading function; and thus the general law announced throughout this paper, that function, and not blood or creed, is the basis on which Indian castes have been formed, receives in the present case a stronger exemplification than in the case of castes previously described. Banjara, the name of the forest trader, is derived from *banij*, "merchant;" or it might be a variant of *banchára*, "one whose way is in the forest": and this is the best description of the function peculiar to this caste. Kunjra, the green-grocer, is from *kunj*, a fruit-garden or vegetable garden. Bhunja, the grain-parcher, is from the root *bhun*, to roast or parch. Raunia, more fully written "Ravaniya," is from *ravan*, which means "the crying or hawking of wares for sale." Kuta, the seller of husked rice, is from *kutna*, to beat out. Bilwar is probably a contraction of *bela-war*, being derived from *bela*, a money-bag. Bhurtia, the retail dealer and petty usurer, is from *bharti-karna*, the lending of small sums for short periods. Lohia is derived from *loha*, iron, for which men of this caste barter grain and other wares. Kasondhan or Kasarbani (names of now distinct but once identical castes) are derived respectively from *kansa*, bell-metal, and *dhan*, wealth, or *bani*, seller. Orh or Rora is probably from *ol*, "one who stands security for a loan." Agrahari and Agarwála are probably from *agari* or *agar*, a kind of fragrant wood which is sold as a perfume. Bohra is a contraction of *beohara*, "one engaged in *beohar* or business." Khattri is a variant, or (to speak more correctly), the modern Hindi pronunciation, of Kshatriya, an offshoot

of the warrior caste which took to the pursuit of money-making in preference to that of fighting. Among the remaining names two have a religious sense—Vishnoi and Maheshwari. The remaining names are perhaps derived from places.

80. The Banjara is the least civilized of the trading castes, and I have therefore placed him at the bottom of the list. As a trader he stands in the same relation to other trading castes that the hunter does to the other landed castes. His speciality consists in conveying merchandize on the backs of bullocks through trackless forest paths where any other class of trader would be lost. To this industry he has added two more—the pursuit of cattle-grazing, which connects him with the nomad or pastoral state, and the pursuit of robbery and rapine, which connects him with the hunting or savage state. The tribe professes to be descended from an illustrious marauder whom they call Mithu Bukhia. But what has really kept them together and made them look like a separate aboriginal tribe is not community of origin, but unity of function and character; for it is well known that any man (or woman), of whatever tribe or caste, can become a Banjara and take his place among their ranks, provided he is willing to comply with the conditions of admission. Banjaras do not come within the regular line of Hindu castes; for they have a caste or clan system of their own, based upon the mythical fourfold division into Brahman, Kshatriya, Vaisya, and Sudra. They are chiefly to be found in the Tarái or sub-Himálayan districts of Hindustan and in the forests of Central India. It is not at all likely that their clan system will last much longer; for as a predatory or criminal class they are being rapidly put down under British rule, and as a commercial and carrying class their usefulness is slowly, but surely, coming to an end through the extension of railways and the opening out of roads in what remains of the primeval forest. The probability is that the tribe will before long bifurcate, one section devoting itself to the business of milkman aud cattle-grazer, like the Gaddi or Gujar, and the other to that of pedlar or shop-keeper, like the Raunia, &c. The cattle-grazing portion of the tribe will no doubt take to agriculture in course of time, as a great number of Ahírs and Játs have already done. Already, in fact, there is a class of Banjaras called Nayik who have settled down to agriculture in the Benares and Allahabad districts and are rapidly losing the manners and traditions of the tribe. Such is the process by which agricultural communities are developed from cattle-grazers, and cattle-grazers from wandering savages and marauders. Such has been the method of caste-formation in the plains of India.

81. The Kunjra or green-grocer has passed beyond the wandering and predatory stage peculiar to the Banjara, though his status is still very low. He goes from door to door selling fruit and vegetables, which he carries on his head in a basket; for he rarely keeps a shop. He raises no crops himself, but retails produce raised by men of the gardening and fruit-growing castes; and not unfrequently he buys a crop on the ground before it is ripe, running the risk of loss should the crop turn out a bad one. The money required for such purchases is almost invariably borrowed from some petty local usurer, and in consequence of the risk incurred a very high rate of interest is exacted. Another way in which a Kunjra attempts to eke out a livelihood is by gathering for sale and for his own consumption the wild fruits of the earth, such as the plum, the fig, the mango, the custard-apple, and many more. This indicates, what is the fact, that he is not far removed above the status of those wandering and semi-savage tribes whose natural home is the forest and to whom he is closely related in blood. The caste is now almost exclusively Muhammadan, but, as the name which it still bears implies, it was originally Hindu. This Hindu original was made up of families or clans taken from low tribes, such as Pasis, Arakhs, Khatiks, &c. (*vide* group II.A), who still live partly by the collection of wild fruits and vegetables and still adopt occasionally the trade of green-grocer, but without detaching themselves from the tribes or castes to which they belong. Men of the Kanjar tribe, which ranks much lower even than Pasis, &c., adopt the trade of green-grocer whenever they become Muhammadan and assume the title of Mewafarosh, the Persian name for fruit-seller.

The name Mewafarosh is sometimes used as a synonym for Kunjra. It is not difficult, then, to see from what class of men the green-grocer caste has sprung, and from which it is being even now recruited. The trade is considered so low that no Hindu or Muhammadan of any respectable caste will enter it.

82. The caste of Bhunja or grain-parcher is much more respectable, though still low as compared with the castes that follow. The Bhunja stands on about the same level as the Kahár or waterman, of whom he is a near offshoot. Kahárs still gather the wild rice which grows on the banks of swamps and rivers, and in my account of the agricultural caste called Kándu I gave reasons for supposing that the first rice-growers in India were men of the fishing or watermen tribes. This supposition is confirmed by the fact that the Bhunja, the Kándu, and the Kahár have many traditions in common, and that the three castes are sometimes confounded, because the Kándu and the Kahár sometimes engage in the same trade as that of the Bhunja. There are two forms in which parched grain is sold—one in the whole state, and the other in the form of a powder or flour called *sattu*, which consists of parched gram mixed with parched rice or parched barley. The Bhunja never mixes this flour with water, but invariably sells it in a dry state. The buyer or consumer must add water drawn by his own *lota* or brass pitcher, and even then the rules of Indian caste do not allow him to eat it anywhere but on a *chauka* or prepared cooking-floor. The art of the Bhunja as compared with that of the Halwai or confectioner is so extremely simple that I have classed the former as a trader rather than an artisan. For there is some art and some trade in almost every form of industry, and castes must be classified according to that element which predominates.

83. The five castes named immediately below the Bhunja in para. 77 are for the most part pedlars or small retail dealers, who as a rule do not keep regular shops. Their status, therefore, ranks generally below that of the castes which follow. But there is nothing to prevent them from rising to the position of the highest merchant or banker, if their business is sufficiently prosperous.

The Raunia (which means literally a crier) moves in a circle of some eight or ten villages surrounding his own; and if he cannot get cash for his grain, he barters it for spices, tobacco, sugar, condensed treacle, &c. In these days he is seldom able to live by trade alone, and in the intervals of business he raises his own crops. But trade, and trade only, was his original function.

The Kuta or Kutámali is one who unhusks rice and takes it about for sale in baskets or on the backs of bullocks. He also cultivates at times, like the Raunia and for the same reason.

The Bilwar is one who acts as the weigher of any kind of market produce that is not sold by measure, and this has led to his becoming himself a salesman. He frequently takes work as a *dallál* or broker; and if the buyer and seller cannot come to terms, he mediates between them and sometimes advances the rupee or pice which seals the bargain.

The Bhartiya is a pedlar who deals chiefly in spices and grain and lends small sums on usury.

The Lohiya is chiefly known as one who barters tobacco, salt, parched grain, or uncooked grain for discarded iron, discarded clothes, old cotton, waste paper, discarded books, &c. The articles thus taken in exchange are retailed for cash to any who can make use of them.

84. There is nothing particular to add respecting the seven castes whose names stand next in the list given in para. 77. Some of them are petty dealers like the preceding; others are men of wealth like the castes which follow; but the majority are men of moderate means, who keep regular shops for the sale of cloth, silk, spices, scents, pickles, salt, sugar, grain of all kinds, &c. As was stated above, any man of whatever caste may deal in any kind of commodity that he prefers. It is true that many of the specific kinds of trade have received specific names, but these names

must not be taken to signify that there are castes corresponding to them. Thus a spice-seller is called Pasari ; a perfume-seller, Gandhi ; a druggist or medicine-seller, Attar ; a cloth-seller, Bazaz ; a seller of groceries, such as salt, sugar, ghi, flour, is called Parchun ; a seller of stationery and other small wares, such as needles, pins, knives, reels of cotton, &c., is called Bisati. If each of these specialities had given rise to a corresponding caste, the subject of the trading castes would have been much simpler than we find it, and this would have been more in keeping with the principle on which Indian castes have been generally founded. The mistake has not unfrequently been made of supposing that the names of specific trades represent corresponding castes. For instance, in the census report now under review "Gandhi" or "perfume-seller" has been entered among the list of castes ; and the same mistake was made by the late Mr. Sherring, who counted not only Gandhi, but Bisati as separate castes in his chapter on traders (see Vol. 1, *Tribes and Castes*, page 302). In point of fact, any member of the twenty castes named in para. 77 except the three first may set up a scent shop and thus become a Gandhi if he pleases ; and not only he, but Brahmans and men of many other castes may do the same. There are two castes, *viz.*, Kasondhan and Kasarbani, whose original speciality (if we are to trust the etymology of the names) was the sale of brass utensils not made by themselves. This speciality still clings to them to some extent, but it has not prevented them from dealing in any other commodities that they please ; and there are many members of these castes in whose shops nothing in the shape of a brass vessel would ever be found.

85. The five castes named last in this list are, generally speaking, the wealthiest, and hence in social status they generally rank the highest. It is from these castes that most of the native bankers are drawn ; and in all civilized countries capitalists and financiers are among the most influential members of the community. Comte, in the picture of an ideal state which he drew in his *Positive Politique*, placed bankers at the head of what he called the secular power, on account of the widespread influence which such men exercise in the direction of industry. Certainly in India the Khattri ranks almost as high as the highest Brahman and considerably higher than many who have assumed the Brahmanical title.

86. The Agrahari and Agarwála must have been originally one—sections of one and the same caste, which quarrelled on some trifling qesstion connected with cooking or eating and have remained separate ever since. I have derived the name from *agar* or *agari*, a kind of scent. But the etymology usually given is either "Agra," the city, or "Agroha," a small town on the borders of Hariana. Another etymology is that they are sprung from an ancestor called Agar Sen. The Agarwála is as a rule a wealthy and prosperous caste. Many are bankers and usurers. Some keep large grain shops, others deal largely in gold and silver jewellery and keep Sonárs in their employment for this purpose.

87. The Bohra seldom keeps a shop, and is almost universally known as an usurer, in which character he is celebrated for his unscrupulous and relentless rapacity. He is by origin a Brahman. But as usury is demed to be irreconcileable with priestly pretensions, he has been forced to detach himself from the parent stem, and to found a new caste. It is said that to prove his Brahmanical descent and yet to show his contempt for the caste which he has forsaken, he associates with Mahá-Brahmans or funeral priests—a class of men whom all other Hindus avoid as unclean. It is said, too, that in the eastern presidency some Bohras have become Muhammadan.

88. The Khattri is the highest and most important of all the trading castes in India. The name is merely the modern pronunciation of the ancient "Kshatriya," and hence the origin of the caste should not be "an ethnological puzzle," as it is termed by the late Mr. Sherring. Every tradition connects them with the great warrior and ruling caste ; and as men of the ruling caste must necessarily be in the way of accumulating more wealth than their subjects, it is not surprising that certain

families should have abandoned the military life and formed a fresh caste of their own devoted exclusively to commercial pursuits. Khattris are much more strict in the observance of Hindu rites than their warlike and land-holding cousins, the Chattris. In this respect they are superior to many men who profess to be Brahmans. A Brahman of the Saraswat tribe will eat food cooked by a Khattri, but not by a Chattri; and there are hordes of Brahmans with whom a Khattri would disdain to associate. Khattris commence the study of the Vedas or other religious books at the orthodox age of eight, whereas many Chattris and Brahmans never commence at all. In the Panjab the priests or *gurus* of the Sikhs (if the Sikhs can be said to have any priesthood at all) are chiefly Khattris. The Khattri is almost the only Indian trader who is known outside his own country. The greater part of the trade of Afghanistan is in his hands, and he was seen by Vambery in Central Asia, throwing offerings on the eternal flame, which burns, self-kindled and self-fed, at Baku.

89. There are two more circumstances connected with the trading castes which deserve a passing notice. One is that they are the only section in the whole of the Indian community in which Jainism, once the rival creed to Hinduism, has held its ground. In every other caste or system of castes Jainism has entirely perished, and yet historians are agreed that most of the men who were converted to Buddhism or Jainism in its early days were from the lower castes or from tribes who had no caste. I can only ascribe this phenomenon to the fact that the sedentary life of the banker and merchant gives more leisure for the study of religion, this being almost the only subject to which the leisured classes in India have paid any serious attention. Hence while the industrial and less reflective classes were entirely won back to Brahmanism several centuries ago, the commercial and studious classes are to this day disputing among themselves the claims of the rival creeds, as their ancestors were doing some two thousand years before them.

90. The other circumstance to be noticed is that some of the highest of these commercial castes, especially the Khattri, the Agarwál, and the Dhusar, and the Jain caste of Oswal, have a much stronger dash of Aryan blood than any other castes in Upper India. If there is any marked exception to the theory announced in para. 10 of "the unity of the Indian race," it is to be found in these castes. The Khattri pilgrim whom Vambery met at Baku is called by him "the yellow-faced Hindu." Vambery would certainly not have used such an expression of the average Brahman or the average Chattri, and yet these are the two castes which have been described by most writers as pre-eminently Aryan, which shows on what very loose grounds the Aryan theory has been held. At the Sanskrit school in Ayodhya, which is attended exclusively by Brahmans, there are representatives of this caste from many different parts of India—Lucknow, Gonda, Kheri, Unao, Agra, Allahabad, Mirzapur, Chupra, Tirhoot, Darbhanga, Muzaffarpur, Gorakhpur, Patna, Mainpuri, Thaneswar, Malwa, Guzerat, Orissa, Gaya, and Travancore: and yet almost every face is as dark as that of the average Hindu, to whatever caste he may belong, nor is there anything at all refined or Aryan-looking in the features. On the other hand there is a "Khattri Patshala" in Lucknow which is attended almost exclusively by boys of the banker castes—Khattris, Agarwáls, Oswals, &c.—and here almost every face is comparatively fair, while the features are as refined as those of the Parsi or Cashmiri, both of whom are undoubtedly descended, with little or no admixture of foreign blood, from the ancient Aryan. It seems, then, that the moneyed and commercial castes of the present day are descended from old Kshatriya families, who were much less ready to admit outsiders within their ranks than the priestly and warrior clans, who thrive by expansion rather than by exclusiveness. An aristocratic moneyed class possessing no political power like the Chattri and no priestly power like the Brahman, and having nothing but personal wealth to rely upon for the maintenance of their social dignity and importance, would be more than usually careful to preserve the purity of their blood. But whatever the correct explanation may be, I do not consider that the exceptionally fair complexion of a few of the trading castes clashes with the general hypothesis on which the present theory of caste has been based, *viz.*, the unity of the

Indian race. As I stated in para. 10, traces of an admixture of alien blood must be expected in isolated cases, just as the blue eye of the fair-skinned Lombard peeps out at times among the swarthy inhabitants of Italy. Individual instances of Aryan atavism are not uncommon even among the lowest of Indian castes, such as the Chamár or the Bhangi, who for thousands of generations past have been exposed to the scorching effects of a tropical sun; nor is the dark skin, though comparatively rare, a thing unknown in the Khattri caste, which has for an equally long period lived under the shelter of strongly-roofed houses. The main contention urged in this paper remains unshaken, that the Indian race is practically one in blood, character, traditions, and sympathies, and that caste is not a question of blood, but of function.

91. It remains to show how far the names given in my own table (group IV) differ from those which were entered in the census list of castes :—

(*a*) Kuta and Kotamali, against which 207 and 3,232 persons have been recorded, are, I have reason to believe, different names of one and the same caste; I have therefore combined the figures under the name of Kuta.

(*b*) Ronia, Ramaiya, and Rawa, against which 38,105, 3,369, and 33 persons have been recorded, are, I believe, one and the same caste, and I have included them all together under the name of Raunia. The root of these names is *ravan*, which means "using the voice." Hence *ravaniya* means a trader who cries his wares; and in a previous census this caste was actually entered under the name "Ravaniya." By substituting *u* for *v* the name becomes Ronia or Raunia; by another slight change it becomes Ramaiya; and by a contraction of the last syllable it becomes Rawá. It is impossible in any case that there can be a caste of only 33 persons.

(*c*) Gandhi, against which 66 persons have been recorded, is not a caste, as I have explained already in para. 84.

(*d*) Rehti, against which only 289 persons have been recorded, cannot be a separate caste, and I learn that it is a sub-class of Khattris, amongst whom I have therefore included them.

(*e*) Baniya has 1,204,130 persons recorded against it. But Baniya is no more a caste than Chirimar or fowler, Karigar or skilled workman, Kishan or ploughman, &c. It is simply a generic name signifying "trader" and is applied to any man, of any caste whatever, who is engaged in trade, even to a Brahman or a Chattri.

(*f*) No mention has been made in the census of the castes of Vishnoi, Rastogi, Unaya, Maheshwari, Dhusar, Agrahari, Agarwál. All of these appear to have been thrown in under the casteless name of Baniya.

(*g*) Kolapuri is, I learn, the same as Kasarwani. The name is evidently derived from the town of Kolapur.

92. *The serving castes.*—We now come to the series of castes to which I have given the name of serving and which are enumerated in group V. Their speciality consists in ministering to the wants of men, bodily and mental; and their rank in social scale depends upon the nature of the service rendered. From the list given below—in which, as in previous lists, the names of castes are mentioned in the order of dignity, beginning with the lowest—it will be seen that the ranks of these castes coincide very closely with those of the corresponding classes in our own country, so far as such classes can be said to exist :—

I.—Bhangi ...	Scavenger.
II.—Dhobi ...	Washerman.
III.—Kahár ...	Water-carrier and house servant.
IV.—Napit or Nai	Barber and surgeon.
V.—Páwariya, Dhári, Dom Mirási, and Kathak	Singer and musician.
VI.—Bhát ...	Bard and genealogist.
VII.—Káyasth	Estate manager and writer.

The broad line of distinction among these castes turns upon the question whether they are literate or illiterate. Roughly speaking, the first four are illiterate and minister to the bodily wants of men; the three last are literate and minister to their mental wants.

93. Each of the above castes represents a clearly-defined social unit, and the names by which they are designated are descriptive of the functions which have called them into existence. Bhangi, the name of the scavenger or sweeper caste, is derived from *bhang*, in allusion to the impurity caused by the sweeper's touch or presence : Khakrob, the Persian name of this caste, signifies "dirt-brusher." Dhobi, the washerman, is from *dhona*, to wash or make clean. Kahár, the water-carrier, is from two words, *ka* or *kam*, water, and *hár*, carrier : hence another, but less common, name for the caste is Kamhár. Napit, the barber, is an abridgement from *snápita*, which signifies "one who causes you to take a bath," in allusion to the invariable custom which compels a Hindu to bathe immediately after the barber has been plying his art. Páwaria, the musician and singer, is derived from *pánwará*, the cloth or carpeting on which men of this caste sing and play. Dhari, the name of a similar caste, is derived from *dhárná*, to raise the voice to a high pitch. Kathak, the name of another musician caste, is derived from *kath*, to use the voice, or *kathá*, a dramatic story. Bhát, the bard and genealogist, is from *bhatta*, a learned man, a man of research. Kayasth, the writer caste, means literally a personal attendant—that is, one who acts as private secretary, amanuensis, or confidential accountant to his employer. This caste has acquired a preferential claim to the exercise of certain other literary functions which are not altogether implied in its name.

94. The lowest of all the serving castes is the Bhangi or sweeper. He is a near offshoot from the savage Dom or Chandál, whom in group I. I have placed among the casteless tribes, and whom Manu fitly described, some two thousand years ago, in the following words :—"Their abode must be out of the town ; they must not have the use of entire vessels ; their sole wealth must be dogs and asses ; * * * * continually must they roam from place to place" (Chapter X., verse 52). To this day the Bhangi, faithful to the traditions of his origin, takes charge of his master's dogs, and like them eats what he can get from the leavings of his master's table. The function which has specially called him into existence as an Indian caste, and detached him as such from the ancestral tribe, is that of sweeping houses and streets and removing everything that is dirty or unclean. He is himself, therefore, the type of all uncleanness ; and to persons of the higher castes his touch, even his presence, is considered a pollution. This is why he has received the name of Bhangi: for *bhang* means literally interruption, breaking, damaging ; and whatever a man is doing, if he is touched by a sweeper, he must at once leave off doing it and go and bathe. It is thus a common custom amongst Hindus, if they wish to remove an intruder or to annoy a neighbour, or to compel some one to listen to their demands, to send the sweeper at him, especially at such times when it is least convenient to him to be disturbed. Many Bhangis have turned Muhammadans, and in the Panjab some have become Sikhs ; but no respectable Muhammadans or Sikhs will allow him to eat with them, although both of these creeds distinctly avow the equality of all men. His change of religion has, therefore, profited him nothing. He is still the Bhangi, or "one whose impurity disturbs you." I used to think that the name Bhangi was derived from the intoxicating drug called *bhanga*, and known to Europeans as Indian hemp. But as the sweeper caste is not more addicted to the use of this noxious plant than any other, the previous explanation is more likely to be right. There is another name of the caste, Chuhra, known chiefly in villages and in districts west of the Ganges, which probably means "vermin-catcher."

As the broom does not always afford sufficient scope for his energies or for his maintenance, he practises many of the callings inherited from his near ancestor, the savage Dom, with whom, however, he now disdains to associate. He makes baskets and brooms for sale and for his own use, digs vermin out of the earth for food, draws sinews out of carcasses for fixing the weaver's brush or the peasant's winnowing-pan, takes off the hides of dead kids and goats, manufactures drums with their skins, and plays on the rustic flute called *shahnái*. By the lower castes he is sometimes hired out as a musician to enliven the celebration of a marriage ceremony. On occasions of public festivity he mounts a temporary platform made of bamboos and beats the drum and blows the flute for the delectation of the people and for his own fee. He is notoriously addicted to thieving and drunkenness and to the violent treatment of his own women. If other means of living fail, his daughters are sent out to earn money as prostitutes. He will accept of alms on days of eclipse, when the demon of darkness is abroad. He is supposed to have some secret understanding with Sitalá, the goddess of small-pox; and to many classes of the community, Muhammadan as well as Hindu, he is the recognized hereditary priest of that abhorred goddess. Such is the typical Bhangi of the Hindu village. But some families of this caste have in recent years acquired much higher tastes and notions. Those who have served in Europeans' houses (for it is here chiefly that the higher tastes have been formed) are gradually developing into a separate caste. Such persons will only intermarry among themselves and decline to associate with their rougher caste-fellows. Some of the women have become lady's maids and have accompanied their mistresses to England, where they pass muster with English maid-servants.

The patron saint of Bhangis is Lal Guru (called by Muhammadans Lal Beg), the prince of scavengers. Hence Hindu sweepers are called Lal Gurus, and Muhammadan ones Lal Begis. Another Muhammadan name is Mehtar, which means literally "prince," a title of respect conferred upon the head of a clan, and hence transferred to the caste in general. Both Hindu and Muhammadan sweepers worship their patron saint in the same kind of way and on the same occasions. His presence is symbolized by a pole and flag. Swine are sacrified in his honor to the strains of the flute and the loud beating of the drum.

95. The Dhobi, or washerman, represents an impure caste, but one many degrees higher than that of the Bhangi, from whom he has sprung. Both are descended from the Dom, "whose sole wealth," according to Manu, "must be dogs and asses." The Indian washerman has always been associated with the indigenous ass, which carries the soiled clothes down to the bank of the river or tank and takes them back clean to the house. No Hindu of any caste, even the lowest, will wash his own clothes; and so the Dhobi has been formed into a caste which shall bear the impurities of all. He is not admitted into the inside of a Hindu temple, and this at once places him on the same social level as that of the "castes allied to the hunting state" and the lowest castes of artisans. His work, however, brings him into continual contact with one of the purest of elements, and the quiet nature of his occupation has taught him a certain refinement of manner. For these reasons he is far less despised than his Bhangi cousin. He has left off eating pigs, as the Bhangi himself has left off eating dogs, while their common ancestor, the Dom or Chandál, still eats both. The washerman is as necessary an element in the constitution of the Hindu township as the watchman, the hide-tanner, the blacksmith, the potter, and the carpenter already described, and he is remunerated, as they are, by a portion of the produce of each half-yearly harvest. On days of child-birth, and on the day when the mother first leaves her room, he receives a special fee in cash or kind: for the garments and wrappings worn till then are believed to be something more than physically impure, and no one but a Dhobi can make them fit for future use. Many families of this caste have become Muhammadan, but this has not materially improved their social status; nor, in spite of the prohibitions of their adopted creed, has it checked their propensity to drunkenness.

96. The Kahár is the general house-servant in respectable Hindu families. His primary function is that of drawing and bringing water for the bath or the table, and this has led to his being employed for various other uses, such as taking care of clothes, dusting the rooms, kneading the chapáti preparatory to cooking it, carrying the palanquin, &c. The two castes previously named—the Bhangi and the Dhobi—are sprung from hunting tribes of the stamp of Dom or Chandál. The Kahár, on the

other hand, is sprung from fishing tribes, such as the *Gaud*, the Dhuria, the Dhimar, and others mentioned in group II. B. As was stated in para. 22 *(e)*, it is not unusual to speak loosely of all the fishing tribes as Kahárs, because any man from among these tribes may take employment as a water-bearer, if he can find a master. Properly speaking, however, the name Kahár belongs only to those families which seceded long ago from their ancestral tribes, abandoned the hereditary industry of fishing, and formed a new and distinct caste devoted exclusively to domestic service. The best evidence of the existence of such a caste is that it has a Muhammadan counterpart—the Bhisti, whose functions in a Muhammadan household are precisely similar to those of a Kahár in a Hindu establishment. The only difference between them is that the Kahár invariably carries water on his shoulders in a pitcher, while the Bhisti carries it across his back in a leather bag, called a *masak*, which is made of the hide of a bullock or large goat. Orthodox Hindus will not even bathe in such water, much less drink it; for they consider the contact of leather a pollution to such a pure element as water. In European houses the Kahár (who is called bearer, a contraction for water-bearer) is used for general house-work, and the Bhisti for drawing water. In Southern India the name for the corresponding caste is Bhoi, which has been corrupted by Europeans into the Madrassi "boy." Both the Kahár and the Bhisti are respectable and orderly castes and are seldom or never seen inside a jail. The worst legacy that the former has inherited from the ancestral fisherman is his propensity to drunkenness. A man convicted of *directly* stealing his master's property, (for indirect gains at his master's expense are not condemned), is expelled from his caste, and can only be re-admitted on payment of the fine or giving the banquet decreed by the caste assembly.

97. The Nápit, or hair-cutter, is, like the Dhobi, an essential element in the constitution of the Hindu township. No village community could exist without him. All Hindu castes who are respectable enough to be admitted inside a temple (and even castes lower than these, if they can pay the fee) employ him for certain ceremonial observances connected with infancy, burials, and marriages, and most of these ceremonies are enforced by religious sanctions.

Every child after the age of six months or a year undergoes the ceremony of having its head for the first time touched with the razor. This is a ceremony of no little importance in the eyes of a Hindu and is called *chura karan*. It is performed in the presence of some deity, or rather in that of his image, who is believed henceforth to take the child under his special patronage. The cutting off of the birth-hair is believed to remove the last trace of the congenital taint inherited from the maternal womb, and hence the ceremony has the same siginficance as that of a baptismal or lustral rite. The custom of cutting off the birth-hair has been widely practised among backward races elsewhere, and is not at all confined to the natives of India. The germs of the barber caste may, therefore, have existed in times before the Aryan had appeared.

In funeral ceremonies the Nápit plays an important part. He shaves the head and pares the nails of the dead preparatary to cremation. He shaves the head of the man who puts the first light to the pyre. Ten days afterwards he shaves the head of every member of the household. By this time, after taking a final bath, they are purified of the contagion of death.

In the celebration of marriage ceremonies he acts as the Brahman's assistant, and to the lowest castes or tribes who cannot employ a Brahman he is himself the matrimonial priest. The important part he plays in marriage ceremonies has led to his becoming the match-maker among all the respectable castes. It is he who hunts out the boy, finds out whether his clan or caste is marriageable with that of the girl, settles the price to be paid on both sides, takes the horoscopes to the Brahman to be compared, so as to see if the stars are favourable, carries the presents from one house to the other, and so forth. His function as match-maker is not an unimportant one in a state of society in which the rules of caste have imposed endless restrictions on the freedom of marriage.

Shaving is not the only service that he is expected to render to his constituents. He is the ear-cleaner, nail-cutter, cupper and bleeder, &c. In short, he performs any kind of operation on the body of man that requires a sharp knife, from shaving a beard to lancing a boil. He might therefore be fitly styled a barber-surgeon. In this double capacity he is the exact counterpart of the barber-surgeons of mediæval Europe, out of whom the modern medical profession has sprung. The Muhammadan Nápits (who are called Hajjam) are said to be more skilful in surgical operations than Hindu ones. Like Kamángars (see para. 63), they are largely employed in setting dislocated bones.

His wife acts as nurse to the mother and child for the last six days of the confinement. During the first six days they are in charge of the midwife—some woman of the less respected castes of Chamár, Dhánuk, or others.

98. The castes of musician and singer fall naturally into two main classes—the Muhammadan and the Hindu; and the list may be shown as follows :—

Páwariya	... ...	Muhammadan.
Dhari	... ...	Muhammadan.
Dom Mirasi	... ...	Muhammadan.
Kathak	... ...	Hindu.

The names by which the former are called, being of Hindi and not of Persian origin, are alone enough to show, even if other evidence were wanting, that these castes were originally Hindu; and this is my reason for recognizing them as a part or product of the general Hindu system, as I have done in the parallel cases of Kunjra, Kamángar, and Tirgar, all of which are now Muhammadan. In fact there are but few Hindu castes to which there is no Muhammadan counterpart; and in some cases this counterpart has become the larger element of the two, while in others it has ousted the Hindu element altogether. It would thus be impossible to give a complete outline of Hindu castes without including those in which the Hindu element has now either partially or wholly disappeared.

The Páwariya caste has one special function. On the twelfth day after the birth of a child, when the mother receives her final bath before leaving the lying-in chamber and puts on a new wedding bracelet, and when all the pottery ware of the household is broken up and replaced by a new set, the Páwariya comes uninvited to the house with two or three comrades of his own class, female as well as male, and sings songs of gratulation to the strains of a fiddle. The fiddle is called the *kingri*, and from this instrument the caste has also been called Kingriya. The instrument is played with a bow and consists of strings of sinew or steel stretched over a hollowed gourd or calabash (*tomri*) as the sounding-board. In return for this unasked attention the performers receive presents of grain or money and clothes, which last they afterwards sell to some Rauniya or other pedlar, if they have no need of them.

The Dhari caste (which appears in the census report under the less common name of Dhariwal) is less specialized than the preceding and more migratory. They go from place to place, wherever they can find employment, and sing and play at marriages and sometimes at Hindu temples. Their chief instruments are the double drum called *mridang* and the *tambura*, a kind of guitar which is played with the fingers. Both men and women perform on these instruments.

The Dom, or as he prefers to be called the Dom Mirási, is one who is especially attached to a certain circle of houses as the family musician and jester. The word Mirási means "hereditary", and the caste has been so called because the son inherits his father's connexion. The instruments most commonly used by the men and women of this fraternity are the light drum (*dholak*), and brass cups or cymbals called *majira*. The men, too, sometimes play the fiddle called *kingri*. The women dance, but only before the ladies of the zenana; and they are sometimes regularly entertained as jesters to help these ladies to kill the time and reconcile them to their domestic prisons. Of each of these three castes it must be said that the women do not dance before men and hence they are reputed to be chaste: for no woman who is not a prostitute will dance in the presence of the opposite sex, though singing and playing are not equally condemned.

No doubt need exist as to the source from which these castes have sprung, or as to what their character was before they became Muhammadan. They are offshoots from the wandering and casteless tribes, such as Dom, Kanjar, Kanchan, &c., whom I have placed in group I, and from the lowest castes of Hindus, such as Pasi, Arakh, &c., whom I have placed in group IIA. All these tribes and castes are addicted to singing, dancing and playing on the drum, the fiddle, the guitar, &c. It would be easy to show that similar instruments were found in use among most modern savages elsewhere, when the first Europeans visited them; and as I have lately mentioned in reference to the Bhangi or sweeper (see para. 94), music and dancing are among the means by which he ekes out a livelihood at the present day. Now the Bhangi is certainly an offshoot from the savage Dom, and this very name—Dom—has clung to the Mirási caste up to the present day. Another link in the connection is the fact that the Páwariya caste to this day, in the intervals of business, maintains itself by the manufacture of fans, palm-leaf umbrellas, baskets, &c.—the very industry in which the Dom and kindred tribes are known to excel. Nothing could be more natural, or more in accordance with the method by which Indian castes have been generally formed, than that certain families or clans from these tribes should have detached themselves from the ancestral stem and formed a new combination devoted especially to music, singing, and dancing.

There is even a well-attested tradition as to the means by which they became converted to Islam. It was in response, as the story goes, to an invitation from Amir Khusru, the poet and musician, who lived in the reign of Ala-ud-din Khilji, A.D. 1295. Up to that day, it is said, there were no regular musician clans or castes who could take service in Muhammadan houses, and whose women could be admitted within the zenanas. The conversion of these clans to Islam has greatly raised them in social estimation. The Dom Mirási has acquired a refinement of manner and expression which places him in marked contrast with the savage ancestor to whom he is directly related in blood. Not knowing what the word Mirási means, he has contracted it into Mir, a synonym for Sayyad. So while the one is an outcaste, eating carrion and dogs, the other is claiming to be a descendant of the great Prophet of Mecca.

In the census report Dom the Musician has been mixed up with Dom the Savage, as is clear from the description of the occupation written against the name Dom: "bamboo basket-making, singing, and dancing." Mr. Williams, however, drew attention to the difference in Oudh Census Report, Vol. I, page 83, where he says "there appears to be no connection between these Doms (the Muhammadan musicians) and the low outcaste tribe of Hindus known by the same name, whose employment is that of making ropes and mats." He is right in drawing a marked distinction between these two tribes *as they now are*, but mistaken in supposing that they have no ancestral connection. The development of the various castes out of the primeval savage is, as I think, the only hypothesis on which the formation of castes and their gradations in relation to each other in the scale of respectability can be explained.

99. The Hindu caste of musician called Kathak is entirely distinct, both in origin and character, from the preceding Muhammadan ones. While the latter have ascended from the Dom and became Muhammadan, the Kathak has descended from the Brahman and remained a stanch Hindu. In the early or Vedic days of Hinduism there were four classes of priests or sacrificers—the lowest or Adhvaryu who slaughtered the victim, the Udgatri who chanted the hymns, the Hotri who

threw the offering on the flame, and the Brahman who superintended the entire ceremony. But the bloody sacrifices of the Vedic age fell into disrepute through the teaching of Buddha; with the spread of Hinduism further east the Vedic ritual went out of use, the Vedic hymns were forgotten, and the order of priests who chaunted them (the Udgatri) ceased as such to exist. The Kathak caste is the descendant of this extinct order. The tradition of their origin has been preserved in various ways. They still wear the *janeo* or sacred thread; and in saluting any one they do not make a bow, as other castes do, but pronounce the *Asirbad* or blessing like Brahmans. Though they have ceased to chaunt the Sama Veda in the presence of bloodstained altars, as their ancestors did in the earliest times, they are still employed to chaunt sacred melodies before idols or other symbols in the temples. The modulations of the voice are now, as then, accompanied with certain gesticulations of the arm and movements of the body which are tantamount to dancing. They dance before the idol, as King David danced before the Ark as it was being led up to Jerusalem.

But in these degenerate days some of the functions exercised by the Kathak are much less dignified than those associated with religion or religions worship. The men are hired out to play and dance and sing at marriage festivals before large and mixed audiences; and their own wives occasionally, but rarely, sing in public. The men are generally accompanied on such occasions by women of loose reputation, who dance and sing before persons of the opposite sex, shaking the castanets. Such women are generally of the low and profligate tribe called Kanchan, whom in group I. I have included among the outcaste or casteless tribes. They frequently take lessons in dancing and singing at the Kathak's house and even from the Kathak's own wife. This is a remarkable instance of extremes meeting. A Brahmanical caste like the Kathak has become associated with the lowest women in India, while the lowest savage in India—the Dom—has risen to the rank of a Mirásí and calls himself a Sayyad or descendant of the Prophet.

The caste of Kathak is slowly, but it seems surely, dying out. The casteless tribes, such as Kanchan, the low-caste Hindus, such as Bhangi, and the Muhammadan castes described in the previous paragraph, appear to provide all that the community requires in the way of dancing, singing and music, and they charge lower fees.

100. The Bhat is another caste which, like the Kathak, is an offshoot from the ancient Brahman. This caste, however, has sprung, not from an order of priests like the Kathak, but from those secularized Brahmans who frequented the courts of princes and the camps of warriors, recited their praises in public, and kept records of their genealogies. Such, without much variation, is the function of the Bhat at the present day. The ancient epic known as the Mahábhárata speaks of a band of bards and eulogists marching in front of Yudisthira as he made his progress from the field of Kuru-kshetra towards Hastinapur. But these very men are spoken of in the same poem as Brahmans. Nothing could be more natural than that, as time went on, these courtier priests should have become hereditary bards, who seceded from the parent stem and founded a new caste bound together by mutual interests and sympathies.

No Bhat for several centuries past has pretended to call himself a Brahman, nor would such pretensions be recognized anywhere in India. But there are many circumstances which recall the tradition of his origin. The most important of the subdivisions of this caste is called Birm-Bhat, which is evidently a corruption of Brahma. There are some Brahmans, especially of the Gaur tribe, who still exercise the function of bard and genealogist, though the Bhat is never permitted to exercise the function of priest. Among all the lower classes of the population the Bhat is still called Maháraj or great king, a title which is generally conceded only to Brahmans. The caste still wears the *janeo* or sacred cord. But the strongest proof of all lies in the survival of certain titles connected with the celebration of sacrifices—a purely Brahmanical function. The prince, chieftain, or landlord, who patronizes the Bhat and entertains him as his family bard is called Yajaman, or "he who gives the sacrifice," while the Bhat himself is called *Yagwá*, *Jajak*, or *Jachak*, or "the priest by whom the sacrifice is performed." Such words recall the day, now passed away for ever, when costly public sacrifices were given by kings and rulers as thanksgivings for some great deliverance or in celebration of some great public event, and when the praises of the giver were solemnly recited before the audience by the superintending priest.

A distinction sprang up, after the caste had been formed, between the Birm-Bhat, who merely recited the praises of ancestors at weddings and other festive occasions, and the Yagwa-Bhat, who kept the family records of births, deaths, and marriages. The former are of more migratory habits and are hired only for the occasion, while the latter have an hereditary circle of constituents, to whom they pay periodical visits, receiving the usual fee in return. Most of the great Chattri families still keep their Jagwa-Bhat or genealogist, but the practice is becoming less common every year, and the Bhat has been falling lower and lower with the declining power of the Chattris, for whose sake they came into existence. In these days a high place allotted at a darbar held by some Viceroy or Lieutenant-Governor does more to ennoble a native chief and to stamp the respectability of his family than the pompous recitations of a Bhat at a marriage festival. Some members of the caste have now taken to the plough; but they are mostly known at the present day as rapacious and conceited mendicants, too proud to work, but not too proud to beg. The period of their greatest prosperity was that in which their services were most needed, *viz.*, when the great nomad and savage chieftains of mediæval India, sprung as they were from the numerous indigenous tribes whose names they still bear were rising into the ranks of Chattris, and when men, publicly recognized as the bards and genealogists of the great, were required to give official testimony to the alleged purity of their descent from some illustrions saint or warrior who lived in the heroic age. It is no wonder that the Bhat is dreaded by Chattris to this day on account of the power he possesses to disclose a family secret or make them the subjects of public ridicule.

The caste of Bhat, like that of Kathak, appears to be gradually dying out in the plains of Hindustan. In Rajputana it is still numerous and flourishing.

101. The last and at the present day the highest of the serving castes is the Kayasth or writer. There is no reason to doubt that this caste is chiefly an offshoot from Chattris. According to the legend told in the Skanda Purana they are descended from the posthumous son of Chandra Sen, the great Kshatriya king, whose widow had fled for refuge into a hermitage after he himself and all other Kshatriyas had been slain by Parasu Rama. The life of the widow was spared on condition that the son to be born from her should renounce the calling of the warrior and take to that of the writer. Kayasths have from time immemorial been allowed to wear the sacred cord, and many of them wear it still. The name of Thakur or lord, which is by courtesy the title of Chattris, as Pandit or Maháraj is that of Brahmans, is not uncommon among men of the Kayasth caste. Local traditions are not wanting of Kayasths who have won distinction as warriors and leaders of military bands. It was decreed in certain law books that the Kayasth appointed by the king as his accountant or secretary "must be one versed in the Shastras or sacred literature," which shows that he was not a man of the so-called Sudra or servile class, as his detractors have tried to prove. It is not difficult to conceive that princes and the owners of landed estates generally would prefer to appoint their own younger sons, or nephews, or any other near relatives, to whom they had no land to give, but on whose honesty they could rely, as their estate-managers and accountants, and that families or clans engaged in such work for several generations in succession would gradually become detached from the parent caste and found a new one of their own. Kshatriyas and Chattris have always been addicted to a love of flesh diet and the use of spirituous liquors, one of the points in which they differ from Brahmans—and this, too, is one of the characteristics of the Kayasth caste.

The original function, then, of the Kayasth caste was that of estate-manager, and this function they have retained up to the present day through all changes of government—from the ancient Hindu raja to the various Muhammadan dynasties, and from these to the English rule. From the earliest known times every Hindu township had an accountant or estate-manager on its staff of functionaries, just as it had its watchman, messenger, potter, ironsmith, carpenter, washerman, barber-surgeon, astrologer, &c. His work consisted in keeping the rent-roll on behalf of landlord, exacting the rents, drawing up leases for tenants, apportioning income and expenditure among co-sharers of estates, &c., and his work as patwári or accountant is much the same even at the present day. The substitution of Muhammadan for Hindu rule made little or no difference in his status. But under British rule his position has become somewhat complicated, and he scarcely knows now whether he is the servant of Government or of the landlord. He is in point of fact something of both, especially as the Government is now beginning to guarantee him a fixed salary. The alphabet or character which he uses in all his registers and accounts is a running hand, called Kaithi, derived from Nágri, the character pre-eminently used by Brahmans. In the North-Western Provinces he has been forbidden to use this character in the rent-rolls intended to be filed in the treasury offices, and Nágri or Urdu have been prescribed in its place. In Oudh, however, Kaithi is still permitted. In both provinces, and in fact throughout Upper India, Kaithi is in all private transactions more widely used than any other vernacular character both by Hindus and Muhammadans.

The Kayasth has not always served in the humble capacity of village accountant. From the earliest times there was a higher and more ambitious class, who served as secretaries and finance ministers in the courts of kings. In the *Smriti*, or collection of laws, ascribed to Vrihaspati, it is said that "a king has ten constituent parts, *viz.*, himself, the chief justice, the counsellers, the *Smriti* or laws, the accountant, the writer, the gold, the fire, the water, and the attendants." Now the chief justice and the counsellors were Brahmans, but the accountant and the writer were Kayasths. In the same code it is said: "the accountant makes calculations, and the secretary takes down the proceedings of trials." The same code says in another place: "Two persons must be appointed by the king, a secretary and an accountant, who are skilled in the expounding of words and meanings, adepts at counting, upright, and learned in the different dialects." Quotations to this effect might be multiplied.

Thus from the very first there were two classes of Kayasths—one the accountant of the village commune or township; and the other the scribe, finance minister, or accountant in the king's court. After the Hindu dynasties had been succeeded by Muhammadan ones, Kayasths of the latter class devoted themselves to the study of Persian and abjured the ancestral Kaithi, while Kaithi still remained, and remains, the favourite character of the patwári or village accountant. This is why Kayasths of a certain class are distinguished above all other Hindu castes for their proficiency in the Persian language. Having thus secured the patronage of their new masters, the Muhammadans, they gradually ousted the Brahmans from those posts which they had been accustomed to occupy as judges, counsellors, &c., under the old Hindu dynasties, and the decline of the political power of the Brahmans can be largely ascribed to this fact.

Under British rule the Kayasths of this class have shown an equal readiness to learn the English language and adapt themselves to the new order of things. There is no caste in Upper India so largely represented in the revenue offices, the courts of justice, and in the literary professions, such as pleader or native barrister. These Anglicized Kayasths are now, in their turn, recoiling against Persian, as their forefathers did against Kaithi, and are seeking to revive the study of Hindi and Sanskrit literature.

All Kayasths, of whatever section or class, revere the memory of a patron saint called Chitragupta, whose twelve sons are considered to be the founders of twelve great Kayasth families, as the twelve sons of Jacob founded the twelve tribes of Israel. The legend of Chitragupta is that he sprang out of the body of the Supreme Being, Brahmá, while he (Brahmá) was meditating on some means by which the good and bad actions of men could be registered. He is thus the recording angel of the Hindu pantheon—a function suggested by the fact already alluded to, that the Kayasth in the court of a Hindu king was "the secretary who took down the proceedings of trials."

102. Among the list of serving or professional castes it may seem strange that no niche exists for the physician, whose function as a preparer and administerer of medicines is quite distinct from that of the Nápit or barber-surgeon, and is considered much more respectable. There *was*, however, a caste of physician called Baidya, a name derived from *vidya* or science : hence Baidya meant "a man of science." The caste still exists, I am told, in Behár and the Lower Provinces. But it has died out in Hindustan, owing to the superior reputation of Muhammadan physicians called Hakims, which name also means "man of science." All Hindus of respectable castes, as well as Muhammadans, who can afford to pay the fee, employ an Hakim, or take their complaints to some native doctor trained in English medicine. It is very probable that many of the Hakims of the present day are descended from Baidyas, who adopted the creed of Islám several centuries ago, while the Muhammadans were still in power and their reputation for medicine at its height.

Among the lower, poorer, and more ignorant classes of the population, whether Hindu or Muhammadan, a different practice exists. Such persons begin by leaving their illnesses to nature, and when this fails, resort to the numerous traditional remedies that are current among the people, or send offerings to temples, or employ an Ojha or Nyotya—that is, an exorcist—to expel the evil spirit. Moreover, there is a class of quacks calling themselves Baidyas, who wander about from village to village and sell vegetable drugs prepared from certain trees and herbs which possess medicinal properties. The vagrant and casteless tribes whom I have included in group I. are specially clever in the knowledge of the properties of herbs. It is they who supply the shops of the attár or druggist with many of the native medicines. There is a Banmánush now in the Central Jail, Lucknow, who boasts that he is a regular medical practitioner among a certain circle of villages near which his gang resides. The fact that these men call themselves Baidya shows that there was once a respected caste which they aspire to imitate and to which they profess to belong.

The name by which the physician caste is called in Manu's Code is Ambastha (see chapter III, 152 ; IV, 212 220 ; X, 8, 13, 47). His account of their origin implies that they were an offshoot from Brahmans, though in his own day they were quite a distinct caste. There are a few learned Hindus at the present day who study the Sanskrit works on medicine and who are called Baidyas by profession. But these men are not Baidyas by caste, but Brahmans. There are four such men in Lucknow and many more in Benares.

103. The differences between the names occurring alphabetically in the census report and those shown in my own table (group V) are the following:—

(*a*) Chera is entered in the census table as a sweeper caste of nine persons !. I have included these amongst Bhangis. Perhaps Chera is a misprint for Chuhra, the name commonly given to the sweeper caste in Hindu villages.

(*b* No mention is made in the census report of the serving caste of Kahár or water-bearer, which, as I have explained already in para. 96, should be separated from the fishing tribes or castes, out of which the serving caste was formed.

(*c*) The Páwariya caste is not mentioned in the census report ; but mention is made of a caste called Paria, which, I presume, is intended for this.

(*d*) The caste of Dom Mirási is not mentioned in the census report. The omission has been alluded to already in para. 98.

(*e*) Bádi, against which 995 persons have been recorded, is shown as a separate caste. But Bádi is merely a synonym for Birm or Brahma-Bhát, and means literally "reciter," a correct description of the function of the Brahma-Bhat as distinct from that of the Jagwa-Bhat (see para. 100). Moreover, Bádi is wrongly described in the census report as a singer and dancer. He is in fact neither, but a reciter of family histories.

(*f*) Ráj Bhat, against which 249 names have been recorded, is not a separate caste, but, like the preceding, a section of Bháts. The Ráj-Bháts and the Bádis have all been included under the name of Bhát in my own statement.

(*g*) No mention is made of the caste of Kathak in the tables of the census report.

140. *The priestly castes.*—We come now to the group or series which closes the long list of Indian castes proper and which in point of social rank stands higher than all that have gone before—those connected with religion. These castes may be almost summed up in a single word—Brahman. The Brahman caste is the coping-stone to which all the other stones of the social arch converge, the model upon which all the other castes were formed, and in a certain sense (as will be shown hereafter) the cause of their existence. But the word "Brahman," whatever its original sense may have been, is now a term of rather vague import. It denotes not one, but a multitude of castes or sub-castes, which are almost as distinct from each other as those of any other series or group previously described ; and if they are called by the generic name of Brahman, it must not be understood that they intermarry or eat together, as if they constituted a single caste, but merely that they have some connection, direct or indirect, with religion, the common element, and have sprung out of a common germ. The lowest of these Brahmanical castes are despised by some Brahmans themselves and are held in very little respect by the upper castes of the outside community; but by the lower and more ignorant classes almost every Brahman, whatever his rank or status may be among his own brethren, is regarded with a feeling of instinctive awe, such as no other caste in the Indian community can ever expect to inspire.

105. According to the census report under review the total number of Brahmans in the North-West and Oudh (all kinds included) amounts to no less than 4,690,850, or about 12 per cent. of the total indigenous population of the province, Hindu and Muhammadan. Distinct altogether from the Brahman, yet closely connected with him in character and representing tenets and modes of life sanctioned by Brahmanical authority and example, is the Goshayen, whose caste numbers altogether 118,308 persons. Distinct both from the Goshayen and the Brahman, yet in some respects resembling both, there are many different orders of religious mendicants, who profess to have retired from the world, and to have done so for the sake of studying or practising one aspect or another of the many-sided creed, of which Brahmans have been the principal authors. These, according to the census, number 226,122 persons. The Brahman, then, is by far the most numerous as well as the most important of the religious fraternities, and the attempt which we must now make to sketch his origin and functions will take up a disproportionate amount of space in this paper—an emblem of the caste itself, which has appropriated far too large a share of the time, wealth, and attention of the rest of the community.

106. The original function which called the Brahman into existence and formed him into a distinct social unit was the performance of sacrifice. It was so with the caste of Levite among the people of Israel, and has been so with every other order of priesthood throughout the world founded on a deistic basis. As regards the Brahman or Indian priest, this is abundantly clear from the ancient Vedic hymn-books or *sanhitas*, from the Vedic liturgies or *Brahmanas* (all of which deal exclusively with sacrifice), from the ancient law-books or *Smritis*. from the two great national epics (the Ramayána and the Mahábhárata), and from many of the Puráns or ancient

histories. The name "Bráhman" shows clearly enough that the origin of the caste. so termed was sacerdotal—that is, functional, and not tribal. One of the numerous names by which a sacrificial prayer was called in the Vedas is *brahma* (neuter), and a man who composed or recited such prayers was called *brahma* (masculine) At the outset any man, to whatever tribe he belonged, or whatever his occupation might be, could be his own priest, and no such thing as a distinct caste possessing the exclusive monopoly of performing sacrifices existed. The original ceremonial practised by the first Aryan settlers in India was very simple and intelligible as compared with what it afterwards became in an age less devoted to the attractions of war and more prone to listen to the gloomy suggestions of priestcraft. The divinities worshipped by the earliest Hindus were the various elements, powers, or departments of nature, whom they personified into a class of divine spirits or deities and invoked under such names as Indra, the sky ; Váyu, the wind ; Agni, fire ; Rudra, the tempest ; Vishnu, the sun ; Prithivi, the earth ; Chandra, the moon ; Ushas, the dawn ; Varuna, the water, &c., &c. As the worshipper was brought face to face with the elements and forces of the world around him, and was not bound to distinguish between the physical agents themselves and the unseen spirits or deities who were supposed to preside over them, he felt no necessity for the presence of idols or temples. The only temple required by such a creed was the sacrificial floor, and the air itself sufficed for the sanctuary of the Devas or "bright beings" who ruled the several departments of the universe. An altar was erected under the open sky, wine was freely poured out, butter was thrown on the mounting flame ; and while the invocations were being recited and the flesh of the victim roasted, the unseen deities of the air were invited to come down and lick the blood, inhale the fumes of wine, and taste the savoury smoke that ascended from the altar. No priestly caste was needed for such a simple ceremony; and there is abundant evidence of sacrifices having been performed and invocations composed and uttered by the military chiefs, who led their people out to the field of battle. Gradually, however, when the warlike instinct had begun to yield to the literary and religious, and the hymns were collected into liturgies, the art of sacrifice became much more highly developed than before. As time went on, it became more and more difficult, and at last impossible, for the king or his ministers to master the elaborate procedure which the Devas had now begun to demand ; and as the slightest error in the performance was believed to be fatal to its efficacy, a class of men came into existence who made a special study of the prescribed rituals and transmitted such knowledge to their posterity. As Brahma (masculine) meant sacrificer in general, without any distinction of tribe or class, so (by the well-known rule of etymology with which every Sanskrit scholar is familiar), the word Bráhmana meant the son or descendant of a Brahma—that is, one who had inherited a knowledge of the sacrificial art from his fathers and forefathers. This was the origin of the word Brahman, and in this way the nucleus of the Brahmanical caste was formed. Thus the Brahman is no exception to, but rather the strongest verification of, the theory maintained and exemplified throughout this paper, that function, and function only, was the foundation of Indian caste.

107. It is not surprising that an exclusive priestly caste should have thus been gradually formed, when we reflect on the extraordinary effects ascribed by the Hindus of that age to the power of sacrifice which Brahmans, and Brahmans only, could call into action. The sacrifice was the food of the gods, and as the gods were the powers of nature personified, it was the sacrifice which sustained the fabric of the universe. In the Atharva Veda even the sacrificial ladles were said to support heaven and earth: "the Juhu has established the sky, the Upabrit the atmosphere, and the Dhruva the stable earth" (Atharva Veda, XVIII, 4, 5); and similar powers are ascribed to the sacrificial grass (*kusha*) and to the sacrificial cow (Vasá). The exclamation "Sváhá!" uttered by the priest as the *homa* offering was thrown on the fire was converted into a goddess and declared to be the wife of Agni, the consecrated flame of the altar. In a later production (Manu's Code) the sacrifice is said to "support the whole animal and vegetable world, since the oblation of clarified butter duly cast into the flame ascends in smoke to the sun; from the sun, it falls in rain; from rain comes

vegetable food ; and from such food animals derive their subsistence" (Chapter III, 76). In a still later production, the Bhagavat Gitá or divine song, the power of sacrifice is described in the following terms: "Prajapati of old created beings with their rites of sacrifice, and said—"Hereby shall you propagate yourselves; this shall be to you the cow of plenty. Sustain with this the god and the gods will sustain you: supporting each other in turn, you shall obtain the highest happiness. Fed with sacrifice, the gods shall give you the food that you desire. He that gives them nothing and eats the food which they give is a thief indeed. Good men, who eat the leavings of the sacrifice, are loosed from their guilt ; but they that cook for themselves alone, and not for the gods, eat sin." It is no wonder, then, that the Brahman, through whom alone the sacrifice could be made to yield its promised fruits, was looked upon as a being possessed of superhuman powers and as one who held the keys of life and death in his hands—that every one demanded his blessing as he passed—that his curse was believed to penetrate to endless distances in time and space—that "no greater crime" (to use the language of Manu, Chapter VIII, 381) was known on earth "than the slaying of a Brahman"—that all other castes and classes were declared to have been made to protect or serve him—and that at the close of the long struggle for supremacy between the king and the priest, the latter was able at last to establish a theocracy more powerful and more lasting than any other that the world has yet witnessed. The final victory of the priest over the warrior was signalized in Indian legend by the slaughter of the whole Kshatriya race by Parasu Ráma, the armed champion of the Brahmans.

108. The art of sacrifice received its highest development in the sacerdotal tracts or liturgies called *Brahmanas*, which were compiled by and for Brahmans as guides to the performance of the great sacrificial ceremonies. The three orders of priests, answering to the three Vedas and their respective Brahmanas, were the Adhvaryu, who did the manual work connected with the sacrifice as prescribed in the Yajur-Veda; the Udgátri, who chaunted the sacrificial prayers collected in the Sáma Veda; and the Hotri, or follower of the Rig Veda, who recited, not chaunted, the appointed prayers in strict accordance with the difficult rules of accentuation and pronunciation. The slightest error or omission in the performance required an expiatory rite—a principle observed, but to a less degree, in the monasteries of Europe at the present day, where a mistake in the singing of any part of the divine office entails upon the offender the ceremony of kneeling down before his superior in a conspicuous place as a form of penance or atonement. To prevent such mistakes and to superintend the other three orders of priests, a fourth order was established with a fourth Veda (the Atharvan), and this functionary was called the Brahman proper. Thus the name Brahman came to be considered the highest title of priest; and when the names of the other three orders died out with the disappearance of the Vedic sacrifices, it was the Brahman who gave his name to the entire fraternity. Thus in the code of Manu the only word used for a man of the sacerdotal caste is Brahman.

109. There was one more development in the signification of the word Brahman which must be noticed in passing. It was laid down in Manu's Code that a Brahman's life should be parcelled out into four distinct periods or stages : firstly, that of a religious student or Brahmachári ; secondly, that of a married householder or Grihastha ; thirdly, that of a forest hermit or Banaprastha ; fourthly, that of an ascetic or Sannyási. In the last two stages the recluse was directed to discontinue the sacrifices performed during the preceding period and devote all his intellectual energies to the study of Brahma, the Supreme Spirit. The books in which these speculations have been recorded are called Upanishads, and these treatises close what is known to Hindus as *Sruti* or the canon of Vedic revelation. Hence some native commentators have said that the Veda consists of two parts—one teaching Yagya, or the art of sacrifice, and the other Brahma, or the mystery of the creative spirit. Now "Brahma" (neuter), as we showed in para. 106, was one of the names for a sacrificial prayer. It is derived from the root *brih*, which signifies to grow, to expand. As a prayer offered in sacrifice was believed to transcend the bounds of space and support the whole animal and

vegetable world, so in the speculations about the origin of the world the same word was used to signify the cosmic soul, the world-evolving spirit, the plastic power that causes all the changes and processes of nature, being itself causeless and unchangeable. The contemplation and study of this Supreme Spirit, Brahma, gave a higher meaning to the word Brahman than that of a mere sacrificer. "Whoever looks for Brahmahood elsewhere than in the Divine Spirit should be abandoned by the Brahmans" (quoted in *Max Müller's Sanskrit Literature, page 23*). Elsewhere it is said that the visionary sage is alone the true Brahman: "Whatever kind of Brahman he may have before been, he becomes a veritable Brahman now" (*Gough's Upanishads, page 162*). The following sloka is taken from a commentary on Manu's Code :—

Janmaná jayate Súdrah, sanskárád Dwijayo bhavet,
Vedapáthir bhaved Bipro, Brahmajnánád Bráhmanah.

The meaning of which is that by natural birth a man is merely a Sudra (that is, unregenerated and corrupt); by the ceremony of initiation he is regenerated and becomes a "twice-born;" by reading the Vedas he becomes a partial Brahman; but only by a knowledge of the Supreme Spirit, Brahma, does he become a full Brahman.

110. Having thus briefly shown the origin of the word Brahman and described the functions which first brought the caste into existence, we can now turn to the *modern* Brahman, with whom alone in this place we are immediately concerned. As the object of this paper is to describe the functions of the different castes and to classify the castes and sub-castes accordingly, I shall attempt in the following remarks to apply the same principle to the Brahman caste also—a task which is rendered the more difficult since, so far as I know, no systematic account has ever before been given or attempted of the functions practised by Brahmans at the present day. The genealogy and sub-divisions of the Brahmanical tribes so called have been described in great detail by the late Mr. Sherring in *Hindu Tribes and Castes*, Vol. I. He has shown how all Brahmans are supposed to have sprung from the seven great Rishis or sages of the Vedic age; how 56 different *gotras* or orders are said to have sprung out of these sages; how the said orders are classified according to the Veda (Rig, Sáma, Yajur, or Atharvan), which they are supposed to follow; how Brahmans are further sub-divided into *kuls* or clans; and lastly, how the clans are sub-divided into *shákhás* or branches. His account, which covers 113 pages, is made up chiefly of lists of proper names. As this subject has been so fully treated already, I propose to leave it altogether alone and to confine myself to the object with which alone this paper is concerned—a description of the functions of the modern Brahman. I hold, too, that the elaborate genealogical scheme described by Mr. Sherring and accepted by Brahmans themselves contains little, if any, historical truth, its very foundation—the seven sages—being mythical. Moreover, there are many sub-castes of Brahmans whose pedigree as Brahmans is said to be spurious, but whom it is necessary to include as members of the great Brahman fraternity, because they are regarded as such by the general Hindu community.

111. The following scheme shows how the Brahmans of the present day may be classified according to function. Some of these names represent separate castes or sub-castes—that is, distinct social units—which never marry or give their daughters in marriage outside their own ranks; others represent hereditary titles which must once have been names of separate castes, but are no longer so at the present time; others represent neither separate castes nor hereditary titles, but functions only :—

I {
- Hotri—Sacrificer (*Brahmanas and Kalpa Sutras*).
- Biduá—Consecrator of idols (*Karam Kánd and Sáma Ved*).
- Achárya—Superintendent of ceremonies (*Kalpa Sutras, Dharm Shastras, &c*)
- Dikshit—Initiator of the twice-born (*Karam Kánd*).
- Pathak—Private tutor of ditto (*Shastras or sciences*).

II
- Jyotishi—Astrologer (*Jyotish, astronomy and mathematics*).
- Pauránik—Reciter of ancient histories (*Purans and epics*).
- Purohit—Family priest (*Grihya Sutras aud Karam Kánd*).
- Pánde—Village schoolmaster (*Vernacular dia'ects and Ganit.*)

III
- Ojha—Sorcerer—(*Tantra and Kalika Purána*).
- Pandá—Temple priest (*Dash Karam*).
- Gangaputra—River priest (*Dash Karam*).
- Joshi—Fortune-teller (*Sámudrika*).
- Mahá-Brahman—Funeral priest (*Garur Purána*).

In the previous groups of castes I have mentioned the lowest first and the highest last. In the present group, however, I have reversed the order, because it was more convenient to begin with the ancient or Vedic Brahman and make a gradual descent to those who are further removed from this standard, but represent most nearly the religious life of the present day. Against each kind of Brahman I have mentioned the names of some of the books with which his function is specially connected. But it must not be supposed that all or even most of the Brahmans concerned are really acquainted with their respective books or with any portion of them. Except in a few places of exceptional note, like Ayodhya, Benares, Mathura, &c., Sanskrit is becoming more and more obsolete in Upper India, and most of the Brahmans named under heading III are now totally illiterate.

112. The Hotri is the only class of Brahman still left whose title and function recall the animal sacrifices of the Vedic age, and even this function is rapidly becoming obsolete in Upper India. The sacrifices of horses and cows, so famous in the Vedas and the great Hindu epics, are among the five things which have been declared unlawful in the *Káli yuga*, or present age of the world. This is distinctly laid down in the following sloka taken from Parásara's Code :—

Aswamedham, gavám lambhyam, sannyástham, pala-paitrikam,
Devarát sutotpattim, kalau pancha bibarjayet.

"There are five things which a man should avoid in the Kali-yuga—the horse sacrifice, the cow sacrifice, the ascetic stage of life, the flesh offering to the souls of the dead, and the raising of a son (to a deceased elder brother) from a younger brother." As the cow and the horse can no longer be used as victims, the modern Hotri is reduced to the less pretentious sacrifice of a goat; and even when this is performed, it is seldom now done according to the Vedic rites and ceremonies. The last instance of a Vedic goat-sacrifice was performed in Benares about twenty-six years ago. The account which I have received of it is as follows :—

A certain Brahman from Southern India, who had inherited the charge of an eternal fire from a remote and distinguished ancestry, had let the fire go out. In order to relight it and make a suitable atonement for the crime he had committed, he determined to celebrate a great sacrifice, and collected from among all the Hindu rájas who could be induced to contribute a sum of about Rs. 30,000 for the purpose. The ceremony lasted for twenty-one days. All this time Brahmans were being fed in thousands, offerings of *homa* were being thrown upon the altar, and *mantras* or sacred words were repeated with each offering. The goat intended for the sacrifice which was to crown the work was stalled in an enclosure set apart as the sacrificial floor; and the greatest attention, amounting almost to worship, was paid to it till the day of sacrifice came round. As the goat was being led up to the altar, its neck was garlanded with flowers, and red powder was showered on its head. The most learned and distinguished Brahmans who could be found were summoned from hundreds of miles round to take part in this Vedic sacrifice. The spot on which the goat was at last killed for the immolation was screened off, so that no profane eyes might behold what the Brahmans were doing or witness the relighting of the extinguished fire from the flame of the sacrifice. On receiving his fire relighted, the man was taken to the Ganges to be bathed by the Achárya or presiding priest; and such was the sanctity ascribed to the water in which he had been washed that almost the whole city of

Benares turned out to get a drop or two thrown at them by the hands of the priest. It is said that no such sacrifice had been performed before within the memory of any man living, nor is it expected that such will ever be performed again.

The substance of the *homa* offering which has given rise to the name of Hotri is made of ghí, rice, barley, til or oilseed, raisins, cocoanut, &c., all mixed up together. In large sacrifices such as the above, or at times when some other religious ceremony is performed with more than usual solemnity and cost, many maunds of this sacrificial matter are collected, and priests succeed each other in turns throwing dribblets of it on the flame and reciting texts from the Vedas. At the time when the homa is thrown on the fire twigs from certain trees or plants are thrown in with it,—*viz.*, from the pípal or fig-tree, the *palasa*, the mango, the catechu, the thorn-apple, the *kusha* grass, and the banyan. These six are collectively called *samidh*.

There is one more function left to the Hotri which may be traced to the Vedic age—the recitation of long passages from the Vedic hymns. This is done at times when new temples are opened, or when large feasts are given to Brahmans, and sometimes in the private houses of rich men. A Hotri is sometimes employed by men, who are wealthy enough to engage his services, to stand before an idol and recite extracts from the Vedas on their behalf. Such repetition is believed to benefit the soul of the man who pays for it.

113. The Biduá is the class of priest specially employed to consecrate images, wells, tanks, and mango orchards. His name is derived from *vid*, "to know," and appears to be a corruption of the word *vidyá*, an ancient synonym for Veda. The point in common between the Biduá and the Hotri is that both have the reputation of being acquainted with portions of the ancient Vedas, and hence the one is sometimes employed for the same purposes as the other. The original functions, however, are distinct. The Hotri performs or professes to perform what still remains of the old Vedic sacrifice, while the Biduá consecrates images and idols, to which the religion of the Vedic age was an entire stranger.

An image or any other symbol, such as a lingam, intended to represent the presence of a deity, is worth nothing more than the material it is made of, until it has undergone the process of consecration. The effect of this ceremony is to draw the deity down into the image or symbol, and to keep him there, so that henceforth the image and the deity become virtually one; for "the Aryan brother" does not make the distinction between the visible symbol and the unseen divinity, with which his admirers have sometimes credited him. The manner of the consecration is much the same for all Hindu deities alike, but the number of days spent on its performance depends upon the degree of dignity which the deity is supposed to possess. The idol or other symbol intended for consecration undergoes various forms of ablution. First it is bathed in water taken from some sacred river, as the Ganges, the Narbada, the Sarju, &c., or any of these combined, if the water can be procured. Then it is bathed in the *panchamrita*, or "five drinks of immortality," *viz.*, milk, cream, melted butter, honey, and sugar dissolved in holy water, first in each of these liquids separately, and afterwards in the five combined. The image is then finally washed once more in sacred water. The niche in the wall, or the block in the middle of the temple, on which the image or symbol is made to stand, undergoes the same ablutions as those applied to the idol. When the idol and its standing-place have been duly consecrated, the temple is *ipso facto* consecrated also.

Wells, tanks, and orchards are consecrated in much the same way as idols. No one is allowed to bathe in the tank, or drink water from the well, or eat of the fruit of the orchard, till the above liquids have been thrown into them. It is chiefly in the case of wells and tanks, which have been constructed from motives of public benefaction, that these rites of consecration are performed.

An essential part of the ceremony in each case consists in feeding a horde of Brahmans and in making a *homa* offering to the gods similar to that already described in paragraph 112. At such times a vast number of deities or unseen guests are invited to attend—(1) the nine planets (including the sun and moon) called Navagrahá ; (2) the twenty-seven lunar mansions called the Nakshatras ; (3) the constellation of the seven Rishis or sages called Sapta Rishi ; (4) the three hundred and thirty million deities who make up the vast pantheon of Hinduism ; (5) the Pitris or souls of departed ancestors, who make up another vast multitude almost equal to that of the gods ; (6) the ten Digpals who are said to preside over the ten points of the compass ; and (7) the sacred rivers of India and of the celestial firmament. For each of these seven groups a separate place, and a separate dish, very small in amount, are assigned, and they are invited to come down and taste, or at least smell, the offering made to them. The smallness of the feast thus prepared for the gods presents a strange contrast to the huge viands placed before the hungry Brahmans, who are regaled with a fresh meal every day as long as the ceremony of consecration lasts.

114. The Achárya (or as the name is now commonly spelt, Acharja) is the highest kind of priest in modern India. His place in the religious ceremonies of the present day is similar to that once held by the Brahman proper in the celebration of the Vedic sacrifices (see para. 108). The special function of the Acharja is to guide and superintend the Hotri and the Biduá, and his name is derived from *áchára*, which means "rule or direction." If any great religious ceremony is to be held in which Hotris, Biduás, and others are required, there must be one man to preside and give the necessary directions, and this man is called Achárya. His supervision is specially needed during the constant repetition of the *homa* offerings and the recitation of the appropriate Vedic texts. It is he, and he alone, who knows how to summon the hosts of divinities who are invited to partake of the offering, and how to send them back into the sky contented and propitiated.

There are very few Brahmans at the present day whose attainments in Sanskrit are sufficiently varied and accurate to enable them to discharge the office of Achárys. The highest title which can be given to a Brahman is to call him an Achárya, and this is the title which has been selected by the Educational Department in these provinces to be given to those students who pass the most difficult examination in the Benares Sanskrit College.

115. The priest specially employed to initiate a Hindu boy into the performance of his religious duties and to give him "the second birth" is called a Dikshit. The word is simply a contraction of Dikshitri or Dikshitá, which signifies "one who initiates"; and hence it does not mean "initiated," as Mr. Sherring and others have supposed (*Hindu Tribes and Castes*, Vol. I, page 9). It is only boys of the upper castes (that is, those who are called the twice-born) who are entitled to the privilege of *diksha*. But Brahmanism has for the last two hundred years and more been steadily decending into lower and lower strata of the population, absorbing one indigenous tribe after another ; and hence the possession of this privilege cannot now be considered a mark of "twice-born" ancestry.

The orthodox age for undergoing the rite of *diksha* or initiation is on the completion of the seventh year. The Hindu book of ceremonies known as *karam kánd* calls it the eighth, but the figure is raised to eight by counting the nine months preceding birth as an additional year. At the present day the orthodox age is not always observed, and a boy can be initiated a year or two later, if it suits the convenience of the parents to postpone incurring the expenditure which these rites entail. A boy, whatever his parentage may be, is not a full Hindu until the *diksha* has been performed. Up till then he is little better than a Sudra or unregenerated person. But on and after that day he incurs the religious responsibilities to which his parents have all along intended to dedicate him, as a Christian boy does by the double rite of baptism and confirmation. Girls are never "initiated" as boys are ; and thus a high-caste woman who marries a man of the Sudra rank cannot but become a Sudra herself. This, I suspect, is the real explanation of the abhorrence felt by Hindus to a woman being married into a caste lower than her own. The same abhorrence has never been felt to a twice-born man marrying or cohabiting with a Sudra woman, for the woman can rise to the rank of her husband ; but as she has never been initiated, she cannot raise the husband to her own. Thus in Manu's Code a Brahman was allowed to take a Sudra woman into his house ; but if a Sudra man married a Brahman woman, the son became a Chandál—"a sinful and abominable wretch."

The entire ceremony of *diksha* lasts some eight or nine days. Throughout these days the boy is put upon a very strict diet and undergoes a rigorous course of ablutions. He is bathed regularly at certain hours; after the bath mustard powder and oil are rubbed on his body; and he then undergoes a second bath to wash them off again. All this time he should wear nothing by day or night but a string made of the sacred grass called *kusha*, which is tied round his waist, and to which a narrow cloth called *langoti* is attached, fastened between his legs before and behind. Meanwhile the usual *homa* offerings are thrown on consecrated fire by priests of the Hotri class, who have been summoned for this purpose. When the last and greatest of the *homa* offerings has been made, the sacred thread (*upavit* or *janeo*) is thrown over the left shoulder of the boy by the Dikshit, and the first act of the ceremony of initiation is completed. The Dikshit then throws a cloth over his own and the boy's head, and under cover of this cloth he instils into his ears (in an under tone, so that no profane ears may catch what he says) the Gayatri and all the other sacred verses which a Hindu should utter on stated occasions every day of his life. The repetition of all these verses, and especially of the Gayatri, which is repeated first, constitutes the closing ceremony by which the boy is formally initiated into the rites of Hinduism. The boy must have heard and seen something of these rites beforehand through living with his parents; but until he has been formally initiated, and this by a Brahman competent to discharge the office, he is a mere heathen. For some weeks after the conclusion of the ceremony the Dikshit remains with the novitiate, so as to help him to perform the several daily rites and make him sufficiently perfect to be left to himself; and after leaving him, he continues to be his spiritual adviser for the rest of his life, whenever such advice may be required.

There is no space to enter minutely into the rites which make up the daily religious life of a Hindu, and for the teaching of which the Dikshit priest is specially employed. Certain verses have to be repeated and certain ceremonies performed every day before eating, drinking, and sleeping. In fact there is scarcely anything that a Hindu can do but he finds the cloud or sunshine of religion darkening or illuminating his path. The most important, perhaps, of the daily rites are the morning, evening, and midday oblations, which are collectively called the Trikal Sandhyá. Every morning in his life a man must rise before sunrise and bathe. While the sun is still half visible above the horizon, he must re-enter the river or tank and first throw up an offering of water with the palms of his hands (both palms being joined together) to the gods, the sages, and the souls of ancestors, and then make a final offering of water to the sun (*arka*). After making the offering to the sun, he must repeat the Gayatri one hundred and eight times. The same ceremony is performed with very slight changes at midday and again in the evening. Each ceremony is called Sandhya, or the junction; sunrise and sunset being the hours when day and night meet, and midday the hour when the easterly sun meets the western.

116. Priests who devote themselves to the teaching of the young have been called Páthak or Upádhay, the former name being best known in Upper India and the latter in the Lower Provinces. Both words mean literally "teacher."

The function of the Páthak begins where that of the Dikshit or initiator ends. In the old Hindu discipline the life of a twice-born or initiated person was parcelled out, as we showed in a former paragraph, into four successive stages or *avasthas*. The first of these was that of student or Brahmachári, and this was spent under the care of the Páthak or Upádhay. The Páthak, then, was a very important functionary in the days when Hinduism was strong and when the people were strictly orthodox. It devolved upon him to train the character of the young after the Brahmanical model and lay the foundations of a religious life. He instructed his pupils partly in the Vedas or religious poetry, but chiefly in the Shastras or so-called books of science. The office of Páthak, like that of almost every functionary in India, from the sweeper to the priest, is often hereditary among a certain circle of families. The sons of his constituents go to his house to receive daily instruction, and the sons of poorer Brahmans, who have no Páthak of their own, are encouraged to attend with them. All tuition is nominally gratis. In fact the Páthak is not only debarred from receiving monthly tuitional fees, but he is even expected to feed and maintain his pupils for nothing. They in return perform many kinds of menial offices for him, such as washing his feet, spreading his bed, drawing water from the well, driving his cows out to pasture, milking them when they come in, &c., nor do they disdain to eat the leavings which come from his table. There are two different ways in which a Páthak is maintained. Sometimes a rája or other rich man provides him with land, the rent of which keeps him above want and enables him to feed his pupils. Such endowments are not uncommon at the present time in Upper India, and in some cases such lands are exempted from paying rent or tax to the British Government. Another way in which the Páthak is maintained is by donations, called *guru dakshana*, which are given him by his wealthier pupils after they have completed their education and come into their patrimonial estates. The custom is for the ex-pupil to go to his former teacher and ask him what he would like to have, and whatever the teacher may say the ex-pupil is bound in honor to give.

117. The five kinds of functions described thus far, *viz.*, those of the Hotri, Biduá, Acharja, Dikshit, and Páthak, are the highest and most respected in which a Brahman can engage. It is only the "twice-born" classes or castes who have occasion to employ Brahmans for such purposes, and this is the main reason why the functions corresponding are held in such high repute. The case is different, however, with the functions which we have now to describe. These stand on a lower level than the preceding, because they are not less frequently exercised on behalf of castes or classes of the population, who are below the rank of "twice-born." The principle of "condescending to men of low estate," which constitutes the ideal of the Christian and Buddhist creeds, is entirely alien to the spirit of Brahmanism and was strictly prohibited by Brahman law-givers themselves (see Manu's Code, Chapter III, 65, and IV, 61, 81, 99). A Brahman who does anything to help or enlighten a low-caste man lowers himself by so doing, and the only motive that can lead him to commit such an impropriety is the fee which he exacts in return. Nevertheless, the practice of officiating for low-caste men is constantly on the increase, and such Brahmans now make up the bulk of the Indian priesthood.

118. The Jyotishi is a Brahman specially versed in astrology. This function consists in interpreting the will of the stars to his clients. His name is derived from *jyotish*, the Vedic name for astronomy, a science which formed one of the six Vedangas, or branches of Vedic exegesis.

The object for which astronomy was studied in ancient India, and which gave the first impulse to such studies, differed essentially from the uses to which such knowledge is now applied. Its sole purpose in the Vedic age was to fix the days and hours of the great periodic sacrifices. In India, as elsewhere, the earliest mode of measuring time was by the changes of the moon; and the asterisms lying in the moon's path were called Nakshatras or lunar mansions. Even in the earliest hymns these asterisms have not only received proper names but have been personified, and are invoked as deities to grant progeny and other blessings to their worshippers. In the first book of the Rig Veda mention is made of the thirteenth or intercalary month, and in certain hymns of the Yajur Veda this month is invoked as a deity under the name of Anhasaspati. In the later epic poems the Nakshatras are declared to be the wives of the moon-god, and the daughters of Daksha, one of the old names for the Creator. The Vedic name for astronomer was Nakshatra-darsa, "one who studied and observed the lunar mansions," and fixed thereby the dates of the periodic sacrifices.

The modern name for astronomer is *jyotishi*. After the old system of Vedic sacrifices had died out, the functions of the astronomer took an entirely different turn.

He became an astrologer rather than an astronomer, and this is the only light in which he can be now regarded. The Nakshatras are still, as before, looked upon as divine persons. But a much greater degree of prominence has been given to the influence which they are supposed to exercise on the events of human life. Every Hindu who is not an infidel (and total loss of faith is rare in Upper India, even among men educated in European sciences) believes that his fate is written in the stars; and as the moon and stars must inevitably run their courses, it is no wonder that Hindus are firm believers in fatalism. But to every evil influence which a star is expected to inflict there is a *shánti* or propitiatory ceremony attached, the object of which is to diminish, if not to avert, the calamity; and it rests with the astrologer to find out what evil the stars are about to inflict and to apply the remedy. The consulting of the Nakshatras plays as important a part in the life of a Hindu as even the institution of caste, and nothing serious can be done or undertaken till the stars have been declared favourable.

After the birth of a child, the first thing that the father does is to go to the *jyotishi* and tell him as exactly he can the hour in which the child was born. The *jyotishi* then consults the stars and casts the horoscope, from which the fate in store for the child is determined. If the astrologer's forecast turns out to be wrong, and he is twitted by the parent for having proved a false prophet, the astrologer taxes him in return with not having told him the hour of birth correctly, a pretext which can be easily set up in a country where clocks and watches are not in common use. At times of sickness or any other calamity the astrologer is consulted as to whether there is any evil star in the ascendant by which the calamity is caused. If the answer is in the affirmative (as of course it always is), the man seeking advice is told to make some offering in cash or kind in order to appease the hostile star; and as the astrologer is the recognised exponent of the star's feelings and wishes, he appropriates, and is expected to appropriate, the propitiatory offering. Thus the offering made to the star becomes part of the astrologer's fee. Sometimes, if a man is applying for a situation or for a higher salary, or seeks to secure success in some particular undertaking, a bribe is offered to the star (through the astrologer with whom the star is in league) to help him to gain his end. Not being able to whip the stars, as some nations have whipped their frogs in order to hasten the fall of the tropical rains, they use the astrologer as the medium for bribing them.

For settling betrothals and for the performance of marriage ceremonies the services of the astrologer are indispensable. When the family barber or Nápit has selected a boy whom he considers a suitable match for some girl of the same caste (see above para. 97), no contract can be made between the parents till the astrologer has been consulted as to whether the stars of the boy are not inimical to those of the girl. Nor is this even enough. He must also find out what the castes of the boy and the girl were in the former state of existence. If both were of the same caste in this pre-existent state, the betrothal contract can be made, so long as the stars are not otherwise hostile. But if it turns out that the caste of the boy in a former state was below that of the girl, the betrothal is disallowed. Brahmans have framed all these rules entirely to their own advantage. A man who was a Brahman in a former state may marry any girl who in a former state belonged to some caste below his own, but the rule is never reversed. Some idea may be formed of the obstructions which can be thrown in the way of marriage amongst Hindus, when it is known that compatibility of caste in a former state of existence is only one out of the thirty-six conditions that must be complied with before a betrothal can be declared valid. The most enlightened Hindus of the present day are generally compelled to comply with these conditions, however much they may desire to discard them.

An auspicious day must be selected by the astrologer for almost everything that can happen in a man's or woman's life—for the day of marriage, for every part of the marriage ceremony, for starting on a journey, for putting the first plough to the soil, &c. A woman cannot put on a new set of bangles until she has learnt that the stars are favourable, and an orthodox man will not put on a new garment unless he is assured that the day is lucky for first wearing it. It is matter of history that when Ala-ud-din Khilji was marching upon Nadiya, the great centre of Brahmanism in Bengal, the Hindu rája was ordered to wait for nine hours before marching out to meet him, because until then the stars were declared to be unfavourable. Meanwhile the Musalman forces entered the city, and the rája had to flee for his life. On the other hand, there is a Hindu proverb to the effect that necessity has no laws, even though the stars may be against it:—*Ghari men ghar jare, Arhái ghari bhadra.* That is, "if the house will catch fire in twenty-four minutes, an hour (hence) is an unlucky moment for action."

In the constitution of the Hindu township the astrologer is a most important functionary, and men of all castes, whatever their rank may be in the social scale, look to him for the interpretation of the stars in every domestic event or industrial undertaking. As the *jyotishi* does not confine himself to the "twice-born" castes, but officiates for men of low estate, provided they can pay him, he has been and is one of the chief means by which the casteless tribes have been brought within the pale of Hinduism; and this is a process which is continually going on before our eyes. The Hotri and Biduá cannot recite Vedas, or perform the *homa* sacrifice, or consecrate idols, for any but the "twice-born" castes; and it is only in those families which have established a similar title to the rank of twice-born, that the Dikshit (initiator) or the Páthak (private tutor) will consent to serve. But the astrologer does not refuse his services to any man who offers him a fee proportioned to his means; and among the various functions that come within the sphere of a modern Hindu priest there is none that appeals more directly to the minds of ignorant and superstitious men. It seems, indeed, that belief in the influence of the stars upon human destiny has been one of the universal instincts of mankind; and the *jyotishi* comes armed with a reputation for mystic knowledge which to the simple mind of the savage or low-caste man is at once convincing. One of the first symptoms of a savage tribe becoming Brahmanized is that they have begun to consult the astrologer. The astrologer, then, has played and is playing a very active part in drawing the indigenous or non-Brahmanized tribes within the net of Hinduism, and the intercourse which he is thus tempted to hold with the unregenerated masses has, as we have just shown, made his office appear less respectable in the eyes of other Brahmans. All castes, however, hold him in awe, and it is impossible to foresee the day which will witness their escape from his thraldom. Muhammadans have almost as much faith in his pretensions as Hindus.

119. The Pauránik, as his name implies, is one who makes it his calling to read out the Puranas, or ancient histories so called, in the presence of mixed audiences. Women as well as men attend such readings; but if they belong to the upper castes, they are screened off by a curtain. The manuscript or printed paper from which the reading is made is called *a poti* (a corruption from the Sanskrit *pustak*); for nothing so profane as a book bound in leather is used on such occasions. The *poti* is worshipped as a fetish. Before the reading is commenced, the man in whose house the entertainment is held bows before the *poti*, makes it an offering of rice, sandal-wood powder, flowers, &c., just as he would make before an idol; and if he is a man of approved piety, he repeats this offering every morning, so long as the reading lasts. Even the priest who reads receives something like divine homage; for his forehead is painted with sandal-wood powder and he is crowned, like an idol, with a chaplet of flowers. One or two hours are set apart every evening for the reading, and sometimes three months are spent before the *poti* is finished. At the close of the performance every member of the audience presents an offering to the *poti*, as to a divinity or idol—an offering of cash, or grain, or a piece of cloth, each giving according to his means. After these offerings have remained a little time in front of the *poti*, the Pauránik takes them up and appropriates them as his own fee—an arrangement which is recognised as perfectly correct and legitimate by the donors present. The reader is believed to impersonate, for the time being at least, not only the book, but the gods and demi-gods whose actions it records; and as neither the book nor the gods appropriate the offering, it is rightly made over to the priest who represents them.

It is chiefly in the rainy season, when there is less scope for occupation in the open air, that these readings are held. They take the same place in Hindu social life as that of the Sunday sermon or week-day lecture in Europe. No one but a Brahman can exercise this function. He may be a worse reader than a Kayasth, or a Chattri or even a common Kahár, but this matters nothing. Spoken by a layman the words lose their imputed sanctity; spoken by a Brahman, they illuminate the soul of the listener, even if he understands little or nothing of their meaning. Pious men, who have the means, sometimes keep a Paurának to read to them every day of the year.

There is one more fact deserving of notice in regard to the Paurának before we part with him. Like the *jyotishi,* he has been and is largely instrumental in converting the indigenous tribes and ignorant classes of the population to Hinduism. To read anything sacred within the hearing of a Sudra, much more within that of an outcaste, is a practice against which Brahmans are cautioned in Manu's Code, on pain of incurring the most terrific consequences in the future life. But when the Brahman begins to weigh the wants of the present life against the threats or promises of an uncertain future, he not unfrequently decides in favor of the former, and the terrors of hell have proved far less effective than the attractions of pice. It is seldom that a camp of Kanjars or Nats, or other casteless and wandering tribes, can remain for several months together on the same spot, but some Brahman finds them out and opens his Purána and commences to read aloud before an ignorant and gaping audience. This is often the first step taken by an Indian savage towards entering within the fold of Hinduism. It is easy to conceive how in ancient times small roving bands of cattle-grazers, such as Ahírs, Gujars or Gaddis, and afterwards hunting bands of Pásis, Bhars, Arakhs, and many more, were thus caught as it were by the hungry Brahman, and detained in the outskirts of the village, till they became part of the regular inhabitants and, having abandoned their own tribes, formed the nucleus of what are now known as the lower castes. It is thus that Kanjars, Doms, Thárus, &c., are now being drawn within the net, from which to those once caught there is no escape.

120. The office of Purohit or family priest was one of much distinction in ancient times; but there is now very little dignity attaching to it. The name simply means "superintendent," "master of the ceremonies." It was one of the oldest names, probably older even than "Brahman," for a professional priest. For it was the custom of kings in the Vedic age to employ some man, versed in the sacrificial art, to perform the sacrifices for them, and this functionary was called Purohit. The violent contests between Vasishta and Visvamitra, two of the most distinguished prelates of the Vedic age, for the post of professional priest in the court of king Sudas, show how much importance was attached to the office in those days.

The office of Purohit seems to have been hereditary from the first, and this is one of the chief reasons why it has become so insignificant in modern times. A man who is certain of his appointment and of being able to bequeath it to his son will not take the trouble to go through the severe course of training to which Brahmans desirous of rising in their profession are ordinarily subjected, and hence the family priest became as lazy and illiterate as we now find him. In these days a purohit can seldom discharge any but the most petty offices for his master, such as presenting the daily offering to the family gods, or performing the usual rite when the first plough is put into the soil or when the harvest is being brought in. On great occasions, such as the performance of a marriage ceremony, or the dedication of a temple, or the consultation of the stars, or the initiation of a son, the Achárya, or Biduá, or Jyotishi, or Dikshit are called in, although such offices would come well within the duties of a family priest, if he were competent to perform them. On these occasions, he renders what help he can under the guidance of the Achárya or other invited priest, particularly in doing the preparatory or (as we should call it) the "dirty" work. At the appointed season he assists his master in paying the annual offering (*sraddha*) to the souls of the dead. If his master has been keeping a fast, the purohit is ready enough to act the part of the Brahman, who, according to Hindu rules, must be fed first before the fast can be broken. If his master has a private shrine in his house, he acts as the temple-priest, tending the lamps and sweeping the floor. If his master is seeking to get his daughter betrothed, he helps the barber to find out some suitable boy. If his master is taking a journey, the purohit sometimes goes with him to act as cook ; for no caste in India will refuse to take food cooked by a Brahman. If his master wishes to give a feast to Brahmans on some periodical or other festival, the purohit invariably offers his services both as caterer and as consumer. At all religious ceremonies, should the master be unable to attend, the purohit can act as his proxy. He can go on a pilgrimage for his master to some distant shrine, fast for him at home, and even bathe for him in some sacred stream or tank.

Every orthodox Hindu is glad to keep a purohit if he can afford the cost, just as the Israelites of old esteemed themselves fortunate if they had a Levite on their establishment. Every reader will remember the story of Micah, who, having met with a stray Levite, said unto him—"Dwell with me and be unto me a father and a priest," and duly installed him in the office. Then said Micah—"Now know I that the Lord will do me good, seeing that I have a Levite to be my priest" (*Judges*, xxvii,13).

But the functions of purohit are not now limited, as they once were, to the twice-born castes. There are certain classes of Brahmans, calling themselves purohits, who have established priestly relations with the inferior tribes and castes, and visit them when the occasion arises, receiving gifts in return. There are, for example, Chamárwa Brahmans, and even Dom Brahmans, who give certain help to the tribes corresponding at times of marriage, &c. A savage, who has gone so far as to consult an astrologer or hear a Paurának read to him, will generally go a step further, if he remains long enough in the same place, and attach himself to some Brahman who will act as his purohit or family priest whenever his services are required. When this stage has been reached, the captivity of the man is no longer a matter of doubt. Henceforth he becomes a Hindu, attends the great public festivals, bathes in the holy waters, visits the sacred shrines, and, though he may not be allowed to enter a temple, he can employ the temple-priest to place his offering on the idol. It is thus that the indigenous tribes of India have one after another been drawn into the net of Hinduism, until, in Upper India at least, there are scarcely any more tribes to be caught.

121. The Pánde (like the Páthak or Upádhay described in para. 116) is a teacher of the young, but of a much lower stamp. The name is derived from *pandá*, science or knowledge ; and hence Pandit has become the title of a Brahman deeply versed in Sanskrit. Perhaps, then, originally the functions of the Pánde were scarcely, if at all, inferior to those of the Páthak : but for some centuries past this has not been the case. The Pánde does not now teach Sanskrit, but only Hindi. His tuitional course is not merely religious, but secular also ; for it includes the elementary arithmetic (*ganit*) used in the native markets, and the quick running hand known as Kaithi. He is in fact "the village schoolmaster," and as such held an important place in the ranks of the Hindu township. His school was less exclusive than that of the Páthak ; for the latter received only twice-born pupils, most of whom were Brahmans ; while the former did not refuse admission to boys below the rank of twice-born, provided these were not of castes whom it was a pollution to touch. The Sanskrit patshalas, which we now see around us, and which are becoming fewer every year, are the legacy of Páthaks, while the Hindi patshalas which have survived in larger numbers are the legacy of Pándes. The existence of these two classes of schools is the sole foundation for the assertion which has been made of late, that India possessed in former times a complete system of indigenous schools open to all classes of the community.

Men of the Kayasth caste have now acquired a large share of the function once monopolised by Pándes. Yet all such Kayasths are called *gurus* or spiritual guides, a title which, properly speaking, could be applied only to a Brahman.

122. The Ojha Brahman is one who is specially versed in the practice of spells and charms. Most of these rites are described in the books called *tantras;* and hence a Brahman who deals in them is sometimes called by the name of Tantrik, that is, wizard or sorcerer. It is difficult for outsiders to investigate the mysteries of Indian magic; for the interpretation of the tantras is more esoteric than that of any other branch of Sanskrit literature; and it is obviously to the interest of the sorcerer caste to keep their knowledge as much as possible to themselves. To this, more than to any other class of Brahman, the well-known couplet given below is applicable:—

Devadhinam jagat sarvam, mantradhinascha devatah.
Te mantrah Brahmanádhinah, tasma Brahmano devata.

"The whole world is in the power of the gods, and the gods are in the power of magic; magic is in the power of the Brahman, and therefore the Brahman is himself the god":—a true description of a priest who professes to control the higher powers by magical words and deeds and to compel them to interfere in the affairs of men according to his own wishes.

The word *tantra* is of Sanskrit origin and means "a string or system" of ceremonial rites. But the name Ojha (by which the Brahman wizard is most commonly known) is derived from the word *ojh,* which signifies "entrail," and is of a purely indigenous or non-Sanskrit source—indicating, what is the fact, that the art of sorcery, though in a ruder and less cultivated form, is well known to those savage and casteless tribes of India which are still outside the pale of Brahmanism, and that Brahmans themselves acquired the art from the aboriginal races. The aboriginal sorcerer is called Ojha because he examines the entrails of the victim immediately after it has been slain, while the Brahman sorcerer does not. In spite of this, however, the name Ojha has fastened itself upon the Brahman also.

The office of sorcerer, within the Brahman caste at least, is strictly hereditary, and thus every man belonging to this class of Brahman is a potential wizard. Yet a severe and prolonged probation must be undergone before a man is competent to commence practice; for he cannot get the deity into his power by the more right of hereditary claims. He must go through a course of *path* and *jap,* the former of which consists in reading aloud, and the latter in silently repeating, the name of the deity to be conquered a million times, more or less, according to the nature of the spell to be acquired. Special hours are assigned for this performance, special postures of the body, special diet, and a specially appointed space, beyond which the probationer is not allowed to go until the process of initiation is finished. Special texts, too, are associated with special spells, and spells have been classified under four main headings, which are as follows:—

(1) *Máran,* or putting a man to death.

(2) *Uchhátan,* or getting him out of the way without killing him.

(3) *Vashikaran,* or getting him into one's power so as to use him as a tool.

(4) *Akarshan,* or drawing him towards you from a distance.

Under each of these main heads there is a variety of sub-headings which need not be here enumerated. Different deities are attached to different spells, and it is though the medium of the deity attached to each spell that the sorcerer is believed to work. All of these deities, however, are at bottom really one; for they are mere variations of Káli, the wife of Mahadev and the dreaded goddess of death. In the Hindu pantheon there are ten main forms of this goddess besides several minor ones, and these ten forms are known collectively by the name of Dashmakávidyá. Each separate form, however, is treated as a distinct personality. The average sorcerer contents himself with captivating three or four only of these as his accomplices. But men of exceptionally high training or ambition aim at acquiring a mastery over the entire group. Saraswati, the goddess of learning and wife of Brahmá the Creator, and Lakshmi, the goddess of wealth and wife of Vishnu the Preserver, are sometimes invoked by the sorcerer in conjunction with Káli, the wife of Mahádev the Destroyer; but this is only done in cases where wisdom or wealth happen to be the objects specially sought for, and even then these benign goddesses lose something of their usual gentleness through being associated with such a hideous divinity as Káli. Those Hindus who worship the female powers (Sakti), to the neglect of the male triad known as Brahmá, Vishnu, and Mahádev, are called Sáktyas, and to such men the *tantras* are the favourite scriptures, and the Ojha or Tantrik Brahman is the favourite priest.

Brahmans of the Ojha caste are also called Panchmakári, because the conditions under which they perform their rites are expressed in five words, each of which begins with *m* : *mánsa*, or eating flesh ; *madra*, or drinking wine ; *mantra*, or repeating magical words ; *mudrá*, or putting the limbs and fingers in certain postures ; and *maithun*, or the association of the wife with the husband. As the sole object of worship is a goddess, and as none but the female powers of creation are recognized by Brahmans of this class, the ceremonies are considered null and void, unless the wife of the priest takes part in them and repeats in act and word everything that he himself does and says. If the priest happens to be far away from his house, or if for any reason his wife cannot accompany him, or if he happens to have no wife at the time when his services are wanted, he engages a prostitute and lives with her as her husband for such time as the ceremonies last. This arrangement answers the purpose equally well ; for the efficacy of the ceremonies is not impaired so long as some woman living in conjugal or *quasi*-conjugal union with the man takes part in it.

In some parts of India the female principle is worshipped, not merely by name and with the help of symbols, but in the person of the woman herself, and at some of the temples of Káli, especially those in Assam and Bengal, promiscuous intercourse is said to form part of the orgies.

There is scarcely any reason for doubt that Brahmans of the Tantrik or Ojha caste are to a large extent descended from aboriginal priests, specimens of whom abound even at the present day among the indigenous and un-Brahmanized tribes of Upper India, such as Doms, Thárus, Kanjars, Nats, &c. Even among these tribes the function of sorcerer has a tendency to become hereditary ; but when such tribes become converted to Hinduism, the hereditary principle which Hinduism has so consistently enforced in every other case would be openly avowed and confirmed, and thus the aboriginal priest would naturally rise to the status of Brahman. The Ojha Brahman is so utterly unlike the Brahman of Manu's Code in manners and character, and so very like the Ojha of the aboriginal tribes from whom he has borrowed his name, that it is impossible to avoid the conclusion that the one is descended from the other. Both lean upon the same goddess, Káli ; both undergo a severe course of physical and mental discipline before she will consent to use them as the instruments of her power ; both indulge largely in flesh diet, in intoxicating liquor, and in free intercourse with women ; both shed the blood of animals before the idol which they worship ; both expel devils from the sick or drive them into those who are whole ; both use magic, spells, and charms. The difference between them lies in the fact that the Brahman sorcerer has reduced his art to a written code or system (*tantra*), while the aboriginal sorcerer has remained a coarse and illiterate savage. But even among those practitioners who from time immemorial have been credited with the name and rank of Brahman, and who are employed as such by the respectable castes of Hindus, there are some who are quite illiterate. Between these and the aboriginal priest no substantial difference exists.

Almost all Brahmans of the Maithil tribe (as distinct from those of the Saraswat, Kanaujia, Jijhotiya, and Gaur tribes) practise the function of Ojha ; and it would seem that Bengal had no Brahmans of any other stamp until the time of Adhiswar, king of Gaur, who lived in A.D. 900, and invited (as the legend says) five distinguished priests from Kanyá Kubja (Kanauj) to enlighten his people and himself in the milder creed of Brahman and Vishnu. These five priests became the founders of the great Kanaujia families in Bengal, and introduced a new class of rites and tenets distinct from those of the Maithil Brahmans, who trace their origin to Mithila or Behar.

The late Mr. Sherring, after giving a brief account of the Ojha Brahmans of Benares (which, however, is more true of the aboriginal than of the Brahmanical sorcerer for whom it is intended) concludes with saying: "Formerly the Ojha was always a Brahman, but his profession has become so profitable that sharp, clever, shrewd men in all the Hindu castes have taken to it." This is quite incorrect. It implies that Brahmans were the first inventors of sorcery, and that the art has since been filtrating downwards from them to the castes immediately below, and from these again to castes still lower. The truth lies in the opposite direction, as we have already explained. Moreover, it is wrong to say that Ojhas can be found "in *all* the Hindu castes." They are only to be found in the very lowest—that is, in those backward and despised communities whom I have placed in this paper in the class of hunting and fishing castes and in the ranks of the lower artisan and serving castes. As these tribes were the last to be brought within the pale of Hindu castes, their Hinduism is still of the faintest possible type, and hence they have not yet altogether discarded men of their own tribes as priests or sorcerers. But as soon as a caste begins to rise in the social scale, that is, to make a nearer approach towards Hinduism proper—the aboriginal priest disappears, and Brahmans of the various orders and degrees take the entire superintendence of divine matters into their own hands. No such thing as an Ojha could be found or has ever been heard of among Chattris, Khattris, Kayasths or other castes holding an equally high status, nor among the agricultural and higher artisan castes who come immediately below them in rank. It would be almost, if not quite, as difficult to find an Ojha among the pastoral castes, such as Ahír, Gújar, &c., who rank immediately below the agricultural. The only castes then, who have retained their own sorcerers, and do not employ Brahmans for this purpose, are those which constitute the lowest stratum of the population, *viz.*, the hunters, trappers, fishermen, scavengers, basket-makers, hide-skinners, &c., who are the least removed from primeval savagery and the furthest removed from the Hindu model.

No worship can be paid to Káli, the patron goddess of the Ojhas, without the shedding of blood. The animal now chiefly sacrificed by the low caste or aboriginal priest is the pig, that by the Ojha Brahman the goat. But the Tantrik sacrifice of the goat must not be confounded with the Vedic one alluded to above in para. 112. The ceremonies are totally different. There are, as is well known, two sets of *mantras* or sacred texts in Hinduism, one of which is called Vedic and the other Tantrik, and the latter only can be used in the goat sacrifice in honor of Káli. Moreover, the Vedic sacrifice can only be performed by Brahmans of the highest stamp (the Hotri and Achárya), who would disdain to associate with an Ojha, and only in honor of the older divinities of Hinduism, amongst whom Káli and her consort, Shiva, had no place.

The Kálika Purána, which is the chief authority for the rites to be paid to Káli, prescribes many kinds of animals besides the goat or pig, as fit to be sacrificed in her honor; and the list is such as to show the savage or non-Aryan origin of Káli herself: "birds, tortoises, crocodiles, hogs, goats, buffaloes, guanas, porcupines, and the nine kinds of deer, yaks, black antelopes, crows, lions, fishes, the blood of one's body, and camels are the sacrificial animals." But the list of victims does not stop here. The same Purána breaks out into a rhapsody of delight on the merits of human blood:—"O man, through my good fortune, thou hast appeared as a victim; therefore I salute thee, though multiform and of the form of a victim.

Thou by gratifying Chandiká destroyest all evils incident to the giver. Thou, a victim, who appearest as a sacrifice meet for the Vaishnavi, hast my salutations. Victims were created by the self-born himself for sacrificial rites. I shall slaughter thee to-day, and slaughter at a sacrifice is no murder." The practice of sacrificing men or children to Káli was once widely practised by the Ojha Brahmans in all parts of Hindustan and Bengal, and perhaps even now it has not entirely died out. "Persons are not wanting," says Dr. Rajendra Lal Mitra, "who suspect that there are still nooks and corners in India where human victims are occasionally slaughtered for the gratification of the Devi;" and he adds that "there is scarcely a respectable house in all Bengal the mistress of which has not at one time or other shed her own blood under the notion of satisfying the goddess by the operation" (*Indo-Aryans* Vol. II., para. 111). The writer is here alluding to customs which prevail among Hindus of respectable castes; but I have reason to think that the shedding of human blood has survived among the non-Hindu tribes also. In the course of the enquiries made by myself amongst the casteless tribes of Upper India, such as Kanjars and others, the hesitation with which answers were given respecting the kinds of victims offered to their tutelar goddess, Mari, Chandrika, Kálika, &c., all of whom are merely variations of the now Hinduized Káli, leads me to suspect that human sacrifices are still offered by the aboriginal priest in places where the act is not likely to be discovered.

123. The Pandá is an inferior class of Bráhman, whose special function consists in taking charge of temples and assisting visitors to present their offerings to the shrine. He might be simply defined as a temple-priest. The word *Pandá* means science, and is the same as that from which Pánde or schoolmaster and Pandit or learned men are derived. But the name Pandá as applied to temple-priests has now become a misnomer; for all such men are totally illiterate—inferior in this respect to priests of the Ojha caste, amongst whom literary ability may not unfrequently be found, though here, too, it is decidedly on the wane. Temple-priests subsist for the most part on the offerings made to the idol at whose temple they preside. Such offerings may consist of money, grain, cloth, vegetables, fruits, live animals, such as the goat, the horse, and even the elephant. All of these are appropriated by the temple-priest, who in some cases, if his temple is much frequented, becomes very wealthy. The popularity of a temple depends, not on the degree of attention which the priest prays to it, but on its reputation for sanctity or antiquity, and on the rank of the god to whom it is dedicated. A Pandá, who has amassed wealth through the offerings made at his temple, seldom remains there himself, but hires out some poorer Brahman to act as his proxy. If, however, he hears that some rája or other rich man is about to visit the temple, he takes good care to be there himself and secure the largest share of the liberal offering or fee that is expected. Almost every Pandá has a distinct circle of clients living at various distances from his own house or temple, and sometimes at a distance of one hundred miles or more. He endeavours to pay each of them a visit at intervals of one or two years, in expectation of the fee which clients so visited are accustomed to give. No Pandá is ever allowed to visit another Pandá's clients. Nor may the client himself pay his devotions to any temple other than that at which his own Pandá presides, unless it be to a temple dedicated to some other divinity.

The Pandá is not able, however, to appropriate all the offerings made at his temple to his own individual use. He is expected out of these offerings to keep the temple in repair, in case no pious layman comes forward to relieve him of the burden. He is expected in any case to supply the clarified butter or oil with which in some temples an ever-burning lamp is fed, to provide the daily offerings of cooked food with which the hunger of the idol is supposed to be satisfied, to sweep out the interior of the temple, and to provide the bell which he rings at the stated hours of worship.

Every temple in India, until it is deserted and offerings cease to be made to it, is furnished with an attendant priest. If the temple is attached to a private house and is not open to the general public, the purohit or family priest may discharge the necessary functions, or some Pandá may be appointed from without. In a public temple the Pandá first placed in charge of it by the founder acquires through long custom a prescriptive right to appropriate all the profits which he can make out of it, and to bequeath this right to his children and grand-children. So entirely is this right regarded as the private property of the priest who has acquired it, that he can use it as security for a loan, or sell it to any other Brahman, or to a Goshâyen, or even to a layman ; and the layman would in this case put some Brahman there as his servant to receive the profits which the temple may bring in to him.

The office of Pandá is not considered respectable by other Brahmans or by the upper castes of laymen. One reason of this is that the majority of the temples of which Pandás are in charge are dedicated to Mahadev; and it is an old maxim amongst Hindus of the upper castes, that offerings made to the lingam (the figure by which the presence of Mahadev is symbolized) will bring evil to any one who receives them, though they will bring good to the giver. It is said that when Daksha's altar was overthrown by Mahadev, the former uttered a curse that any offering paid to the lingam would prove an evil rather than a blessing to the priest who received it—a legend which corroborates the assertion made in the previous paragraph, that Mahadev was an aboriginal god, whom Brahmans for that reason at first declined to honor, but whom they were afterwards compelled to admit as the third member of the Triad in consequence of the ever-increasing absorption of the aboriginal tribes. In the Vedic hymns, where the Aryan side of Hinduism is specially represented, Daksha appears as one of the numerous forms of the Creator, while Mahadev or Shiva is never once mentioned. It is only by the upper castes of Hindus that the Pandá is not respected : for the lower castes, who make up the great majority of the people, esteem him very highly as the mediator between themselves and their favourite divinity, Mahádev. Men whose caste is so low that they are not allowed to go inside a temple employ the Pandá to place their offerings on the shrine.

The most celebrated of the shrines in Upper India and elsewhere have distinct families of Pandás attached to them, and the local groups made up of such families might truly be said to constitute separate castes ; for they marry only among themselves and carefully exclude outsiders from participation in the privileges which they have secured. There are, for example, the Pandás of Gaya, who are called Gayawáls; the priests of Mathura, who have taken the title of Chaube ; similar castes of Pandás at the great temples in Benares, at Vindhyachal near Mirzapur, at Jwála Mukhi in the Kangra valley, at the temple of Káli in Calcutta, at the temple of Kámákshi in Assam, at the celebrated temple of Mahádev in Golagokaran, and at many of the holy places of Ayodhya.

One of the duties of the Pandá is to sacrifice goats to Káli—a function which he shares with the Ojha Brahman whom we have already described.

124. The Gangaputra or Ghatiya (for the two names are synonymous) might be called a river-priest. The former name means "son of the Ganges," and the latter "one who sits on the ghát or bank." His special function consists in helping pilgrims to bathe in some sacred stream or tank during the appointed periodical festivals. His rank among Brahmans is about equal to that of Pandá; and their duties are very similar, except that the one presides at temples and the other at bathing-places. As the Pandá provides the oil and lamps required for the idol and sometimes repairs the temple itself and assists the visitor to present his offering, so the Gangaputra repairs the steps leading down to the water, spreads a carpet or mat for the bathers, and takes charge of their clothes and shoes till they come out of the water. There are some Brahmans who combine the functions of river-priest and temple-priest in one;

such for example are the Chaubes of Mathura, the Gayawáls of Buddha Gaya, the Prágwáls of Allahabad, and others.

The Gangaputra, like the Pandá, is totally illiterate. The bather is supposed to have a *mantra* or sacred text recited over him by the priest as he descends into the water. But many of the priests cannot repeat even this. The pilgrim is generally satisfied, so long as he gets a dip into the holy water and pays a fee to the Brahman. By so doing he propitiates the water and washes away his sins. River-priests as a class are distinguished for their lazy and licentious mode of life; but this does not diminish their influence among the community at large. The pilgrim on arriving at the sacred tank or river is at once pounced upon by some priest who has been watching his approach, and is guided implicitly by what this man tells him to do. The stairs leading down to the water are parcelled out in certain lots, each of which is claimed by some particular priest as his hereditary property; and if one priest is found poaching in another's preserves, the encroachment may lead to riot and even to bloodshed. The property in a *ghát* or bathing-stair can be given as a dowry, or sold, or mortgaged, or sub-divided between brothers, and in short treated like any other kind of private property. Such property is even recognized in the Government courts; for both Pandás and Gangaputras will appeal to these courts for redress, when they think that their rights are being encroached upon by men of their own fraternity.

It is specially important in the eyes of orthodox Hindus to bathe in the Ganges or some other sacred river on days of eclipse; and it is at the same time especially degrading to Brahmans to accept of fees or alms on days when the demon of darkness is abroad. But the Gangaputra has no scruples on this account, and this is an additional reason why he holds such a low rank among other Brahmans. On the eclipse of the moon, the most lucky site, at which a person can bathe in the Ganges, is Benares; and on the eclipses of the sun, Kuruksetra. The most appropriate kind of donation to be given on days of either eclipse is a cow; but those who are unable to afford such a costly offering give presents of grain, or cloth, or money. It is believed that anything given on a day of eclipse will be returned a hundredfold to the giver. Hence Hindus esteem themselves fortunate in having been provided with a priest of the Brahman order, who will accept of donations on such inauspicious days.

Another function for which the services of the Gangaputra are often employed consists in the assistance rendered to ignorant and illiterate men in making the annual offering to the souls of ancestors. An offering of water and of the cake or ball of rice called *pinda* is paid once a year in the month of Kuár (partly September and partly October): this offering is repeated for fifteen days continuously and is called *sráddha,* while the days set apart for paying the offering are called *pitri-paksha.* The priest leads his clients into the water, shows them what to do, and utters the appropriate text if he knows it, or invents one if he does not. Men who are educated do not seek his assistance, but they do not withhold the customary fee for the privilege of using his ghát or bathing-stair.

125. The Joshi is a caste of Brahman who professes the art of telling fortunes. The name is merely a contraction of Jyotishi, "astrologer." His art, though somewhat akin to that of the astrologer, is not by any means the same; but writers have been apt to confound them. For instance, in the North-West Provinces Gazetteer, Vol. VIII, Part II., page 1, it is said: "Joshi is a class of Brahmans who follow astrology as a profession and earn a subsistence by casting nativities." This is true not of the Joshi, but of the Jyotishi; for the Joshi never casts nativities and is not really an astrologer. Again, in the same Gazetteer, Vol, V, page 583, it is said that "the trade of the Jyotishi is fortune-telling or astrology. The planet Sanichar or Saturday is their favourite deity, &c." These remarks apply to the Joshi, but not to the Jyotishi; for the Jyotishi is not under the patronage of the planet Saturn, whereas the Joshi is. The difference between the two men is this: the Jyotishi tells fortunes by the stars, while the Joshi

does so by the lines and other marks on the palms of the hands, on the face, and on the body generally. The nearest term, then, to express the Joshi's art is palmistry, while the exact term expressive of the art of the Jyotishi is astrology.

Another mistake has sometimes been made in supposing that the Joshi is a mere migratory impostor of the gypsy stamp, having no historical foundation for the function which he affects to practise. The supposed analogy between the Joshi and the gypsy is entirely groundless. The art of palmistry is a very old one in India and has a literature of its own. The caste, too, has as good a pedigree as any other caste in India. Nor is the art of palmistry more absurd than that of astrology, which is generally practised by high-caste Brahmans. The old name for palmistry was Samudrika, and in ancient times one who specially devoted himself to its study was called Samudriki. It was considered to be a collateral branch of the single science of Jyotish, and this is the reason why the caste is now called by the name of Joshi.

The Joshi of modern times has become totally illiterate; yet he is generally to be seen with a manual of palmistry in his hand of which he knows nothing. The highest castes of Hindus refuse even at times to consider him a Brahman; but he regards himself as one, and is so regarded by about eighty per cent. of the population. Moreover, he wears the sacred thread, and has worn it from a remote ancestry: and he is by no means the only Brahman with whom other Brahmans refuse to associate. The fee which he receives for delivering his oracle (the wording of which, like those of Delphi, is always studiously ambiguous) is generally a supply of grain sufficient for one day's consumption. But if one of his clients happens to fall in with some stroke of good luck, the Joshi at once pays him a visit and attempts to convince him that it has occurred in fulfilment of his prediction, and demands a special fee for having proved such a wise and auspicious prophet. Each Joshi has a select circle of constituents, who live in villages surrounding his own at a distance of about ten or twelve miles, and no other Joshi is allowed to visit them. In the hill districts of Kumaun, where some of the old Hindu customs have retained something of their pristine vigour, the Joshi is more respected than he is in the plains; and in Kumaun he is not so illiterate. In those districts many of the clerks in the Government offices are of the Joshi caste, and Pandit Mathura Dat, late head-master of the anglo-vernacular school of Jalaun, might be quoted as an example of a Joshi who has done credit to his fraternity. The name Bhanreriya or "gabbler" has been sometimes given to men of this caste, on account of the fluent readiness with which they read the fate of a person after examining his hands and face.

The art of the Joshi has (as was stated) a certain connection with astrology, and, so far as I can learn, the connection is as follows:—In the Hindu system of astronomy there are said to be nine planets, *viz.*, the five regular planets, the sun and moon, and the two demons of the eclipse. The collective name for these nine planets is Navagraha (*nava* meaning "nine" and *graha* "planet"). These planets, like the stars of the lunar zodiac, are believed to exercise an extraordinary influence upon human destiny. Three are said to be auspicious and are called Subhagraha; three others are said to be less auspicious and are called Pápagraha; while the three last are said to be cruel or malignant and are called Krúragraha. The scheme stands thus:—

Subhagraha ...	Guruwár	Thursday (Jupiter).
	Somwár	Monday (the Moon).
	Sukrawár	Friday (Venus).
Pápagraha ...	Bhaumwár	Tuesday (Mars).
	Budhawár	Wednesday (Mercury).
	Adityawár (Itwár) ...	Sunday (the Sun).
Krúragraha ...	Shanaischar (Sanichar) ...	Saturday.
	Ráhu, Ketu	Demons of the eclipse.

It is with the last three planets alone that the Joshi is in league. The offerings made to these malignant powers and transmitted to them through their appointed priest, the Joshi, consist of oil, the black pulse called *urd*, pieces of iron, black cloth, &c.

The colour black is the appropriate emblem of these deities of darkness, and oil for relieving the darkness is the appropriate offering. It is customary for the Joshi to receive such gifts on the Saturday.

126. The last and lowest caste of Brahman is the funeral-priest, who, in consequence of the aversion with which he is regarded by all classes of the community, is contemptuously termed Mahá-Brahman or Mahá-Patra, "the great priest or the great vessel." He is sometimes called the Karataka or Vulture Brahman, because priests of this caste flock like vultures round the carcasses of the dead. Nevertheless, the function which the Mahá-Brahman performs, as will be seen below, is a very important one in the eyes of Hindus; and the very highest castes, though they consider it a pollution to touch him, cannot dispense with his services. Such are the strange inconsistencies of the supernatural creeds: the Mahá-Brahman is indispensable for discharging the pious offices due to the dead, and yet he is loathed for the very reason that he performs them.

Amongst Hindus, as amongst all other people whose religious beliefs are in the savage or barbarous stage, the soul of the dead is supposed to suffer from hunger and thirst, and to need the same conveniences that it enjoyed in the body which it lately occupied. To this sentiment, for example, must be ascribed the atrocious rite of *sati* or the burning of the widow alive upon the pyre of her husband, so that she may accompany him to the world beyond. This rite has long been suppressed by the British Government; but a series of less mischievous rites has survived of which *sati* was only one link in the chain. On the day after a person has died the survivors hang an earthen vessel called *ghant* from a tree—a pipal tree, if one can be found. This vessel is replenished every morning and evening with water, while a small lighted lamp, intended to give light to the departed soul, is placed on the top of it. A small hole is bored at the bottom, so that the water may trickle out to appease the thirst of the dead. The vessel continues to hang and to discharge water for ten, twelve, fifteen or thirty days, according to the rank of the caste to which the deceased belonged. But the operation would be of no avail, unless the Mahá-Brahman himself suspended and consecrated the vessel. All this while every member of the deceased's family is considered unclean, and must bathe every morning at some particular hour and as near as possible to the place where the vessel is hanging. The Mahá-Bráhman is always present at such times, and, after placing a bunch of dry *kusha* grass on the ground, causes every mourner or bather to throw upon it an offering of water and a handful of black *til* seed for the refreshment of the departed soul. The name of this ceremony is called *tilanjuli*, because the til and water are thrown from the joined palms of the hand (*anjuli*). For assisting at this daily ceremony the Mahá-Bráhman receives every day enough cooked or uncooked grain to keep him for the day. After the ten, twelve, fifteen, or thirty days have expired, the Mahá-Bráhman goes to the tree where the vessel is hanging, and, after breaking it in the presence of the assembled mourners, is presented by them with every kind of thing that the departed soul is likely to require in the next life, such as tobacco, grain, clothes, carpets, pillows, bedsteads, shoes, walking-stick, the *hukka* or native pipe, cooking utensils, &c. If the deceased's survivors can bear the cost, they provide a new batch of all such articles, besides giving (as all must do, whether rich or poor) the old clothes, the old pillows, the bedstead, the cow or buffalo, the plough-cattle, the palanquin, &c., which the deceased was specially accustomed to use. If a Rája or rich man dies, the Mahá-Bráhman receives even his horse and elephant. The meaning of all this is that the departed soul requires, or is believed to require, after death everything that he used during life, and that the Mahá-Brahman is the medium through whom they are supposed to reach him. In every country but India such things are buried in the same tomb with the body; and it is chiefly through the contents found in the interiors of tombs that the arts and inventions known to the ancestors of mankind have been discovered by archæologists. But in India no tombs are erected. The bodies of the dead are burnt, and the ashes are thrown on the rivers; while the Mahá-Brahman acts the part of the tomb, being himself the living tomb which receives the gifts intended for the happiness of the dead. A better example could scarcely be quoted of the extent to which Brahmans have traded on the instincts natural to the human mind and turned them entirely to their own advantage.

On the twelfth day immediately following the cremation of the corpse a horde of Mahá-Brahmans is summoned to eat a banquet, and on the thirteenth day other Brahmans belonging to different classes are invited for the same purpose. Thus the feast to the dead, which in every other country is eaten by the kinsmen of the departed, is in India eaten by Brahmans.

The Mahá-Brahman as a class is totally illiterate: he can seldom even repeat correctly the texts which are supposed to be uttered during the different stages of the ceremonial.

127. This completes the long list of priestly functions exercised by the modern Brahman. It must now be shown to what extent these several functions have given rise to corresponding castes or sub-castes within the Brahmanical aggregate.

Among the nine different functions described under headings 1 and 2 in para. III, there is none that now represents a caste or sub-caste in the strict sense of the term. But as Dikshit, Páthak, and Pánde are and have long been the hereditary titles of corresponding classes, and as each of these classes still prefers to marry within its own ranks if suitable connections can be found, it is more than probable that each of them was once actually a caste or sub-caste—that is, a body of men exercising a function peculiar to itself and allowing none of its members, either male or female, to marry outside its own fraternity. Achárya is an hereditary title in Bengal. Jyotishi must once have been a distinct caste in Upper India; for otherwise the name Joshi, by which the kindred caste of palmisters is called, could not have come into existence. Among the names descriptive of the function of sacrifice there are two, *viz.*, Bajpay and Jijhotiya, which are almost synonyms of Hotri. The former is the hereditary title of a certain Brahmanical class which like Dikshit, Páthak, Pande, &c., must once have represented a separate sub-caste. Jijhotiya is the name of a distinct Brahmanical caste, with which no other caste will intermarry, dwelling chiefly in the plains between the Ganges and the hills of Central India.

Among the five different functions named under heading 3 in the same paragraph, there is none that does not represent a corresponding caste in the strictest sense of the term. The Ojhas, the Pandás, the Gangaputras, the Joshis, and the Mahá-Brahmans, are all entirely distinct units—distinct not only from each other, but from all the other classes of Brahmans named under headings 1 and 2. In the case, then, of these five classes of priests, *viz.*, the sorcerer, the temple-priest, the river-priest, the palmister, and the funeral priest, the law maintained throughout this paper, by which diversity of function gives rise to diversity of caste, is seen in its most perfect operation. Probably, too, its operation would have been not less complete in the case of the other nine functions also, if the field within which they were practised had not been pre-occupied by the ancient system of sub-divisions into *gotras*, orders, clans, and branches, to which allusion was made in paragraph 110. This system had been formed and fully established before the modern developments of Brahmanism had come into existence. It was based, as we have shown, not upon diversity of priestly functions (for in the Vedic age such diversities did not exist), but upon supposed diversity of descent from the seven great Rishis or sages. During the long struggle with Buddhism which followed the close of the Vedic revelation, Brahmans were more than ever careful to preserve every time-honored tradition that existed in regard to the organization of their caste; and hence this system not only survived the conflict with the rival creed, but has lasted to the present day. Thus when the new developments of Brahmanism had taken their present shape, the old system of sub-divisions into *gotras* and clans and branches was too strongly established to admit of new castes, based upon the new diversities of function, being permanently formed.

128. The statistics given in the census report regarding the Brahmanical sub-castes are very incomplete. No separate mention has been made of the Ojha, the Pandá, or the Gangaputra, all of which are (as we have stated) distinct social units. The only sub-castes of whom separate statistics have been given are the Joshi, the Mahá-Brahman, and the Cháraj. The last two, however, are really one and have been shown as such in the accompanying statement (group VI). Charaj is merely a corruption of Achárya, a high sounding title assumed by funeral-priests, not less pretentious than that of Mahá-Brahman or Mahá-Patra.

129. The reader must have been struck with the contrast between the complex developments of Brahmanism which are in force at the present day and the single function of sacrifice which marked its earlier career. But there is one common element which runs through all these various phases of the Brahmanical office. Except in the case of the schoolmaster, *viz.*, the Páthak and Pánde, who were selected from among the Brahman caste merely because Brahmans alone were sufficiently educated and sufficiently sacred to be trusted with the training of the young, every variety of Brahman that I have described in this paper acts as mediator between man and the invisible world; and to this extent the caste is on a par with the priests of other creeds. Thus in Vedic times the Hotri was the mediator between the sacrificer and the Devas or gods who personified the elements. In modern times the Bidua is the medium between the founder of a temple and the deity whom he draws into the idol; the Dikshit between the boy whom he initiates and the gods to whom he dedicates him; the Jyotishi between the man who consults him and the stars whose influence he interprets; the Pauránik between the man who listens to his recitals and the spirit presiding over the book from which he reads; the Ojha between the man who is possessed with a devil and the death-goddess through whom the devil is to be expelled; the Pandá between the man who brings an offering to the shrine and the deity at whose shrine it is made; the Gangaputra between the man who bathes in the sacred pool and the spirit presiding over the water; the Joshi between the terror-stricken suppliant and the demons of the eclipse; the Mahá-Brahman between the living and the souls of the dead; while the Purohit can mediate for his employer in almost any capacity, even to the extent of bathing or fasting for him. Thus the Brahman is a true priest, in whatever direction, except that of schoolmaster, his services have been employed: and even when he acts as schoolmaster, he does not resign his position as priest or messenger of men to the unseen world. That this is the light in which the laymen of all classes regard him is clear from the fact that, in whatever capacity he may be employed at the present day, he is still invariably called *jackak* or sacrificer, while the man for whom he officiates is called *yajaman*, or the man who pays for the sacrifice. Thus the astrologer, the sorcerer, the river-priest, the funeral-priest, &c., &c., are at bottom priests of the sacrifice—messengers through whom the oblations of man are transmitted to the abodes of gods and departed souls.

130. There is one rather peculiar rite by means of which the Brahman is used by all classes of Hindus as messenger between gods and men, and this is by making him eat—a ceremony, which so far as I know, is confined to the Indian priesthood and is altogether unknown in other countries. In the ancient or Vedic age the element on which the flesh and butter of the sacrifice were thrown was fire. But the *Smritis*, or books of canon law (of which Brahmans were, of course, the authors), are never weary of telling us that the Brahman himself is "the flame of the sacrificial mouth," and that if the leavings, that is, the solid parts, of the sacrifice go to any but Brahmans, "the offering is not made to gods (Devas), but to devils (Asuras)." Thus the Brahman is a consuming fire; and provided he eats at any one's expense but his own, he is one of the chief means by which at the present day men of other castes transmit their offerings to the higher powers. So whenever a man wishes to perform some expiatory rite, or to invoke the divine favour upon some new undertaking, or to signalize some important event in his own life, such as a birth, a marriage, or a

funeral, he invariably invites a horde of Brahmans to a banquet. It is not at all essential to the efficacy of such banquets that the Brahmans who are fed should be men of cultivated minds or versed in sacred science or in the practice of priestly offices. Whatever his training or mode of life may be, he is by birth an impersonation of the deity, a messenger between gods and men. "Whether literate or illiterate," says Krishna in the *Bhagavad Gita*, "a Brahman is my own body." To feed a Brahman, therefore, is to feed Krishna or the divine being himself. The object of all sacrifice in the Vedic age was to feed the gods. But as the slaying of animals to any deity except Kali is now practically extinct, the rite of feeding the gods by feeding Brahmans has succeeded to its place.

131. After all that has been said about the functions which in ancient as well as in recent times have been the peculiarities of the Brahman caste, it may cause some surprise to the reader to be told that the most honòrable state in which a Brahman can exist is to live as much as possible for himself and exercise no functions at all for the outside community. Such, however, is the ideal set forth in Manu's Code, and such is the ideal recongnized at the present day.

There are several considerations which commend this view of a Brahman's status to the minds of Hindus. As there is no caste above that of Brahman which can perform religious rights on his behalf, such as he himself is able to perform for others, any time that may be spent on ministering to the wants of others represents a loss of grace and opportunity to himself, and he suffers in holiness and purity accordingly. Again, there is nothing so degrading to a Brahman as service. Devotion to the good of others is a sentiment entirely alien to the spirit of his creed ; for it is a fundamental maxim of the Brahmanical codes to believe that all other races were created to serve himself. But whenever a Brahman undertakes to discharge some priestly function for another, he becomes for the time being the servant of the man who employs him. The Purohit, for example, is the servant of his master for life, and this is one of the chief reasons why the office of hereditary family-priest is considered so degrading. Again, it is impossible for any one who desires to propitiate some deity to do this without presenting an offering in cash or kind ; and this offering is appropriated by the Brahman, who receives it on behalf of the deity, being himself an impersonation of the divine being. But, in spite of all theories to the contrary, the constant acceptation of gifts has a mercenary look, and the receiver loses in dignity as much as the giver gains in grace. The highest status, then, in which a Brahman can live is to stand entirely aloof from the outside world, to be a priest only to himself and family, to lead the model life made up of the daily routine of offerings and ablutions prescribed by the rules of his order, and, when his sons are grown up and married, to retire into a hermitage and meditate till the day of his death on the mystery of Brahmá, the Supreme Spirit.

There are but few Brahmans, however, who can dispense with the emoluments of their calling : and as there was a never-ceasing demand among the general community for religious direction of all kinds, which only a Brahman could give, the author of Manu's Code was generous enough to lay down the rule that there are six *karmas* or works in which the Brahmanical caste may lawfully engage, while to every other twice-born caste there are only three :—

(1) To study the Vedas ; *pathan*.
(2) To teach the Vedas ; *páthan*.
(3) To offer sacrifice ; *yajan*.
(4) To help others to sacrifice ; *yájan*.
(5) To give alms ; *dana*.
(6) To receive alms or fees ; *pratigraha*.

The three duties which any twice-born caste in common with the Brahman may perform are the first, third, and fifth. The three which only a Brahman, and no other caste, may perform are the second, fourth, and sixth ; and he is not allowed to perform any of these, unless he is in want of the necessaries of life. Mr. Sherring makes the curious mistake of saying that " only those Brahmans who perform all these six duties are reckoned perfectly orthodox. Some perform three of them, *viz.*, the first, third, and fifth, and omit the other three ; yet they suffer in rank in consequence" (*Hindu Tribes and Castes*, Vol. I., page 10). Such a statement is directly opposed not only to existing facts but to Manu's Code (X, 103), which runs thus : " From teaching the Veda, from officiating at sacrifices, or from taking presents, though these things are generally disapproved, no sin is committed by priests in distress ; for they are as pure as fire or water."

132. The reader need scarcely be reminded that in the account which we have given of the several functions open to the modern Brahman we have merely considered him as a priest, and taken no account of the fact that many members of the caste are in practice mere laymen, who discharge no priestly functions whatever. Out of the total number of Brahmans recorded in the census of 1881, *viz.*, 4,690,850, the number of males, that is, of potential priests or Levites, is given as 2,443,040. Turning to the details of occupation given in the same census, we find that only 81,318 persons are set down as " Hindu priests." If to these we add 509 more who in another place are shown as astrologers under the rather misleading title of " scientific persons," we get a total of 81,827 (see pages 105 and 106 of Preliminary Dissertation). According to this the proportion of actual priests to the total number of potential ones would be less than 4 per cent., and this is obviously too small to be correct. So far as I can learn from persons likely to be well informed on the subject, Brahmans of the present day might be sub-divided as follows :—

(*a*) Those who live exclusively by the practice of religious functions ; about fifteen per cent.

(*b*.) Those who live partially by such functions, but follow various secular callings in addition ; about twenty-five per cent.

(*c*.) Those who, without performing any of the priestly offices implied in the above, might yet be asked to sit down to a banquet and eat at another's expense ; (for even this must be accounted a priestly function in India) : these make up some twenty per cent. more.

(*d*.) Those who perform no priestly office whatever, not even that of eating : these make up the remaining forty per cent.

133. According to Manu's Code the state of life most becoming to a Brahman was, as we have shown, to be a man of independent means and do nothing but live for himself and for his own soul. But if he was poor, he might earn a subsistence by "assisting to sacrifice, teaching the Vedas, and receiving gifts from a pure-handed giver" (X, 76). But supposing even these did not suffice, " he might live by the duty of a soldier, for that is next in rank" (X, 81) ; or if this failed, " he might subsist as a mercantile man, applying himself to tillage or attendance on cattle" (X, 82). But he might never plough the field with his own hand ; for the " iron-mouthed pieces of wood not only wound the earth, but the creatures dwelling in it" (X, 84). Nor might he ever take up secular work for hire as the servant of another, " for this is *swavritti* or dog-living" (IV, 6).

With the exception of the last, each of the above rules is observed for the most part at the present day. There are certain classes of Brahmans, the Pánde for example, which are distinguished for their military propensities ; and the same may be said of almost all the Brahmans, of whatever class, living in the Baiswara districts of Oudh. Commerce, too, is a favourite occupation of the caste : and there are few, if any, forms of trade in which a Brahman will not engage. Many follow the occupation of milkman and cattle-grazer ; and as the cow is a sacred animal, this is not uncongenial to the instincts of the caste. If Brahmans take to agriculture, as many do, in the capacity of either landlord or tenant they will in some few districts, chiefly in those to the south of the Ganges, plough with their own hands ; but elsewhere they employ Chamárs, Koris, or Ahírs to do this for them ; for they still cherish the tradition that ploughing is forbidden to the caste. As to the "dog-living" or working for hire, all scruple against such a practice appears to have completely died out. Brahmans may now be found in any and every kind of occupation for which wages are paid, except those which would entail ceremonial pollution and consequent loss of caste, such as that of sweeper or washerman. They will act as water-carriers, cooks, cart-drivers, night-watchmen, field-watchmen, messengers, policemen, public singers, dancers, wrestlers, &c. Latterly, too, they have taken largely to thieving and other forms of crime. Grasping and lazy by long hereditary instinct, and not being so liberally supported by the outside community as they consider that they ought to be, they have begun to resort to force; and in Oudh at least they are now one of the chief criminal classes, ranking in this capacity scarcely, if at all, below Pásis.

In spite of all this, every Brahman, even the lowest, is still called Mahárai, or great king. Every other caste still looks to him for his blessing as he passes. The coarsest features, the most abject ignorance, and the most humble occupation do not detract from the fact that in the eyes of the Hindu community he impersonates Brahma, the Supreme Being, and is entitled as such to the homage of mankind. A wretched Brahman once complained to me of the hardness of his lot, that "the God had descended in him in vain."

134. There is one class or rather caste of secularized Brahmans whose hereditary occupation is of such a peculiar nature as to deserve a passing notice. These are the Sanauriyas of Bundelkhand, a caste which claims affinity with the great Sanadhya stock whose chief habitat is the plain between the Ganges and the Jumna. The hereditary function, if it can be called so, of this caste is thieving, but only by daylight. They make no secret of the fact that this is the main industry by which they live, and they even defend it on quasi-religious grounds. They quote a legend which shows that this was the lot assigned to them by Ram Chandra of Ayudhya, the greatest of the incarnations of Vishnu. There is a Hindu proverb to the effect that a theft by a Brahman is a gain rather than a loss to the person robbed :—

"*Girpare Ganga ; Churai Khai Bamhan.*"

That is, property stolen and eaten by a Brahman should be no more regretted than property which has fallen into the Ganges. To eat at another's expense is, as we have shown, a priestly function in India. To give what is eaten voluntarily is of course more meritorious than to have it taken from you by stealth ; but to be robbed by one who impersonates the deity is much better than to be robbed by anyone else. The Sanauriya throws an odour of sanctity over the act by the rule of robbing only in daylight—a rule so jealously observed by the caste that any infringement of it would entail dissmissal from the fraternity. Night is associated in the minds of men with the commission of evil deeds, and the Sanauriya by performing the daily *argh* or oblation of water to the Sun-god and by repeating the Gayatri as other Brahmans do, secures, as he thinks, the countenance of the Sun-god to the predatory life which he is leading.

The goddess who is believed to preside over the peculiar craft of this caste is Kalika. In order to escape detection they have invented a thieves' Latin and a gesture language, with which, however, the police authorities are now beginning to be familiar. They carry their thievish expeditions sometimes as far as to Malabar, Bombay, or the Madras coast, leaving their wives to till the fields in their absence. The person by whom the theft is actually committed is generally a boy under twelve or fourteen years of age ; and such boys are taken regularly into training by the men, who teach them the sleight-of-hand necessary to the difficult art of stealing in broad daylight, and organize all their movements on march.

The Sanauriya is a strict Brahman. He renews his sacred thread annually, as other Brahmans do, in the ceremony called Rakshabandan ; he is a total abstainer from flesh and wine; never destroys life in any form; observes the same ceremonies connected with births, marriages, and deaths that other Brahmans do; worships the cow and the serpent, and when he is sick employs none but Brahman sorcerers to expel the evil spirit from his body. Whenever he meets a man not of the Brahman caste, he pronounces the usual *asirbad* or blessing and receives back the usual salutation of Maháraj, or great king, athough he is known by every one to be a professional thief.

135. The Brahman caste has with that of Chattris become one of the last strongholds of Aryan ethnology, so far as this theory of race has been applied to the Indian people. As the genesis and classification of caste which this paper is attempting to unfold are based on the hypothesis of the unity of the Indian race, I am compelled, before dismissing the subject of Brahmans, to go briefly into the question as to whether any grounds exist for supposing them to be of Aryan as distinct from indigenous or Indian blood. The question has already been discussed in regard to Chattris in para. 37; but as the same line of argument does not apply to Brahmans, their case requires to be separately dealt with.

Originally, when Aryanism first came into vogue, *all* natives of India, of whatever caste, who spoke any form of neo-Sanskrit or Hindi, were for this reason declared to be Aryans; and the phrase "Aryan brother" has passed into a proverb. No one would think of denying that Sanskrit and neo-Sanskrit are Aryan tongues; and if the statement made by Professor Max Müller is correct, that "the evidence of language is irrefragable, and is the only evidence worth listening to with regard to ante-historical periods" (*Ancient Sanskrit Literature*, p. 13, edit. 1859), there is nothing further to be said. But it has become the fashion of late years, amongst writers of the same school, to say that only the upper castes of Hindus are Aryans, all the rest being either aboriginal or mixed. A moment's reflection will show that the linguistic theory as thus applied refutes itself. The very lowest of Indian castes, such as Chamárs, Pásis, Bhars, Arakhs, &c., not to mention tribes still lower in the scale, such as Doms, Kanjars, Haburas, &c., speak Hindi quite as much as Brahmans do, and from time immemorial have known of no other language. If, then, these castes and tribes are not Aryan at all, and the test of language proves to be worthless in their case, it must be equally worthless in the case of the Brahman also.

Convinced, however, that Brahmans at least, whatever the other castes may be, are of Aryan blood, many writers have learnt to speak of them as having fairer complexions and finer features than ordinary Indians, and find in this a further proof of their Aryan descent. Mr. Sherring for example, speaking of the Brahmans of Benares, writes thus:—"Light of complexion, his forehead ample, his countenance of striking significance, his lips thin, his mouth expressive, his carriage noble and almost sublime, the true Brahman * * * is a wonderful specimen of humanity walking on God's earth." We can only meet this statement with a simple denial of the fact. A walk through the class-rooms of the Benares Sanskrit College, in which some four hundred students, all of the Brahman caste and hailing from all parts of India, south as well as north, are assembled, would convince any one who used his eyes that the great majority of Brahmans are not of lighter complexion or of finer and better-bred features than any other caste. The expression of the face may be more intelligent than that of the labourers working in the roads: but expression is the result of culture, and this is quite a distinct thing from diversity of physical type. A stranger visiting India for the first time, and walking through the Benares class-rooms, would never dream of supposing that the students seated before him were distinct in race and blood from the scavengers who swept the roads. But a man who has lived long enough in this country and seen more provinces than one might discern that some difference of feature and general appearance exists among the different students, and that this difference depends on the nationality to which they belong. He would observe, for example, that a Bengali Brahman looks very like other Bengalis, a Hindustani like other Hindustanis, a Mahratti like other Mahrattis, and so on, which proves that the

Brahmans of any given nationality are not of different blood from the rest of their fellow-countrymen. It is not denied that rather fair complexions, recalling the Aryan type, do occasionally show themselves amongst men of the Brahman caste. But similar instances of atavism occur among the lowest castes also, and occur much less frequently among Brahmans than among some of the trading castes. Aryan blood has undoubtedly filtrated to some extent through all classes of the people. If Brahmans have rather a larger share of this than Chamárs, the difference is not so great as to entitle us to speak of the two castes as belonging to different races. The truth, then, appears to be that the Aryans, who entered the river-basins of the Indus and the Ganges *viâ* Cabul and Kashmir, became absorbed after two or three centuries in the pre-existing population, leaving, however, as evidence of their immigration some slight modification of the features and complexion of the native race, a language which has superseded most of the indigenous languages of India (as Latin or neo-Latin has almost ousted the Basque languages of Spain), and a religion which a few centuries later became profoundly modified, or rather completely transformed, by the rites, customs, and beliefs of the aboriginal savage.

Some writers, again, who admit that Brahmans in certain parts are a dark-complexioned race, ascribe this fact to the effect of a long residence under a tropical sun, and believe them to be Aryans notwithstanding. Professor Max Müller for example, in discussing the physiognomy of Brahmans, observes :—" Time, hewever, has worked many changes ; and there are at present Brahmans, particularly in the south of India, as black as Pariahs " (*Chips from a German Worship*, Vol. II., page 323). But the argument has the fatal defect of proving too much. If physical appearance is a mere matter of time and climate, and if through these causes Brahmans have become as dark as the ordinary native, we have nothing but the worthless evidence of language to show that they are Aryans at all. Moreover, the argument is opposed to facts. There are Jews in the south of India who have lived there for more than a thousand years, and are still as fair as the Jews of Palestine : these are called the white Jews. In the same part there is another community of Jews, holding no intercourse with the preceding, who are as dark as the darkest natives and are called the black Jews. The latter have taken wives from the native tribes, while the former have not. The Aryans who settled in the plains of India followed the same course as that adopted by the black Jews, and consequently their blood has been lost in that of the native population. On the other hand, the Aryans who remained in Kashmir and never entered the plains of India at all have retained their Aryan features and complexion to this day.

No one can now be called a Brahman (as every is one aware), unless he can satisfy his neighbours that his parents on both sides were like himself of Brahman parentage. This is what is meant by caste, so far as birth is concerned. Assuming that the priests of the earliest or Vedic age were Aryans, writers have drawn the conclusion that the modern Brahmans, who by the rules of caste are their hereditary descendants, must be Aryans also. But the restrictions of marriage which are *now* imposed by the rules of caste did not begin to exist until at least a thousand years after the Aryans had come into the country, and by this time the Aryan blood had been absorbed beyond recovery into the indigenous. It was not till the time of Manu, that is, about 200 B. C. or later, that the caste rules in regard to marriage were coming into force. Even then, as his own writings show, they were not universally accepted by Brahmans themselves : for he waxes very wroth with certain Brahmans of his own day who persisted in the habit of taking Sudra or low-caste women as their first wives, and dooms them in consequence to the most terrible penalties in the next life (III, 17). It is clear, then, that prior to his time, that is, ever since the Aryan invader had set foot on Indian soil, which must have been more than a thousand years before his Code was compiled, a Brahman or professional priest (for the Brahman *caste* did not then exist), could marry any woman that he liked. The hymns of the Rig Veda Sanhita are said to be "the earliest collection of Aryan poetry;" yet some even of these were composed by a man of "Dasya" or aborignal descent (Max Müller's *Ancient Sanskrit Literature*, page 58). The authors of such hyms were, in the Vedic age, called by the name of Brahman, because a hymn was called *brahma*. But if the author of a hymn could be the son of an aboriginal mother, the word Brahman must have meant something very different in that early age from what it means now. The meaning which Manu laboured to fix upon it, or rather the rule which he laboured to establish as binding upon priests, was that no one could be considered a real Brahman, unless his mother was of that class as well as his father. But as Brahmans of this perfect stamp were not always to be found, he was kind enough to tell his countrymen that, in selecting a priest for making offerings to the gods, they should not enquire too closely into a Brahman's parentage :—"For an oblation to the gods, let not the man who knows what is law scrupulously enquire into the parentage of a Brahman ; but for an oblation prepared for ancestors, let him examine it with strict care" (III, 149). It is quite clear, then, that even in Manu's time, and *a fortiori* in the centuries preceding it, the gods were accustomed to be fed through any priest who was versed in the intricacies of the sacrificial art, and that the acceptability of the offering did not depend upon the parentage, but upon the knowledge, of the officiating priest.

The original distinction of colour which marked the Aryan race from the indigenous is alluded to once or twice in the Vedic hymns, because the event of the Aryan immigration was still comparatively recent and the distinctions themselves may have still existed. But nothing of the kind is ever alluded to in Manu's Code. Indeed, he cautions his Brahman friends against marrying "a girl with reddish hair" (III, 8), because in a dark or Indian race, such as Manu and his fellow-Brahmans had become, red hair is a disease, while to a white or blue-eyed race it is the sign of a healthy temperament.

In the earlier days of Hinduism the great qualification required in a professional priest was, as we have already hinted, not the parentage of his mother, but an accurate knowledge of his father's art, or in other words intellectual ability—ability, that is, to grasp the endless rules and remember the endless texts necessary to the correct performance of the sacrifice. But intellectual quickness, as any one who has lived in India must know, is not a question of colour or race, and a Brahman of the olden time desiring to train a son in his own art would select, from among the sons born to him by his various wives, the one in whom he discerned the greatest aptitude, and no consideration of the tribe or class to which the mother of such a son belonged would deter him from so making his choice. In fact, by the ancient custom of exogamous marriage a woman took the rank of her husband as a matter of course, whatever her own origin might have been. Such was the rule in other parts of the world ; and if this had not been the case in India also, Manu could not have penned such maxims as the following, all of which tell strongly against the very principle of caste which it was the main object of his code to establish :—"Whatever be the qualities of the man with whom a woman is united by lawful marriage, such qualities she also assumes, like a river united with the sea. Akshamála, a woman of the lowest birth, being thus united with Vasishta, and Sarangi, being united with Mandopála, were entitled to very high honour. These and other females of low birth have attained eminence in this world by the good qualities of their lords" (IX, 22-24). Vasishta, as the reader need scarcely be reminded, was one of the most distinguished of the seven great Rishis or sages, and one of the great priests of the Vedic age, from whom Brahmans claim to have sprung. He, then, was the man who took a "woman of the lowest birth" as his wife, and by so doing raised her to very high honour.

Enough has been said, then, to show that long before caste was established in India, the Aryan invader, to whatever class he might belong, was in the habit of taking the women of the country as wives, and that hence no caste, not even that of the Brahman, can claim to have sprung from Aryan ancestors. But apart from all the written evidence that can be quoted in proof of this fact, the marked deterioration of tone and sentiment, which is conspicuous in the later writings of the Vedie age, is alone sufficient to show that the true Aryan race had by that time ceased to exist on Indian soil.

In the *earlier* Vedic poetry the Aryans pourtray themselves in characters that might have fitted the Gaul, the Roman, the Homeric Greek, or the ancient Briton. They are a free and warlike race, fond of wine and the chase, boar-hunters, eaters of beef, and like the ancient Persians, with whom they were closely allied in blood, worshippers of the simple elements or forces of nature—the sun, the moon, the winds, the waters, the storm, &c. But all this becomes changed two or three centuries later. The worship of the personified elements is hardened into a series of dry mechanical rites, which only a professional priest could perform. Vishnu, whom the Aryans had honoured as the propitious and "all-permeating" Sun-god, is transformed into the smoky messenger of the sacrifice, and his elemental significance is forgotten. The repulsive and thoroughly non-Aryan Shiva, descending with matted locks and closed eyes from the mountains of the north, thrusts himself into the Brahmanic scheme, and becomes identified in name, but not in nature, with Rudra, the Storm-god of the Vedic poets. The gloomy superstitions of the savage self-torturing ascetic, of whom this terrific divinity was the model, override the cheerful faith of the old Aryan warriors. The desire, so natural to the human mind, for a personal second life beyond the grave, to be enjoyed in the bright kingdom of Yama among the forefathers of mankind, is superseded by a morbid longing for personal annihilation by absorption into the World-spirit, Brahma. The widow, instead of being led away from the tomb of her deceased husband, as she was in the old Vedic ritual, the text of which was wilfully corrupted by the new class of priests, is now made to burn herself alive on his funeral pyre. A five days' sacrifice of human victims—a rite altogether unknown to the Aryans who migrated into India—is performed once a year to the numerous gods of the changed pantheon. The Aitareya Brahmana, or book of liturgies, discloses to us a Brahman, by name Ajigarta, as the seller and butcher of his own son for the altar of sacrifice. The Mahábhárata alludes to Brahmans who not only sacrificed human victims but eat their flesh. In the same poem we find Bhima the hero thirsting to drink human blood, and Draupadi the heroine married to five brothers—a custom unknown to the Aryan invaders of India, but still practised by certain savage tribes in the south of India. Even the name of Pándu, by which the heroes of the Mahábhárata were called, is suggestive of the savage tribe called by the very same name in the institutes of Manu.

A similar deterioration of race is noticeable in the literature of the period. Speaking of the Brahmanas or liturgic treatises which succeeded to the early age of Vedic poetry, Professor Max Müller (though himself an ardent believer in the Aryan ancestry of the Hindus) remarks :—"These works deserve to be studied as the physician studies the twaddle of idiots and the ravings of madmen. They will disclose to a thoughtful eye the ruins of faded grandeur, the memories of noble aspirations" (*Ancient Sanskrit Literature*, page 389). The writer adds :—"It is most important to the historian that he should know how soon the fresh and healthy growth of a nation can be blighted by priestcraft and superstition. It is most important that we should know that nations are liable to these epidemics in their youth as well as in their dotage." But possibly other writers might see the fact in a different light, not as the premature blighting of a fresh and youthful nation by superstition and priestcraft, but as the absorption of the Aryan blood into that of the pre-existing indigenous savage. Such is the view taken by Mr. Gough in his very interesting volume on the philosophy of the Upanishads, a type of literature far superior to that of the Brahmanas, which have been so strongly condemned by Professor Max Müller. At the close of his work Mr. Gough describes the Upanishads as "the loftiest utterances of Indian intelligence, but the work of a rude age, a deteriorated race, and a barbarous and unprogressive community" (page 268). Again in page 3, speaking of the material out of which the blood of the Brahman theosophist was moulded, he observes :—"The greatest confusion has been introduced into the popular study of Indian matters by the term Aryan. This word has been fertile in every variety of fallacy, theoretical and practical. Before the work of thought begins in India, the invading Aryan tribes have become Indo-Aryans or Hindus. They have been assimilated to and absorbed into the earlier and ruder population, whom they at first fought against as the dark-skinned Dasyus, and then made to till the soil and drudge for them as Sudras."

But this is not all. A great prophet arose in about 500 B.C. who protested against the whole theory of Brahmanical sacrifice and drew most of his converts from the lowest classes of the people. Buddhism, as we know, died out in India after contending for more than ten centuries with the rival creed, and the whole of India at last reverted to Brahmanism. But what could have become of the numerous orders of low-caste priests by whom this long-pending contest was sustained? It is not at all improbable that they were won back into the earlier creed by the bait of admission into Brahmanhood, provided they brought their followers with them; or, what is still more likely, that they themselves imperceptibly slided back into Brahmanism, retaining, however, the rank and title of priest and bequeathing the same to their children. Brahmanism has never been noted as a persecuting or missionary creed. But it has evinced, and still evinces, an extraordinary power of assimilating and absorbing every religious agency that crosses its path. We have seen already how, without any conscious effort, it assimilated hordes of aboriginal magicians or Ojhas, and thus created the large and powerful sect of Hindus called Saktas (see para. 122). It is not less likely that it absorbed in the same way, one after another, the mixed brotherhoods of priests who represented the rival creed of Buddha. The great Brahmanical tribe known as Sarjupari or Sarwaria, and so called because they live to the east of the Sarju or Gogra, belong to the very districts in which Buddhism first arose and where it secured the largest following. Mr. Carnegy is probably right in asserting that they were once Buddhists. They themselves have a legend which connects them with Ramchandra, the great king of Ajudhya, who is said to have transplanted them from the western to the eastern side of the Gogra. But the fact of such a legend having arisen implies that there was something unusual in their origin which the legend was intended to conceal.

Local traditions in Oudh and the North-Western Provinces abound in tales of Brahmans being manufactured out of low-caste men by rájas, when they (the rájas) could not find a sufficiently large number of hereditary Brahmans to attend some sacrifice or feast. For example, the Kunda Brahmans of Partabgarh are said to have been manufactured by Rája Manik Chand, because he was not able to collect the quorum of 125,000 Brahmans to whom he had vowed to make a feast: in this way an Ahir, a Kurmi, or a Bhat found himself dubbed Brahman and invested with the sacred thread, and their descendants are Brahmans to this day" (*Oudh Gazetteer*, I, 305). A similar tale is told of Tirgunait Brahmans in Vol. III, 229; of the Pathaks of Amtara in Vol I., 365; of the Pandi Parwars in the Hardoi district; of the large clan called Sawalikhs in the Gorakhpur and Basti districts, who have nevertheless assumed the high-sounding titles of Dube, Upadhay, Tiwari, Misra, Dikshit, Pánde, Awasthi, and Páthak (*North-Western Provinces Gazetteer*, Vol. VI, 351-2). Only about a century and a half ago a Luniya, or man of the salt-making caste, which ranks decidedly low, was made a Brahman by Raja Bhagwant Rae of Asothar, and this man is the ancestor of the Misra Brahmans of Aijhi (*Gazetteer*, Vol. VIII, Part III, 49). The writer remarks:—"Numerous Brahmans have been co-opted into the caste through the influence of the rajas of Argat and Asothar, when the latter were at the height of their power. To carry out this ceremony a number of Brahmans were collected, among whom the candidate was seated and with whom he fed. Henceforth the man was known as a Brahman of the sub-division into which he had been elected."

If such things could be done within recent times, what could have prevented their being done during the last two thousand years, and especially during the long contest which prevailed between the rival creeds of Brahmanism and Buddhism, and who can now venture to assert that the Brahman of to-day is the lineal descendant of the ancient Aryan invader?

Mr. Growse is among those who consider that Brahmans with Kshatriyas are " in the main descendants of the early Aryan conquerors ;" and as regards the former he observes that " the strength of a community which lays claim to any esoteric knowledge lies in its exclusiveness" (*Mathura*, page 414). But, so far as I can learn, the only class of Brahmans that lays claim to esoteric knowledge is that of the Ojha or sorcerer, and of all the Brahmanical sub-castes this is the one whose origin can be most clearly traced to aboriginal priests.

Brahmanism in indigenous to India. From small beginnings it has gradually won over to its side almost the entire Indian race, and is even now continually gaining fresh victories. I believe that one of the great secrets of its influence lies in the fact that its professional expounders are one in blood, in character, and in sympathies with the general population. It is to me quite inconceivable, and opposed, I believe, to all the teachings of history, that a race of over two hundred million souls could have been brought into the most abject spiritual subjection by a foreign priesthood.

Religious orders.

136. We come finally to the various celibate orders of devotees or religious mendicants, which, though they cannot be called castes in the proper sense of the term, represent one of the classes into which the Hindu population is divided. One of them, too, has become a caste as well as an order, and there is another that threatens to follow. We cannot, therefore, omit them in this paper.

137. For the origin of the celibate orders we must go back to the ancient discipline of the Brahmans described in Manu's Code. The reader is already aware that, according to this Code, the life of a Brahman, or other " twice-born" man, was parcelled out into four distinct stages, the two last of which were that of the *Banaprastha* or forest anchorite and that of the *Sannyasi* or ascetic. These two stages are the model on which the numerous orders of religious celibates have been founded. In the time of Manu, it was only the twice-born castes, and of these chiefly the Brahman, who were entitled to enter into this holy state. But the modern religious orders are recruited from *all* castes, even the lower ones ; and when the ceremony of induction has once been performed, all connection with the former caste is for ever cut off. The Brahman, once admitted into one of these orders, ceases to be a Brahman and ranks no higher and no lower than any other member of the same fraternity. All members alike are supposed to have entered into the state of being dead to the world ; and in the spiritual life thus formed, no less than in the earthly grave, all men are equal. The first disciples of any new order that may be founded are actuated by the same intensity of faith that inspired the founder himself. But as time goes on, faith grows cold, and the enthusiasm of the first converts is not maintained by those who succeed to them. Thus has it been with most of the religious orders in India. The adults who now enter them are for the most part men who have become broken in fortune, or have no relations or descendants living, or have deserted their wives and families, or have lost their caste and cannot gain admission into any other. There is a Hindu proverb intended to signalize the decline of the religious spirit :—

" *Nári mui ghar sampatti nási,*
Mund murái bhae sannyási."

" One whose wife is dead, and who has lost his home and property, having shaved his head, becomes a Sannyasi" (enters a religious order). Another mode by which new adherents are gained is by picking up boys of a tender age, who have been disowned by their parents or have lost them, and training them to become disciples (chela). This is the method which most orders prefer; for it is easier to train children than elderly and broken-down men in the tenets and practices of the sect.

138. For every order of devotee the ceremony of induction is substantially the same. The main difference lies in the fact that each order has its own *gáyatri* or sacred formula recited at the time of initiation. The account given of the induction ceremony in Sherring's *Hindu Tribes and Castes*, Vol. I, page 256, is so very inaccurate as well as incomplete that I must here attempt to describe briefly what it is, so that the remarks which follow may not be misunderstood. In every order there is firstly the *Banáprasth*[illegible] or anchorite stage, which is considered incomplete and preparatory, and seco[illegible] *Sannyási* or ascetic stage, which is complete and final. For the induc[illegible]s into each of these stages a separate ceremony exists.

The [illegible] two days and is as follows:—On the day fixed for the induction (the [illegible] generally selected with reference to some periodical festival set apart in ho[illegible]of the deity to whom the order is specially attached), several prominent members of the order are invited to assemble at a certain place and witness the initiation. The man who has brought the disciple, and who is for this reason called his *guru* or spiritual guide, introduces him as an intending novitiate to the assembled members, and it is he who performs the ceremonies necessary to his induction. Holy water drawn from some sacred stream or tank, or (if such can be procured) water which has been already poured as an offering on the shrine of the tutelar deity of the order, is first thrown on the head of the novitiate in the presence of the congregation. He is then shaved by a barber, only a tuft, called *shikha* or *chundi*, being left on the top of the head. When the shaving is finished, he is congratulated and blessed by the members present; sacred texts appropriate to the tenets of the order are whispered into the ear by the *guru* presiding; and (unless he happens to belong to one of the twice-born castes, in which case he would possess a thread already), the *janeo* or Brahmanical thread is put over his left shoulder. At the same time a large sweetmeat is divided among the assembly, and after the *guru* has eaten most of his own share he causes the novitiate to eat the leavings—an act which renders it impossible for him to return to his former caste and binds him for ever to the *guru* as his disciple or *chela*. On this day he is considered to be a Brahman, and the main object of this part of the ceremony is to make him one. The title which he receives or holds in this capacity is that of Brahmáchari or religious student, this being the first and earliest of the four stages of a Brahman's life. On the second day the tuft is shaved off, not by a barber, but by the *guru* himself, and the sacred thread is cut to pieces and discarded. The object of this is to signify that the novitiate has left the status of Brahman and entered the higher one of *Banaprastha* or forest recluse.

Thus far, however, the novitiate is only an anchorite and not yet a full-blown ascetic or *Sannyasi*. In this incomplete state he may remain, if he chooses, for the next thirty or forty years, though the intention is that the final ceremony which will make him a *Sannyasi* should follow soon afterwards. The preliminary ceremony is performed, as we have seen, by the *guru*; but as the final one is performed by the anchorite himself, it rests with him to choose his own time for doing it. Faith, as we have said, grows cold after the first few generations of disciples are gone; and hence most anchorites at the present day postpone the last act till they are old enough to have outlived all their passions, because by that time it is easier to undergo the severer discipline and self-mortification required by the rules of the order.

This final ceremony is called Vijaya Homa, which signifies "the oblation of victory." It consists of an offering of *homa* prepared after the manner described already in para. 112 and thrown upon consecrated fire. The throwing of this offering into the fire is intended to typify the entire dedication of the soul to the flames of ascetic devotion, the complete "victory" over all earthly passions. Such is the efficacy ascribed to this rite that the bodies of those who have performed it are not burnt after death, as is the custom amongst all other classes of Hindus, but are either buried in the earth or thrown as they are into some river. The Vijaya Homa is itself looked upon as a kind of cremation ceremony; for the body of anyone who has undergone it is supposed to have been reduced to ashes by the flames of his own devotion. This explains, too, the meaning of the word Goshayen, the name by which one of the greatest of the religious orders is called. It is derived from *go* and *swámi or sháyi*, which writers have hitherto translated as "master of cows." But this gives no sense. *Go* is sometimes used in Sanskrit as a collective term for the five senses and the five corresponding organs. Hence the most probable meaning of Goshayen is "one who has mastered his senses." It is a synonym, in fact, of Sannyasi, but has become the proper name of an individual order.

139. The number of religious orders in Upper India is very great. Even in the ascetic state, when self-salvation is supposed to be the one pursuit of life, a Hindu is nothing if he is not a sectarian, attached to some particular deity or tenet in the multifarious creed of Hinduism, and bent upon furthering the interests and influence of the sect to which he has given his allegiance. The census report is altogether silent on the subject of these religious orders and has not one word to say either about those of the Hindu or of the Muhammadan persuasion in section IX of the Preliminary Dissertation on the "Religions of the People." The figures, too, recorded in form VIII are so obviously inaccurate, that no comparison between the results of the last and the preceding census could yield any useful result. The plan upon which I have arranged the religious orders of the Hindus is given below, but only the more important of them are named under their several headings:—

I.—Followers of Shiva, the third god of the Triad—

- Gosháyen.
- Dandi.
- Tridandi.
- Yogi.
- Sannyási proper.
- Shiváchári.
- Brahmáchári.
- Ákáshmukhi.
- Urddbáhu.
- Maunidási.
- Aghori.
- Nága.

II.—Followers of Vishnu, the second god of the Triad, in one or other of his incarnations—

- Bairági.
- Srivishnava.
- Rádhá Vallabhi.
- Nirmali.
- Sukhpanni.
- Satnámi.

III.—Followers of either Shiva or Vishnu, but only according to the teaching of some particular prophet, who showed the *panth* or right way to worship him:—

Gorakhnáthi	Shivite in name as well as in character.
Bharttari	
Baitáli Bhát	
Haríschandi	
Ramávat	Vishnuite in character, but not in name.
Ramánandi	
Charandási	
Raidáspanthi	
Kabirpanthi	
Dádupanthi	
Sadhanpanthi	
Udasi	
Nánakpanthi	
Akáli	
Suthra	
Kukaphanthi	

140. The deity to whom the mendicant orders originally looked as the type and founder of asceticism was the non-Aryan Shiva, and not the Aryan Vishnu. The character, under which the former first made his way into the Brahmanic pantheon as the third and last member of the Triad was that of the model ascetic, with closed eyes and bated breath, frequenting grave-yards, smeared over with the ashes of cow-dung, and wearing matted locks. Such was the character that he wore when he overthrew the altar of Daksha (see para. 123), and thus established his right to the title of Mahádev, or the Great God. The greatest and probably the oldest of the ascetic orders, the Goshayen, is based upon the worship of this divinity. One of the numerous names by which he is called is Jogeshwar, or the Lord of Ascetics. If the followers of Vishnu have founded certain sects of devotees similar to those which bear the name of Shiva, this has been done more out of jealousy for the credit of their

own divinity, Vishnu, than because there was anything in the creed of Vishnu that prescribed the ascetic state.

141. Every one of the above orders has one or more external badges (*bhesh*) by which it can be distinguished from any other. It is only thus that the public can know whether they are distributing their alms to the sect whose doctrines they prefer. Hence the Hindu religious orders have been called by the generic name of Bhésh-dhári or badge-wearer; and this is a more appropriate designation than the name more usually given, "Sannyasi," which for the reasons stated in para. 138 is applicable only to those anchorites who have entered the final stage. Another generic name in common use is Sádhu, which is ambiguous, because it can be applied to any pious man who has not formally entered into the status of a devotee.

The badges assumed by the various sects are much too numerous to be detailed in this place. Almost every sect has three different sets of badges: the *tilak* or device painted on the forehead and elsewhere with sandal-wood powder, clay, &c.; the colour of the cloth worn round the loins; and the staff or pot or shell or other kind of implement carried in the hand. Some too have a peculiar way of wearing the hair; but in one respect all sects are alike, *viz.*, that they never allow their hair to be cut. As regards the *tilak* every Shivite sect paints itself with the figure of a half moon thrice repeated, one under the other, or with some variation of this: this device is called *tripund.* On the other hand every Vishnuite sect paints itself with the symbol called *ramanandi* or some variation of it. The device consists of three parallel lines drawn perpendicularly, the two outside ones being joined at the base by a curved line which does not touch the middle one. The Shivite and Vishnuite sects are further distinguished by the kind of rosary that each of them wears; for every religious mendicant, to whatever order he may belong, must wear a rosary of some kind to enable him to keep account of the number of times that he repeats the name of his deity or the words of the Gayatri or sacred verse peculiar to his order. The Shivite rosary is made of the seeds of a tree called *rudraksh*, or the "eye of Rudra" (Shiva), being so called because there is a mark on the seed shaped like an eye, which the Shivites regard as the symbol of the middle eye of their three-eyed god—the middle eye which is at present closed, but which he will one day open to destroy the world with fire. The Vishnuite rosary consists of beads made of the wood of the *tulsi* plant, this being the plant into which the nymph Tulsi was metamorphosed when she was pursued by Krishna, one of the incarnations of Vishnu.

142. Some orders are further distinguished from others by the austerities which they practise or profess to practise. Some, for example, keep the right arm always erect in the air (*Urddbáhu*). Others keep their faces always turned to the sky and never look down (*Akashmukhi*). Others maintain a perpetual silence (*Maunidasi*). Others touch nothing except at the end of a staff (*Dandi* and *Tridandi*). Others practise holding their breath, or standing on one leg, or keeping one leg fixed behind the neck, or standing between four fires under the scorching sun of April, May, and June, or standing all night in water in the open air in the months of December and January, or exposing themselves day and night to the rain of July, August, and September (*Yogi*). There are some kinds of penance which are common to several different orders. The most severe kinds are those practised by the Shivites proper named in class I. The least severe are those of the Vishnuite *Panthis* of class III.

143. By far the most interesting of the above orders are those enumerated under heading III. The founders of these sects represent the various forms of modern dissent from the letter of Brahmanical teaching. The relation in which they stand to the dominant priesthood might be compared with that of the prophets of Israel to the priests and Levites of the Mosaic law. They were reformers, and the chief aim of their teaching was to protest against the the claim of Brahmans to superior sanctity or to superior spiritual gifts. They came from various different castes, and some of them from very low ones. Raidás, for example, was a Chamár or hide-skinner; Kabir, a Kori

or weaver, and Sadhan, a Khatik or butcher. But Brahmanism has been too strong for them, as it proved to be too strong for Sákyamuni himself some two thousand years ago. The older a sect becomes, the more steadily does it relapse into the fetters from which its founder wished to emancipate the disciples. Speaking of the polity of the church of Rome, Macaulay describes it as "the very masterpiece of human wisdom * * *. She thoroughly understands, what no other church has understood, how to deal with enthusiasts * * *. The Catholic church neither submits to enthusiasm nor proscribes it, but simply uses it." The same might be said of Brahmanism in India; for the effect is not less conspicuous, though a less degree of conscious effort is employed in producing it. Even the Sikh sects, the five named last in the list, some of which are of very recent origin, though they began by proclaiming a deism of the most liberal type, and disavowed any leaning towards either the Hindu Parameshwar or the Musulman Allah, are rapidly falling back into the old ways and taking colour more and more from Brahmanic teaching. A layman of any caste may profess allegiance to some particular *panth* or "way" without at all losing, or desiring to lose, the caste in which he was born, and different men may follow different *panths* within the same caste. Thus a Kayasth may be a Nanak-panthi, or a Charandasi, or a Ramanandi, without ceasing to be a Kayasth. In Hindustan these *panths* have permeated the several classes of the community less widely than in the Panjab. But, so far as their influence has extended, it may be said that, if Hindus are divided socially and industrially by caste, they are divided religiously by the *panths* or schools of modern reformers.

144. Out of all the religious orders in Upper India there is at present only one, *viz.*, the Goshayen, which from a celibate order, as it originally was and as it has still partially remained, has become a caste in the strict sense of the term. Writing of Gosháyens Mr. Sherring says :—" Brahmans, Kshatriyas, Vaisyas, and Sudras may, if they choose, become Goshayens ; but if they do so and unite with the members of this fraternity in eating and drinking, holding full and free intercourse with them, they are cut off for ever from their own tribes. It is this circumstance which constitutes the Goshayens a distinct and legitimate caste, and not merely a religious order" (*Hindu Tribes and Castes*, Vol. I., page 256). Every word of this comment is beside the mark. All the religious orders, and not merely the Goshayen, are so constituted that any person from any caste who enters any such order is cut off for ever from his own tribe. In this respect all the religious orders are alike ; and the very ceremony by which the novitiate is made to eat what his *guru* leaves at the time of induction entails forfeiture of caste and cuts off all possibility of return to it, as we have explained already in paragraph 138. What makes the Goshayen a caste, and not merely a religious order, is the fact that it has ceased to be celibate, while the other orders have remained so. In other words, it has openly admitted marriage among its rules or at least among its customs, and hence it can and does perpetuate and extend itself from within like any other caste, and not merely from without like the other religious orders. The Goshayen, therefore, is both a caste and an order : and in this respect, so far as I know, it has no parallel in India. It is a caste, because it extends itself by natural increase from within; and it is an order, because it admits new adherents from without and because many of its members are celibates.

145. Goshayens have grown into a caste, because they had previously grown into a priesthood, and as priests had acquired property in land, houses, and temples, the possession of which modified the aims and character of the fraternity. The founders and first disciples of the order had no intention of serving as priests to the outside community, or in fact of doing anything else than to wander over the earth as celibates and lead the ascetic life of which Shiva, their patron deity, was the pattern. But the piety of the people compelled them to become priests in the temples of Shiva, whether they liked it or no ; for it is only in the temples of Shiva or his consort, Kali, that priestly functions have been assigned to them. As was explained above (see paragraph 123), it is only Brahmans of an inferior stamp who will accept offerings placed on the lingam or Shivite symbol ; and hence a class of men like

Goshayens, who were believed to have special influence with Shiva, and therefore to be better qualified than any others to receive on his behalf the offerings made to him by the people generally, supplied a public want. Thus, if a Brahman of the Pandá class could not be found to take charge of a Shivite temple, some Goshayen was selected for the office ; and by the rule explained already in paragraph 123 a Goshayen so appointed became thenceforth the owner of the temple and acquired the right of bequeathing all the interests attaching to it to his own successors. By the same rule, too, a Goshayen might purchase such rights from a Brahman ; and in this way many more of the temples of Shiva fell into the hands of Goshayens and remained there. Other Goshayens again, not employed as temple-priests, but leading the model life of an ascetic, have been presented at different times with gifts of land and houses by the pious laymen of the community, partly with a view to presenting a costly offering to the Great God Mahádev through the medium of his chosen servants, and partly for providing a permanent source of charity to the poor and needy, of which the Goshayens would serve as trustees and distributors. Having thus acquired property of a kind which could not be moved, and which therefore compelled them to live in certain fixed places, a large portion of the fraternity ceased to be mere wandering mendicants, begging their bread from place to place, as all originally did and as some are still doing. But settled habitations and the permanent acquisition of wealth lead naturally to the marital instinct and to the desire for heirs, to whom property can be bequeathed. Moreover, the custom of illicit unions with women of the lower classes had long been secretly practised. The postponement of the final ceremony of "Vijaya Homa" led to a gradual relaxation of discipline, especially among the younger men of the order, who had been initiated from early boyhood. Low-caste women were seduced from their houses, and others who had no homes received shelter and were retained as mistresses. When sons and daughters were born, the former might be initiated under the disguise of boy disciples. But daughters could only be given in marriage ; and as no outside caste could accept such girls as wives to their sons, it was necessary to find husbands for them within their own community. Thus marriage became at last an openly recognized rule or custom of the fraternity, and so from a celibate order they became an hereditary caste.

146. The special function, then, of Goshayens, considering them as a caste of priests and not merely as a religious order, is that of serving as priests in the temples of Shiva, and less frequently in those of his consort, Kali. Mr. Sherring observes : "In this part of India they worship Vishnu, though in some other parts they seem to be devoted to Shiva" (*Hindu Tribes and Castes*, Vol. I., page 257). Such a remark implies a fundamental misconception of the facts. They worship Vishnu at times, not because they are Goshayens, but because they are Hindus. But it is the worship of Shiva which has made them what they are. It is only on the Shivarátri, or the great annual festival of Shiva, which takes place in February, that candidates for initiation are inducted into the order. The text whispered into the ear of the novitiate on that occasion is the Rudri, that is, the Shivite Gáyatri, and not the ordinary Gáyatri pronounced in honor of Vishnu, the Vedic Sun-god, which Brahmans and other twice-born castes are expected to repeat daily at sunrise, noon, and sunset. Again, all Goshayens trace their origin to Sankara Achárya, whom they worship as an incarnation of Shiva, just as Ráma, Krishna, and many others are held to be incarnations of Vishnu. Sankara Achárya, as is well known, was the great teacher, who came from Southern India (Malabar) in the eighth or ninth century A.D. and preached the doctrine of Shiva in opposition to that of Buddhism, which in Upper India was then in an advanced stage of decay. The ten branches or sub-divisions of Goshayens fancy that they are descended from the ten eminent disciples on whom his mantle descended when he left the earth. Shivism is therefore the peculiar creed of the Goshayen order or caste, and it is only in the temples of Shiva that they can act as priests. Goshayens of the Kanphata or ear-split class can serve as priests and slayers of victims in the temples of Kali also. A conspicuous example of this is to be seen at the temple

of Devi Patan in the Gonda district, Oudh. In Assam, where the temples of Kali are especially numerous, I have heard that Goshayens are more prominent as temple-priests than Brahmans ; and even in Upper India they must be considered a rival, though still much inferior, caste.

147. The marriage ceremonies of Goshayens are not the same as those of other Hindus. There is a much less degree of formalism attending them, indicating, what is the fact, that the custom of marriage was foreign to the original aims and intention of the order. Probably by degrees the differences of ceremony will dieout, and Goshayen marriages will be attended with as much fuss and expenditure as those of other Hindu castes. A change is coming over the whole spirit of the order. A considerable number of Goshayens have, like Brahmans, become entirely secularized, all pretensions to be either priests or devotees having been abandoned. Like Brahmans, too, they have no speciality of function as a secular caste, but will take up almost any kind of work that comes to their hands, so long there is no ceremonial pollution attaching to it.

148. There is one other celibate order which threatens ere long to become a caste, and by precisely the same process that has made the Goshayens one. This is the order of Bairagis, who hold about the same degree of influence and wealth among the Vishnuite orders that Goshayens hold among the Shivite. Thus far no such thing as marriage is openly recognized amongst them. But they have acquired vested interests in many of the temples and other places sacred to Vishnu or to the deified men and animals who are associated with his history. The great Hanuman Garhi at Ayodhya—the fort of the flying monkey-god who aided Ráma in his invasion of Lanka, which is visited every day of the year by pilgrims from all parts of India—is in the hands of Bairágis. In fact the whole of Ayodhya, the city so sacred to the memory of Ráma and so endeared to the hearts of all Hindus, is overrun by this grasping and mendacious order, who point to one house as the spot where Rama was born, to another as the house in which he played as a child, to another as the courtyard in which his father, Dasharatha, administered justice, and so forth ; and they exact a liberal fee for the information. The same kind of fate has attended many of the other cities or temples sacred to Vishnu or his incarnations, such as Bithor in the Cawnpore district, Brindaban in Muttra, Chitrakuta in Bánda, Misrikh in Sitapur, Dwarka in Gujerat, and many more. Bairágis have acquired, too, a proprietary right in some of the temples of the sun ; for Vishnu in the Vedic age, before he had begun to make himself incarnate in beasts, fish, and men, was merely an impersonation of this luminary. At many of the Surajkunds or Sun-tanks in Upper India, to which patients go to be healed of skin diseases, as Naaman the Syrian went to the Jordan to be healed of his leprosy, an image of the Sun-god may be seen on the bank, with some Bairági seated beside it, ready to receive the offerings made by the visitors. In another way, too, Bairágis are following in the footsteps of Goshayens. They have acquired large properties in land given them by pious laymen as offerings to Vishnu and for the benefit of the poor. The boy disciples whom they initiate into their order are often their own illegitimate sons, and it is to such disciples that they bequeath the lands given to them for a purpose so entirely different. Probably the day is not far distant when marriage will be openly recognized as one of the customs of the order, and the Bairágis will then have become a caste like the Goshayens.

149. The jealousy with which the different orders regard each other is best seen at the Kumbh-ka-Melas or twelfth-year fairs, when crowds of pilgrims assemble from all parts of Upper India to bathe in the Ganges at Allahabad or Hardwár. It is deemed especially fortunate to enter the water when the sun is passing from the zodiac called *kumbh* or pot and entering that of *makar* or crocodile; and violent contests arise as to which order is to have precedence. "The rivalry of the Bairágis and Goshayens culminated in the last day of the fair in 1760 in a pitched battle, which terminated in the defeat of the former, of whom some 1,800 were slain. Again in 1796 the Goshayens, venturing to resist the better-equipped Sikh pilgrims, were

defeated with the loss of five hundred men" (*North-West Provinces Gazetteer*, Vol. II, page 291). As the reader is aware, the Sikh and Bairagi are of the Vishnuite class, while the Goshayen is Shivite. At such battles the honor of their respective deities is at stake. The Goshayens and other Shivite orders claim the right of the first bath, because the Ganges is said to have sprung from the matted locks of Shiva, when he first descended into the plains of India from the peak of Kailása. The Bairagi, Sikh, and other Vishnuite orders claim precedence, because by their creed the Ganges took its rise from the sweat of Vishnu's toes.

150. The statistics to be gathered from the census report as to the religious orders are not a little bewildering. The names that come nearest to this description, together with the figures recorded against each of them, are as follows :—

	Males.	*Females.*
Goshayen	67,079	51,180
Bharti	30	19
Rangaswámi	73	53
Kaparia	380	340
Faqir	123,904	101,372
Total ...	191,466	152,964

The entries against the name Goshayen cause no difficulty : for as this has long been not merely a celibate order, but a marrying caste, no surprise need be felt at the existence of 51,180 females against 67,079 males. The remaining four names taken together include 124,387 males and 101,784 females. But if these four names are intended to stand for the orders of religious devotees, there should be no females at all, or only a very few, such orders being professedly celibate ; whereas the number of females recorded is almost equal to that of the males. If, however, these names are not intended to stand for the celibate orders, then these orders are not shown anywhere in the census report as they should have been. Perhaps faqir, being a Muhammadan name, is intended to stand for the Muhammadan mendicant orders, amongst whom marriage is openly allowed. But if this is so, they ought not to have been included in a list which professes to relate exclusively to Hindus. Again, it is not understood why such obscure and little known orders as Bharti and Rangaswámi, the one consisting of only 49 and the other of 126 souls, should have received separate mention, and no mention be made of orders which are ten times as important and numerous. Again, the description of occupations recorded against faqir, *viz.*, "religious ascetic, beggar," appears to imply that common vagrants or beggars, professing no connection with religion, have been mixed up with devotees to whom begging is a religious duty. It is therefore impossible for me to do anything more than add up the figures recorded against Bharti, Rangaswámi, Kaparia, and Faqir, and call them by the collective name of "other mendicant orders." This has been done in the accompanying tabular statement (group VII.)

151. So far as I can learn from persons likely to be well informed on the subject, the total number of males belonging to the several Hindu orders, within the area of the North-West and Oudh, is not likely to be less than half a million. Individuals from these orders may be seen wandering from place to place in all parts of the country. Groups varying in number from 50 to 150 are collected together in monasteries called *maths* or *akaras* at places of pilgrimage, such as Benares, Allahabad, Chitrakut, Hardwár, Muttra, Ayodhya, &c. Probably most of the Brahmans who are now established at these sacred places as river-priests or temple-priests, under the name of Gangáputra or Pandá, are descended from the illegitimate sons of celibate devotees, who permanently resided in the local monasteries and received the alms and adoration of the people.

152. *General summary.*—We have thus completed the brief survey of Indian castes, which it was the object of this paper to unfold. If we omit the "foreign races not returned by caste" and "unspecified," neither of which have anything

to do with the subject, the number of Hindu tribes and castes recorded in the census report in alphabetical order amounts to 182. From the examination which has now been made this number has been reduced to 101, no less than 81 of those shown in the census report having been found to be either synonyms for castes already recorded, or the same names differently spelt, or names of subdivisions of certain castes, or merely the names of occupations belonging to no caste in particular. On the other hand, the names of twenty-one castes, of which no mention was made in the census, have been added to the original number. Thus the net difference between my own list and that given in the census report amounts to 61.

153. Another result elicited by these enquiries is that the names which were given in the census report in alphabetical order have now been classified according to the function or occupation, by which each caste is distinguished, and on the basis of which it was originally formed. The order in which the several castes have been arranged in the appended statements is believed to coincide inversely with the order in which they came into existence—inversely because our method has been to commence with those which were the last formed, and therefore stand at the bottom of the social scale, and thence to make a gradual ascent to the caste first formed—the Brahman, which stands at the top. Outside the series altogether stand the casteless tribes, the remains of the ancient aboriginal population, out of whose blood the whole series of Indian castes was gradually formed. Each caste or group of castes represents one or other of those progressive stages of culture which have marked the industrial development of mankind not only in India, but in every other country in the world, wherein some advance has been made from primeval savagery to the arts and industries of civilized life. The rank of any caste as high or low depends upon whether the industry represented by the caste belongs to an advanced or backward stage of culture; and thus the natural history of human industries affords the chief clue to the gradations as well as to the formation of Indian castes. Such in rough outline is the theory of caste advocated in these pages. A general summing up of the various castes as thus classified has been given already in paragraph 8, and a more detailed list may be seen in the twelve tabular statements appended to this paper. As the mode of classification here adopted and the theory on which it is based have not, so far as I know, been proposed by any previous writer, a few general remarks will now be offered in further explanation of the principles and causes through the operation of which the great caste system of India is believed to have been formed.

154. In the first place, then, I think it has been clearly proved that the bond of sympathy or interest which first drew together the families or tribal fragments of which a caste is composed, and formed them into a new social unit, was not, as some writers have alleged, community of creed or community of kinship, but community of function. Function, and function only as I think, was the foundation upon which the whole caste system of India was built up. This, too, is the view expressed by the Hindus themselves respecting the origin of their own institution. No doubt most of the accounts given in the sacred literature, respecting the origin of caste, are mythical and absurd, if we take them in their literal sense and make no attempt to extract the kernel concealed in the deistic shell. But rationalistic explanations are not wanting in Hindu writings, as the following examples taken from the Mahábarata show:—"Bhrigu replied:—"There is no (natural) distinction of castes; this world, having been at first created by Brahma purely Brahmanic, became afterwards separated into castes in consequence of men's works'" (*Muir's Sanskrit Texts*, Vol. I, page 144). Again in another chapter of the same poem, describing the condition of men in the *Krita*, or best age of the world, it is said of the four castes "that they had but one Veda and practised one duty, but had separate duties" (Vol. I, page 145); that is, all alike were obedient to the same law of duty, but, subject to that law, exercised separate functions. The author of the Mánava Code gives in his first chapter the usual mythical account of the origin of the four great orders or classes into which the population was said to be divided. He shows, as others had done before him, how the Brahman

issued from the mouth, the Kshatriya from the arms, the Vaisya from the thighs, and the Sudra from the feet of the Supreme Being. But the mythe itself, if we strip it of its theistic colouring, affords the clearest possible testimony to the fact stated in the Mahábhárata, that "the world was separated into castes in consequence of works," and the author of the Code himself can be quoted as his own interpreter :—"For the sake of preserving this universe, that glorious Being (Brahma) ordained separate functions (*prithak karmani*) for those who sprang from his mouth, his arms, his thighs, and his feet" (I, 87). In the next four slokas he describes in some detail what these separate functions are, which I need not however repeat, as they are already well known to the reader. He winds up his account with showing that the Brahman is sprung from the most excellent organ (the head and mouth), because "he is the first-born of castes and possesses the Veda, and is by right the chief of this whole creation" (I, 93). The stress laid in this and in many other passages that might be quoted, upon the fact that the Brahman was the "first born" of the castes, gives an unforeseen support to the theory advocated in this paper, that the Brahman was the first caste that came into existence, and that all the other castes were formed upon this model, extending gradually downwards from the king and warrior to the hunting and fishing tribes, whose status is not much better than that of savages.

155. In the 10th chapter of the Code the author informs us that "several impure classes have been formed by intermixture of marriage" between the four so-called original castes—the Brahman, the Kshatriya, the Vaisya, and the Sudra. After describing in detail the various crosses between the four original breeds, he says : "These, among the various mixed classes, have been described by their several fathers and mothers ; but whether their parentage is known or unknown, they can be discriminated by their respective occupations" (*veditavyah swa-karmabhih*). Thus the fanciful attempt to deduce the inferior classes of the population existing in his own day from intermarriages "in the inverse order" between the four original castes so called is supplemented by the more rational theory which distinguishes one class from another by occupation.

156. The views thus expressed by the Hindus themselves as to the origin of their own institution are entirely borne out by the evidence collected in this paper. The reader will have observed that special pains have been taken, in the account given of each caste, to ascertain the etymology and signification of the name by which it is called : for the signification of caste names is the most trustworthy indication we could possess of the process through which the castes themselves have come into existence. An analysis of all the caste names given in the appended tables, which, omitting those of the casteless tribes and the religious orders which are not castes at all, amount to exactly one hundred, brings out the following result :—

	Functional.	Tribal.	Local or geographical.	Religious.	Not known.	Total.
Hunting castes	4	7	...	...	...	11
Fishing "	4	5	...	...	...	9
Pastoral	5	1	1	...	...	7
Agricultural	7	4	...	...	...	11
Landlord	1	...	...	...	...	1
Artisans, lower	10	...	...	...	...	10
Artisans, upper	15	...	...	...	...	15
Trading	15	...	2	2	1	20
Serving	10	...	...	...	...	10
Priestly	6	...	...	...	...	6
Total ...	77	17	3	2	1	100

The reader will observe, then, that seventy-seven per cent. of the names of the various castes are functional—that is, neither tribal nor local nor religious. He will observe, too, that out of the seventeen tribal names all but five (and even these five exceptions can be explained) belong to the hunting and fishing castes ; and he is already aware that these fraternities are tribes as much as castes. If, then, our theory is correct—that caste was founded on hereditary distinctions of function, independently of all questions relating to tribal origin or descent—the above result is exactly what we should expect to find. These hunting and fishing tribes, being the furthest removed from the arts and industries of civilized life, and therefore still hanging on the outskirts of Hindu society, do not possess any function at all (save that of merely hunting and fishing) as members of the Hindu industrial system ; and consequently there is scarcely any kind of work to which they will not turn their hands, if they can get the chance. But as we ascend the social scale, we find that the functions of the several castes become more and more specialized as well as more refined ; and thus in all such castes functional names have superseded tribal ones.

157. If we look to the conditions of human society in its earliest stages, it is obvious that, in the hunting and fishing states proper, life is so simple and one-sided that scarcely any division of labour is required; and where there is no division of labour there can be no hereditary functions, such as exist in more advanced communities, and no distinct classes of men to perform them. As Plato remarked more than two thousand years ago, " a state only begins to exist when the individual ceases to be self-sufficing and needs the co-operation of many." In other words, it is only when settled, that is, agricultural communities have been formed, that certain hereditary functions, either secular or religious, can be acquired by certain classes of the population. When this point has been reached, the hunting, fishing, and nomad tribes, if they are not altogether absorbed, as most of them are certain to be, into the agricultural and other industrial classes, are expelled from the community as outcastes ; or if they desire to be retained as members of the community, but to adhere to their old occupations of hunting, fishing, and cattle-grazing, they must be content to accept such conditions as are consistent with the welfare and convenience of the more advanced portion of the community. This is exactly what has come to pass in India. The Ahírs, Játs, Gújars, Gaddis, &c., all of whom were originally nomads, and whom I have therefore classed as being " allied to the pastoral state," have now become largely absorbed into the agricultural function, though they have still retained many of the traditions and customs peculiar to the nomad state, and are still in the actual practice of nomadism, wherever agriculture has left them sufficient room. Again the Pasis, Arakhs, Bhars, &c., all of whom not many generations ago were mere hunters and marauders, and whom I have therefore placed under the heading of " allied to the hunting state," have abandoned the migratory life of the original hunter and formed permanent homes on the outskirts of the villages and towns, where they devote themselves to peaceful and industrial pursuits, as far as their opportunities permit. But they still hunt and trap wild animals and birds in the neighbourhood of their huts, and are still waging a secret war against a society which has failed to assimilate them. These make up the last and lowest link in the Hindu industrial chain. Outside this chain, and claiming no affinity with it at present, are the Kanjars, Haburas, Banmánush, &c., who still lead the wandering and predatory life of the unreclaimed savage. These are the outcastes of Indian society—tribes, or rather fragments of tribes, which have lagged behind the rest in the onward march of progress, while their brethren have advanced, at different paces, from one stage of culture to another, impelled and guided by the same laws as those which have governed the industrial development of mankind in every other part of the world.

158. There are several minor castes at the present day which are still in process of formation, and the process admits of direct observation in all its stages. In the case of all these incipient castes it is some peculiarity of craft or industry, and not community of religion or community of kinship, which supplies the motive force. One good example of this has been given already in the case of the Sangtarash or stonecutter (see para. 62). Regarding this and other similarly incomplete castes

Mr. Growse has written as follows:—"These partially developed castes are only recognized in some few districts and totally ignored in others. Thus Mathura is a great centre of the stonecutter's art; but the men who practise it belong to different ranks, and have not adopted the distinctive trade-name of Sangtarash, which seems to be recognized in Aligarh, Hamírpur, and Kumaun. Again, in every market town there are a number of weighmen, who no doubt in each place have special guild regulations of their own; but only in Benares do they appear as a distinct caste, with the name of Palledars. So, too, at Sahåranpur some fruit-sellers, whose trade, it may be presumed, has been encouraged by the large public gardens at that station, have separated themselves from the common herd of Kunjras and decorated their small community with the Persian title of Mewafarosh" (*Mathura*, 415-6). Many other instances might be named of castes which are in the course of formation, and which may or may not become eventually complete. There is the Peshiraj or stone-quarrier, on the sides of the Mirzapur hills, who seems inclined to separate himself from the parent stem of Ahír or cattle-grazer; for it is in the neighbourhood of these stone-quarries that the Ahír finds woods and pasture for his herds. There is the Raj or Maimár, who seems to be gradually developing into a caste of masons, distinct both from the Peshiraj and the Sangtarash. There is the half-formed caste of Beldar or navvy, which shows signs of detaching itself from the parent stem of Lunia or salt-maker; for as the Lunia is no longer allowed by Government to practise the ancestral art of extracting salt from the alkaline soils of the earth, the caste is now turning to other callings, such as well-digging, road-making, &c., and the beldar is one of the results of this change of function. There is the half-formed caste of Chapparband or thatcher—an offshoot from the caste ot Kori or weaver, but an offshoot which has not yet been able to separate itself from the roots of the parent tree. There is the Khemah-doz or tent-sewer, who stands in a similar relation to the parent caste of Darzi or tailor. There is the partially-formed caste of Gadahla, whose special industry consists in driving and rearing the ass, but who belongs at present to the caste of Kumhar or potter. Thus in every example that can be quoted it is some peculiarity of trade or craft which supplies the root of the new plant, and the name assumed by the incipient caste is invariably descriptive of the industry from which the said caste takes its rise. The process of caste-formation which is thus going on before our very eyes is as good an indication as we could have of the process by which the castes already established were formed from the beginning.

159. The same rule will be found to hold good if we examine the process by which individual men and families are seen to pass out of their own into some other caste. It is always through change of function that the first step towards change of caste is taken. A barber, for example, who has taken to carpentry (and the case which I have in mind is not an imaginary one), though he will not be able himself to change caste from Nápit to Barhai, will be able to do so in his descendants; and he himself will go some way towards it by associating with Barhais, attending their annual festivals, observing the trade rules, learning the caste traditions, &c. If he sticks closely to the trade, and if his sons and grandsons follow in his footsteps, they will certainly be called Barhais or carpenters by their neighbours; for the term Barhai, like most other caste terms, stands for an occupation as much as it does for a caste. They, too, will give themselves out to be Barhais, whatever their actual caste at the time may be; for if you ask a native what his caste is, he is very likely to tell you some word descriptive of his occupation—so closely are the two ideas intertwined in his mind. The grandson or great-grandson of this barber-carpenter, if his position is sufficiently prosperous (for everything depends upon this), and if he watches his opportunity and bides his time, will not find much difficulty in forming a matrimonial connection with some family of the carpenter caste; and when this point has been reached, the change of caste from Nápit to Barhai has been completed. Migrations of this nature from one caste to another are perpetually being made. Thus while the castes remain, the personnel of castes is liable to constant changes, through change of individual functions.

160. We hold, then, that the grouping of men by castes or sub-castes is at bottom the same thing as grouping them by crafts, occupations, or functions. It appears, too, that in the minds of the natives themselves it has never meant anything else. We do not concur in what has been lately represented by a writer of note, that the grouping of men by castes consists in "grouping them by their folk or their faith, by kinship or by worship," and that these two institutions "are the roots from which society has grown up all over India," "The essential characteristics," as the same writer says in another place, "of a man's state of life and position among his people, those which settle who he is and where he belongs, are his kinship and his religion; the one or the other, sometimes both * * * *. If, now, having laid hold of these two facts, we look around us in central India and try to perceive how they have been worked out, we shall find the simplest and earliest expression of them in two institutions—the pure clan by descent and the religious order; the brotherhood by blood and the spritual brotherhood; those to whom a common ancestry, and those to whom a common rite or doctrine, is everything." It seems to us that the formation of castes cannot be ascribed to either of these sentiments, and that if we eliminate the element of a common function and substitute in its place that of a common ancestry or a common worship or both, we strip the word "caste" of almost the only meaning that it possesses.

161. We shall have something to say further on as to the relation in which caste, the more recent product, stands to tribe, the earlier one. But we may at once allude to a certain fact, which alone appears to be sufficient proof that castes did not, as many tribes have done, spring up out of the sentiment of a common ancestry. Had this been so, we should at least been able to know who the reputed ancestor was in each case; and every such ancestor would have received some kind of periodical worship from his reputed descendants, as the custom was and is amongst tribes. Instead of this, however, we find that there is no caste which has an ancestor to worship, and that every caste pays regular homage to the tools, instruments, or other objects peculiar to the function out of which it sprang. Thus (omitting the tribes or castes "allied to the hunting state," which, as we have already explained, have no specific function as members of the Hindu industrial community) we find that the boating and fishing castes (see group II B.) sacrifice a goat to every new boat before it is put into the water, and that at the time of the Diwali they make an annual offering, which consists of red powder, oil, a wreath of flowers, and sweetmeats, to every boat they possess. Similarly, all the pastoral castes (see group II C.) pay a kind of worship to their animals by rubbing ochre or red earth (*geru*) on their tails, horns, and foreheads; this is done on the annual festivals of Diwali, Holi, and Nagpanchami. Similarly all the agricultural castes who plough the fields (see group II D.), and those members of other castes who have taken to agriculture as their means of livelihood, pay worship to the plough on the day called *Asári*, when the monsoon sets in and the work of cultivation is renewed. Sugar mixed with melted butter and a few grains of rice mixed in water are thrown upon the plough at the spot where it breaks up the first sod of earth, and thus both the earth and plough receive a share of the offering. The grain-heap is similarly worshipped in the months of March and October, before it is removed from the threshing-floor to the agriculturist's own dwelling. The Tamboli or betel-grower pays similar homage to the betel plant in October, before he begins to pick the leaf; and in July, before planting the new crop, he does homage to the ground prepared for the purpose. On the great annual festival of Dasahra, which is especially sacred to Chattris, all men of this caste (see group II.E.) worship their weapons of war—the sword, shield, matchlock, and bow and arrows, and the animals used in war, the horse and the elephant. Artisan castes of the lower rank (see group III.A.) all worship the tools by which they practise their respective crafts, and chiefly on the Holi, the great annual festival of the inferior castes. The Bansphor worships the knife with which he splits the bamboo and cane; the Chamár or tanner worships the *rápi* or currier's knife; the Bunkar or Kori the apparatus with which cloth is woven; the Teli his oil-press; the Kalwar an earthen jar filled with wine; and

the Kumhar the potter's wheel. Artisan castes of the upper rank (see group III.B.) worship their various tools on the Diwali festival, which to the more respectable castes marks the opening of the new year; the Rangrez worships a jar filled with dye; the Halwai or confectioner does honor to his oven by placing against it a lamp lighted with melted butter. The trading castes (see group IV.) invariably bring out their rupees on the Diwali and worship them as the instruments of their trade. Among the serving or professional castes (see group V.), the Kahár or carrier pays worship to the *bahangi* (which has been anglicized into "bhangy") before placing it for the first time across his shoulder. The Nápit or barber does homage to his razor; musicians to their instruments; the Kayasth or writer caste to the pen and ink. The dates on which periodical worship is paid to tools, &c., are the Holi, the Diwali, or both; the former being New Year's Day to the lower, and the latter to the upper castes. The last and highest of all the castes, the Brahman, observes the annual festival of Rakshabandan (which to the Brahman is New Year's Day) by paying a *homa* offering with much solemnity to the new sacred thread (*janeo* or *upavit*), with which he then invests himself as the badge of his priestly dignity. We find, then, in India a completely organized system of fetish worship, and the fetish of every caste corresponds with the function to which the caste itself is attached.

162. Not one of the castes of Upper India, so far as I can learn, claims descent from a common ancestor, though there are some few which have a patron saint or deity peculiar to themselves. Thus the Kayasth or writer caste has Chitragupta; the Lohar or ironsmith has Visva Karma; the Bhangi or scavenger has Lal Guru; Kahárs or fishing castes have Raja Kidar; and the agricultural caste of Kurmi pays especial honor to Vishnu in his incarnation of the tortoise (*kurma*). The worship paid in each case to the patron saint or deity of the caste only proves more distinctly than before that function was the foundation upon which the caste was formed. For Chitragupta in the Hindu pantheon is the recording angel who writes down the good and evil deeds of man in preparation for the day of judgment, as a Kayasth in a court of justice takes down the depositions of witness. Viswa Karma is merely a Vedic name for the deity in his capacity of artificer or blacksmith. Lal Guru or Lal Beg (Hindu or Muhammadan) was simply a king of sweepers, around whose name some fables have gathered. Raja Kidar is merely a Hindi corruption of Khwaja Khizr, the Musalman god of waters, who showed Alexander the Great where to look for the well of immortality, and who, therefore, became the patron saint of castes whose occupation is with water. Kurma is the mythical tortoise which supports the earth, and is therefore specially deserving of worship by castes who live by the tillage of the soil. Thus in every instance that has been named, it is function, and function only, which, besides making the caste, has determined the character of its patron deity or saint. In all this there is no trace of the worship of a common ancestor. The sentiment of kinship or a common ancestry is likely to spring up, it is true, among a body of men who have been previously united by a common industry and common connubial rights; but this sentiment is the effect, and not the cause, of the formation of caste.

163. The theory that a caste can be regarded as "a religious brotherhood," a body of men, "to whom a common rite or doctrine is everything," appears to be equally groundless. If the reader will again refer to para. 156, he will observe that, in the analysis of caste names there given, there are only two which carry a purely religious meaning. And if he will refer to the general head of "trading castes," group IV., he will find that the two castes referred to are Vishnoi and Maheshwari. Neither of these is mentioned in the list of castes given in the census report; and thus, if I had confined myself to that list and had not made a new one of my own, I could have affirmed that there was not a single caste among those under report which owed its origin to the bond of spiritual brotherhood. But these two exceptions, when we come to examine them, only serve to place the functional theory in a stronger light. The Maheswari caste, as its name implies, must have originally consisted of a body of

traders devoted to the worship of Shiva (Maheshwara). The only bond, however, which has held them together as a distinct social unit is the possession of a common function; for many members have become Vishnuite in creed and many others Jain. If the caste had had no better bond of union than religion, it would have broken up into three distinct parts long ago. The name "Vishnoi," as applied to the caste so called, is a misnomer; for they are Musalmans almost as much as Vishnuites. "They worship," as Sir Henry Elliot has shown, "according to the Hindu ceremonial three times a day, and pray after the Musalman fashion five times a day. They keep twenty-eight holidays during the year and observe the feast of Ramazán. They read both the Quran and Hindu Pothis" (*Supplemental Glossary*, Vol. 1, para. 43). Some Vishnois, too, have become Jains, like the Maheshwaris. Both of the above castes are extremely unimportant; but had their importance been greater, and their religious unity more complete than it is, two solitary exceptions out of such a large number of castes would not have been sufficient to invalidate the functional theory.

164. In the analysis of caste names given in para. 156 I have abstained from including the names of religious orders on the ground that the said orders are celibate sects and not castes or marrying communities. But considerable stress has been laid, by the writer referred to in para. 160, on "the formation of sectarian castes under the complex working of the ideas of kinship and religion combined;" and Professor Müx Muller has been criticized for not having included "sectarian" among the headings under which Indian castes can be grouped. It has been alleged by this writer that "the various sects representing the several phases of Hindu schism, and founded by mystics or devout ascetics, who spiritualize the idolatry and rude superstitions of the vulgar, * * * have almost invariably ended by a new Brahmanic caste or sect;" "that almost all the sects, except those allied to Buddhism and its satellite Jainism, have formed separate castes." The same writer has alleged that "in Northern India there are several of these purely sectarian castes whose origin can be historically traced back to a famous personage, often a good fighter as well as preacher, who is now the semi-divine head centre of the caste. Within at least one of these cástes the idea of affinity has woven during the last three or four centuries a wonderful net-work of separate groups, deriving from the various clans, castes or families of the proselytes, who at sundry times and in divers places have joined the sect." But the Sikhs (for this apparently is the sect referred to) can in no sense be called a caste, nor has any caste arisen out of them. In all questions of inter-marriage the old restrictions and distinctions are observed as closely by Sikhs as by any other of the numerous sects of Hindus, and in weddings and on other domestic occasions the Hindu ritual is followed. In fact the expression "sectarian caste" is almost a contradiction in terms. One essential characteristic of the sects founded by "mystics" is that they (the mystics) are celibate, and celibacy forbids the very principle on which the existence of a caste depends, *viz.*, transmission from father to son. Out of all the thirty-four sects named in paragraph 139 (and the list there given was avowedly incomplete), there is only one, the Goshayen, which has ended in forming a caste, and it has accomplished this only through violating the vows taken by the members on entering the order. The Goshayens, so far as they are a caste at all (for many of the novitiates remain faithful to the vow of chastity to which they bind themselves), are a caste of bastards, and no one would make bastardy the basis of a theory for the explanation of Indian caste. It is worth noticing, however, that the Goshayen had no sooner acquired a function, *viz.*, that of priest in the temples of Shiva or Kali, than he grew into a caste—that is, a marrying or non-celibate community. His case, then, so far from proving that castes can be of sectarian origin, only proves that they are of functional origin; for it is function, and function only, which has made him what he is. Even now, however, the Goshayen is not regarded as a caste by the general community, though he has partially become one in fact. Most natives still call him an *atit*—that is, who has "passed away" and become dead to the world.

165. Caste, then, is a purely secular institution, and religion has had nothing to do with it. Within the same caste, and even within the same *gotra* or sub-division, many different phases of religious belief, popularly known as Panths or ways, may and do co-exist. Thus within the Kashyap gotra of the Kayasth or writer caste, it will be found that some families are Vishnuite, others Shivite, others Sákta ; others again are followers of doctrines founded by the various modern reformers, such as Kabir, Charan Das, Nanak, &c. ; yet all this diversity of belief causes no disruption of the caste as an endogamous unit. Jainism, the satellite of Buddhism, separated itself from the Brahmanic creed and ritual by a much wider interval than Sikhism or any other form of dissent has since done. Yet in the caste of Agarwál there are Jains as well as Hindus, and a Jain father has no scruple whatever against giving his daughter in marriage to a Hindu boy. The writer whose opinions on the formation of clans and castes we have been examining has given the following remarks respecting the alleged formation of castes on the religious basis :—"It appears that a religious body with some distinctive object of worship or singular rule of devotion, has usually (though not invariably) come to split off into a separate group, which, though based upon a common religion, constructs itself upon the plan of a tribe. The common faith or worship forms the outer circle, which has gradually shut off a sect not only from inter-marriage, but even from eating with outsiders ; while inside this circumference the regular circles of affinity have established themselves independently, just as families settle and expand within the pale of a half-grown tribe. Each body of proselytes from different tribes and castes has preserved its identity as a distinct stock, keeping up the fundamental prohibition against marriage within the particular group of common descent. But with some other group of the sect it is essential to marry ; and thus in course of time has been reproduced upon a basis of common belief or worship the original circle of a tribe, beyond which it is impossible to contract a legitimate marriage * * *. Several instances could be given of sects having gradually rounded themselves off into complete castes, neither eating nor marrying with any beyond the pale." So far as I can learn, not a single example of this alleged process, by which a sect becomes rounded off into a caste with a distinct outer circle of marriage based upon a common faith or worship, has ever occurred in India, excepting only in the case of Goshayen ; and this sect, as we have shown, only grew into a caste through bastardy, that is, by violating the very principle on which the sect as a religious brotherhood was founded. Had caste been a religious and not an industrial institution, it would not have been possible for any caste to have survived, as many have done, the conversion of a large part of its members from Hinduism to Islam. A more radical change of feeling and conviction than what is implied in such a conversion as this could scarcely be conceived. Yet the hereditary transmission of functions has survived amongst those Muhammadans who are Hindus by blood and were formerly Hindus by religion.

166. The hereditary transmission of functions from father to son, and the consequent distribution of society into various functional or industrial groups, have not by any means been confined to India. "Nothing indeed," says Comte, "could be more natural at the outset than that by domestic initiation, the easiest and most powerful means of education, employments should descend from fathers to sons ; and it was the only possible training in an age when oral transmission was the sole means of communicating conceptions" (*Positive Philosophy*, Book VI, Chapter 8, page 198). In more than nine-tenths of the industries of India at the present day, oral transmission, through the example and teaching given by the father, is the sole means, both amoug Hindus and Muhammadans, by which a boy can acquire his father's craft, and this is no doubt one reason of the hold which caste has had on the people of this country through all vicissitudes of creeds. Moreover, the possession of transmitted skill and the reputation acquired by the father as a craftsman are often the most valuable legacies which a father can bequeath to his son, and during the father's own lifetime the son is the cheapest and best helpmate that he can secure. Hence there

are few civilized or semi-civilized countries in the world in which caste, in the incipient stage at least, has not existed, and even in the backward races, wherever the germs of specialized industries can be traced, society at once begins to distribute itself in the hereditary groove. We will now quote a few examples in illustration of this position.

The ancient inhabitants of Attica were divided into four hereditary classes, *viz.*, priests, warriors, husbandmen (including herdsmen), and artisans. A similar division prevailed among the Ionians generally, of whom the people of Attica were one particular section. In fact class distinctions and class prejudices permeated the whole frame-work of ancient Greek society, and it was Clisthenes, the founder of the Athenian democracy, who abolished this system in Attica by substituting the qualification of wealth for that of birth and function. The Cretans, as Herodotus tells us, had a caste system of their own, something like the Egyptian, aud he especially alludes to the agricultural and warrior classes. We hear of hereditary priests in Elis, Sparta, and Gela, and of hereditary musicians and painters in many other states. The population of Lacedæmonia was divided into three great castes—the Spartiatœ or citizens of Sparta itself, who monopolized the functions of priest, ruler, and heavy-armed warrior ; the Perioiki, who constituted the tradesmen and artisans of the provincial towns and furnished the inferior infantry; and the Helots, who tilled the fields and did every kind of menial and manual work for the ruling caste. The Lacedæmonians were further sub-divided, as Herodotus tells us, into many minor castes, similar to what we find in India :— " Their heralds, musicians, and cooks inherit the trade of their fathers : the musician must be the son of a musician, the herald of a herald, the cook of a cook. A man with a louder voice cannot come into the profession of herald and oust the herald's sons. Such are the customs of the Lacedæmanians" (Book VI., 60). Plato, in his ideal scheme of a republic, advocates the compulsory division of labour among six hereditary classes—Priests, Warriors, Husbandmen, Artisans, Shepherds, and Hunters; and he quotes the example of the Egyptians as his precedent. It will be seen that this list of castes coincides exactly with the scheme on which I have myself classified the Indian castes in this paper, except that the Trading and Serving castes must be added to make the list of headings complete. As to what the Egyptian caste system precisely was, authorities differ; but the general conclusion to be drawn is that the main divisions were very much what Plato described them to be, and that besides these there was a multitude of minor divisions, such as cowherd, swineherd, merchant, boatman, &c., as is the case in India. The Iberians (the ancient inhabitants of Spain) were, according to Strabo, divided into hereditary classes or castes consisting of kings, warriors, priests, husbandmen, and servants or slaves. In Peru, as Mr. Prescott tells us, before its indigenous civilization was destroyed, "there were certain individuals carefully trained to those occupations which minister to the wants of the more opulent classes. These occupations, like every other calling and office in Peru, always descended from father to son. The division of castes was in this particular as precise as that which existed in Hindustan or Egypt" (*History of Peru*, I, 143). In Cuzco, the old capital of Peru, the priests of the Sun-god, the public registrars, the learned men, and the singers, all transmitted their functions to their sons. In Mexico, as we are told by another historian, " the sons in general learned the trades of their fathers and embraced their professions : thus they perpetuated the arts in families, to the advantage of the State." Among our own ancestors there are traces of a caste system, or of something approximating to one, having once prevailed. The Anglo-Saxon population of England was divided into Ealdermen (the highest class of nobles), Thanes or the inferior nobles, Ceorls or churls (yeomen), and Serfs. Fortunately in the catholic church there was no hereditary class of priests, such as there is in India, to give fixity and permanence to this arrangement : but the minute rules in the old Anglo-Saxon laws defining the conditions under which a ceorl could become a thane, and a thane an ealderman, appear to point to a time when the hereditary nature of function and status was more rigorously enforced. In the Fiji Islands carpenters form a separate caste ; and the skill displayed by these islanders in boat-building, above that of their neighbours, may probably be ascribed to the rule of transmitting acquired skill from father to son. In the same islands each tribe is divided into five classes distinguished from each other by marked diverities of rank ; *viz.*, kings, chiefs, warriors, landholders, and dependants or slaves (*Fiji*, by J. H. DeRicci, page 67). In Abyssinia the people are divided at the present day into four great hereditary classes—the military and nobles, answering to the Indian Chattri or Rajput ; the sacordotal class, answering to the Indian Brahman ; the cultivators of the soil, answering to the Indian Kurmi, &c. ; and the traders, answering to the Indian Baniya. Besides these there are a few tanners, saddlers, and blacksmiths (*Land of Prester John*, by J. C. Hatten, p. 144ff). Something very like caste exists at the present day in Madagascar. The population is divided into the four great classes of nobles, Hovas, Zarahovas, and Andrvas or slaves ; no intermarriage ever takes place between them. As among the Chattris of India, so among the nobles or royal clans of Madagascar " their aristocratic lineage is no bar to their earning their bread as artisans and tradesmen." In the same island we are told that the middle class consists of the Hova freemen, divided into numerous tribes and families, each intermarrying only within its own circle (*Madagascar, Past and Present*, by Miss E. M. Clarke). In a recent article called " Russia Revisited," by Canon McColl, this writer points out that one of the first things needed for the amelioration of the people is " the reform of the caste system which divides society into classes separated from each other by chasms very difficult and often impossible to pass. Nobles, merchants, clergy, are separated by rigorous rules which practically confine each class to its own territory. The nobles again are subdivided into the great nobility and the little nobility, hereditary nobility, and personal nobility. The clergy are divided into black and white—that is, those who must not, and those who must, be married. The merchants are classified in three categories. Then there is the innumerable host of Chinovinks—that is, all the functionaries of the civil service. The army may be regarded as another caste. This caste system breaks up the unity of the nation." With a few changes of words this description would give a fairly correct view of the social condition of India at the present time.

167. Enough, then, has been said to shew that not only in India, but in almost every other country similarly advanced, the several arts and industries, springing up out of those natural divisions of labour which are necessary to the convenience of settled communities, were at the outset and for several centuries following hereditary, and that the first great advance made by nations, after they had emerged from the hunting and nomad states and begun to adopt the modes of life coeval with the agricultural state, was made in this groove. But so long as the hereditary transmission of functions is simply natural and spontaneous, and no artificial rules are invented for its support and continuance, no such thing as caste, in the proper sense of the term, can be said to exist. Mere heredity of function is not the same thing as caste ; or if it can be called by such a name at all, it is caste only in the incipient stage—the foundation without the superstructure. Before anything like a complete conception of caste can be said to have been formed, there are two great questions to be asked and answered:—

(1) In what respect does an hereditary industrial class fall short of a caste properly so called. ?

(2) In what relation does caste stand to the earlier organization of the tribe which it superseded ?

168. With a view to obtaining an answer to the first of these questions, we must go back once more to the time when the Brahman, " the first born of castes"—the model upon which all the other castes were subsequently formed—did not exist as a caste, but mearly as a professional priesthood.

The mode in which a chief or any other personage of Vedic times sought to propitiate the gods was by inviting them to come down and lick the blood of animals slaughtered upon the altar, to smell the odours of flesh roasted on consecrated fire, to imbibe the fumes of the intoxicating Soma, and to hear praises sung in their honor by the bards and sages of the day. So long as the ceremony was simple, no professional priest was required. Even when it had become more lengthy and complicated, a man of any rank or station in life was authorized to perform it, provided he was master of the details necessary to its efficacy. The great example of Visvamitra, who was descended from a long line of kings both of the Bharata and the Kasika families, and yet was appointed domestic priest (purohita) to King Sudas and sacrificing priest (hotri) to King Harischandra, shows that men of royal parentage could not only perform sacrifices for themselves without the help of professional priests, but could officiate as professional priests for others.

But a complicated ceremonial, the efficacy of which depended upon the rigidly exact performance of all its minutest details, could not but lead to the creation ; of a highly-trained priestly class, and such a class would necessarily become hereditary, for there was no other way in which an art so difficult as that of performing a Vedic sacrifice could be acquired except by a long course of instruction under a father's guidance. Moreover, initiation under a competent spiritual guide was the only guarantee to the public, that the man offering his services as priest possessed the authentic tradition of those magical texts, gestures, and intonations, whose virtues called down blessings on the head of the worshipper and made his oblations acceptable to the gods. Among the nine qualifications laid down in one of the Sutras, or books of aphorisms, as necessary in a professional priest, the first and most important was that he must be an *arsheya*—that is, able to trace an unbroken descent for ten generations in the family of some Rishi or inspired sage (*Muir's Sanskrit Texts*, Vol. I, 513).

But the hereditary transmission of a function, whatever the nature of the function may be, depends upon the father only ; for it is the father, and not the mother, who acts the part of instructing the son in the hereditary craft. No question need arise as to the race, stock, or class to which the mother belonged. And in point of fact, no such question was raised in the early days : for by the ancient law of marriage (as the Mánava code itself testifies), the woman could rise to the rank of the man, whatever her own rank might have been, if she was lawfully married to him (Manu's Code, IX, 23). Of all the Rishis or inspired sages of the Vedic age, Vasishta is the one in whose history the future position of the Brahmans is most distinctly foreshadowed. But Vasishta is described in the Mahábhárata as the father of a hundred sons, and as having begotten a son to King Kalináshapáda, whose queen had had no issue through her legitimate husband. He is also described in the Manava Code as having taken to wife Akshamálá, "a woman of the lowest birth." Yet there is no Rishi to whom a Brahman of the present day would more gladly trace his origin than to Vasishta. If we take the rule of "ten generations" quoted above, and if we suppose an extreme case, as we are authorized in doing, that in each of these generations the father was married to some woman of the non-priestly class, then the amount of Rishi blood inherited by the tenth in descent would be in the proportion of only 1 to 512, which is as good as saying that it would be reduced to nothing. And yet all the traditions, rules, and divine precepts of the inspired sage might have been handed down to his tenth descendant quite as faithfully, as if the nine mothers, through whom the series was continued, had been of the purest Rishi blood. In the Vedic age so little was a priest or sage prevented from marrying a woman outside his own class, that even Indra, the highest god of the Vedic pantheon, is said to have allied himself to a Danavi—that is, a woman of the aboriginal race. The legendary discussion between Yudisthira and the serpent, recorded in the Mahbhárata, respecting the origin of Brahmans, draws a striking picture of the freedom that once prevailed in the choice of wives :—"The serpent remarked—'If a man is regarded by you as being a Brahman only in consequence of his function, then birth is vain until action is shown.' Yudisthira replied—'O most sapient serpent, birth is difficult to be discriminated in the present condition of mankind on account of the confusion of all classes. All sorts of men are continually begetting children on all sorts of women. The speech, the mode of propagation, the birth, the death of all mankind are alike' " (*Muir's Sanskrit Texts*, I, 137).

169. Mere hereditary of function, then, is not sufficient by itself to constitute a caste. This can only be accomplished when restraint is put upon the freedom of marriage by establishing and enforcing the rule that no one can inherit the name and function of his father, unless his mother as well as his father was born with the same class. The two things, then, which constitute caste are heredity of function *plus* limitation of marriage. The principle of choosing a wife from some family enjoying an equal rank and exercising the same function is so natural, that it must have been growing into a custom long before it was made compulsory by social penalties. But so long as the opposite practice was permitted, the dignity and privileges attaching to Brahmanhood were at stake: for men could not continue for ever to accept such sophistry as the following :—" Sages who had begotten sons in an indiscriminate way conferred upon them the rank of sages by their own austere fervour " (*Muir's Sanskrit Texts*, Vol. I, 132). If, then, the dignity of Brahmanhood was to be secured against all risks, it was necessary to lay down and enforce the rule that no one could be considered a Brahman, unless he was born one on *both* sides of his parents. Such was the rule insisted on by the author of the Mánava Code. " In all classes," says the Code, (X., 5) " they, and they only, who are born in a direct order of wives *of the same class,* and virgins at the time of marriage, are to be considered as the same in class with their fathers." One of the chief characteristics of Indian caste is contained in the words italicized. If, then, I were asked to define caste in such a way as to discriminate it from a mere hereditary class, I should describe it as a trade-union or professional group, of which no one is entitled to exercise the function and enjoy the privileges, unless he was born within its ranks from *both* parents. The word " caste " is derived from the Portuguese *casta,* which signifies " breed." As purity of birth from both parents is the *differentia* of caste as distinct from class, a more appropriate word could not have been introduced.

170. The effect of such a rule as applied to Brahmans (and it was only for their benefit that the rule was made, Brahmans themselves having of course invented it), was that the essence of Brahmanhood consisted henceforth, not as it originally did in a personal qualification, that is, in the possession of *brahma* or sacred knowledge, but in purity of descent from both parents. Henceforth every man so born was entitled, by the mere claims of birth, to all the privileges and honors due to a professional priest, whether he did or did not discharge the priestly office or possess the sacred knowledge for which alone such privileges were originally conferred. Henceforth no one except a person so born, even if other men born of a different parentage might be more competent, could be allowed to exercise the priestly office for the public or receive gifts in return. " Whether ill or well versed in the Veda," says the Mahábhárata, " whether untrained or trained (in sacred science), Brahmans must never be despised, like fires covered with ashes. Just as the fire does not lose its purity by blazing even in a cemetery, so too, whether learned or unlearned, the Brahman is a great deity. Cities are not rendered magnificent by ramparts, gates, or palaces of various kinds, if they are destitute of these excellent Brahmans " (*Vanaparvam*, 13, 436). It was nothing but the most sordid and selfish ambition that led the Brahmans thus to constitute themselves into a caste, and in the rules laid down in the Mánava Code for defining the relations in which this caste was to stand to the other classes of the community, we are struck with the utter absence of reciprocity—the only element which could have imparted some degree of morality to their pretensions. Provided he married a Brahmani first, a Brahman might take concubines or inferior wives from the Kshatriya, Vaisya, and Sudra classes; but only the children of the Brahman wife could inherit the father's status, and no Kshatriya, Vaisya, or Sudra might marry a Brahman's daughter. Again, if the Brahman were

not able to live by his own profession (that is, by sacrificing for others, teaching sacred science, and receiving gifts in return), he might take up any of the callings belonging to the other classes, provided they were such as not to interfere with his dignity. As the calling of a Kshatriya or warrior was next highest in rank to his own, he was directed to choose this in preference to any other, if his own calling did not maintain him (Manu X., 81). But though he might bear arms and kill a fellow-countryman on the field of battle, he was forbidden to do anything so mean as to plough the earth with his own hands, and an hypocritical scruple was set up on the ground "that the iron-mouthed pieces of wood not only wound the earth, but the creatures dwelling in it" (Manu, X. 84). Again, supposing that he was rich and could dispense with the earnings of his own or any other calling, he was instructed to refrain from acting as priest or teacher to men of other classes who might require his services, because it was more dignified for a man of his parentage to stand aloof from inferior mortals. Hence, as no one except a Brahman could render such services, every other class in the community might go to perdition for all that the Brahman cared. But if the Brahman condescended to act as priest for the other classes, he must be liberally rewarded in return; "for the organs of sense and action, reputation in this life, happiness in the next, life itself, children, and cattle, are all destroyed by a sacrifice offered with trifling gifts to the priests" (XI, 40). On failure of heirs the property of other classes escheated to the king, but that of Brahmans is reserved for men of their own caste (IX, 188-9). A king, "even though dying of hunger," must never take taxes from a Brahman, but a Brahman, if he is in want, must always be fed by the king (VII, 133). If a Brahman was guilty of a capital offence, he was not to be put to death as other criminals were, but simply told to depart elsewhere "with all his property secure and his body unhurt" (VIII, 380). A Brahman was never to be smitten "even with a blade of grass." "A twice-born man who touches a Brahman with intention to hurt him shall be whirled about in the hell of Tamisra for a hundred years" (Manu, IV, 165). Offerings intended for the gods had much better be given to Brahmans, as the latter were visible deities and were certain to accept them, whereas there was an element of doubt as to whether such offerings reached the unseen powers: "an oblation in the mouth of a Brahman is far better than offerings to holy fire: it never drops, it never dries, it is never consumed" (Manu, VII, 84). Hence, as I have shown in another place, one of the chief functions of a Brahman at the present day is to eat at another man's expense. But no Brahman is ever expected to give a banquet to any but men of his own class or caste.

171. When the Brahman had thus set the example of forming himself into an exclusive and highly privileged caste, the other classes in the community were compelled to take what precautions they could for securing such privileges as were within their reach; and they did this not merely in self-defence, but in imitation of a class of men whom they had been accustomed for centuries to regard with the deepest veneration. If Brahmans had been a celibate order, like the Roman Catholic priesthood in Western Europe, or if they had been held in as little respect as are the parochial clergy of Russia, amongst whom marriage is compulsory as it is amongst Brahmans, the example which Brahmans gave of setting up caste barriers, so as to secure their own monopoly against all outsiders, might have had no effect upon the general structure of society. The caste system which has now penetrated into every corner of India might in that case have never come into existence, or would have remained in the incipient and harmless stage, by which a son naturally inherits the craft or function of his father: and India would then have been spared the degradation and disunion, which the Brahman has inflicted on her. But the influence of the Brahmans, at the time when the Mánava Code was compiled, was overwhelming; and this, added to the naturally superstitious character of her own people, has wrought her ruin. "From priority of birth, from superiority of origin, from a more exact knowledge of sacred science, and from a distinction in the sacrificial thread, the Brahman is the

lord of all the classes" (Manu, X, 3). As in the Hindu family " the eldest son is in this world the most respected," and all other members of the household are taught " to behave to him according to law, as children should behave to their father ;" so in the family of castes the Brahman, claiming priority of birth, superiority of origin, and a more perfect knowledge of sacred science, was the " first-born " son, to whom all the other classes looked for guidance, the oracle from which they drew their own inspiration. The principle of caste arrogance, once set in motion by the most influential class in the community, has been extending gradually downwards from the Brahman to those immediately next him in rank, till it has at last taken possession even of those inferior and backward classes who had no privileges or functions that are worth defending. A multitude of castes as thick as a cloud of locusts were thus called into existence at the bidding of the Brahman's wand : —

> As when the potent rod
> Of Amram's son, in Egypt's evil day,
> Waved round the coast, up called a pitchy cloud
> Of locusts, warping on the eastern wind,
> That o'er the realm of impious Pharoah hung
> Like night, and darkened all the land of Nile.—*Paradise Lost, Book I.*

172. One of the best proofs we could have that the Brahman was the founder of the caste system of India, or at least the model upon which all the other castes have attempted to form themselves, is the constant recurrence of the number seven. Brahmans of all kinds, according to their own assertion, are descended from the seven great Rishis or sages who are said to have laid the foundations of sacred science in India. The very lowest castes will tell you that their own communities, too, are made up of seven sub-divisions. Even Kanjars, who are still outside the pale of caste, will give you the same account of the organization of their savage community. Yet there is scarcely a caste or casteless tribe in India which is agreed as to what its seven sub-divisions are ; for the same caste or tribe will give you one list in one place and another in another. The truth is that this compact scheme of seven, which almost every caste or tribe is so fond of repeating, has no foundation in fact. But these various tribes and castes could not have conspired togther to assert a common fiction, if this fiction, almost the only point on which they do not quarrel, had not been drawn from a common source—the Brahman.

173. Two things, as we have shown, were necessary to the formation of a caste, *viz.*, (*a*) some speciality of function, which served as the bond of union among the members and formed them into a distinct *industrial* unit ; and (*b*) the limitation of the right of membership to those who were born within its ranks from both parents, which made them a distinct *social* unit. A large number of industrial classes, possessing some hereditary function, was in existence long before the Brahman caste was formed ; for the Brahman himself was merely an hereditary priest at the outset. The Mánava Code, though it maps out the population of the country on the plan of the old semi-mythical division into Brahman, Kshatriya, Vaisya, and Sudra, adds that there was a large number of other industrial groups, sprung " from the intermixtures of these classes by their marriages with women who ought not to be married ;" and these groups are alluded to incidentally in various parts of the code as potters, fishermen, physicians, usurers, cattle-grazers, boatmen, bards, oilmen, spirit-distillers, bowmakers, shepherds, barbers, goldsmiths, silversmiths, actors, basket-makers, washermen, sweepers, weavers, leather-cutters, musicians, carriers or porters, carpenters, &c. In fact it would be quite possible to classify the industries alluded to in the Mánava Code, including of course those of the Kshatriya and Brahman, on the same plan as that on which the castes of the present day have been classified in this paper ; and in some cases even the names would coincide. All that was needed, then, for the conversion of each of these classes into castes was that it (the class) should follow the example of Brahmans, " the first born of castes" and that of Kshatriyas, the second born, by establishing the same rule within its own ranks which the Brahman and Kshatriya had

already done in theirs, *viz.*, that all intermarriage with outsiders should cease, and that no one should be entitled to the privilege of membership, unless his parentage was of the approved type. There is therefore no mystery about the origin of Indian castes, if we will only accept two facts, (1) that caste was based at the outset on some unity of function, and not, as some writers have affirmed, on unity of creed or unity of kinship, the several functions themselves having been based on those natural divisions of labour which, following each other in an ascending scale from one stage of culture to another, have marked the industrial development of mankind in every part of the world; (2) that the Brahman had acquired an overwhelming ascendancy over the minds of all the other classes of the population, and that these classes, being intensely ignorant and superstitious, had no alternative left to them but to follow the example of their priests. The explanation of Indian caste, then, centres in two great facts; one general and scientific, *viz.*, the progressive development of the various arts and industries according to certain fixed laws, which have been substantially the same everywhere; and the other, special and historical, *viz.*, the extraordinary influence acquired by Brahmans over the ignorant and superstitious masses. It is futile to attempt, as some writers have done, to explain the origin of a great social phenomenon, such as that of Indian caste, on purely general grounds, and without taking into account those idiosyncracies of custom and sentiment which moulded the Indian character and marked the career of the nation in the preceding centuries: for man is pre-eminently an historical being, shaped and fashioned into what he is by the accumulated influences handed down to him by every generation that has gone before. Every nation has had its industrial development, and the process of development has been substantially the same in all. But what nation in the world except India has had its Brahmans? "Through the power of the Brahmans," says the Mahábhárata, "the demons were thrown prostrate in the waters (of the abyss); by the favour of the Brahmans the gods inhabit heaven. The void cannot become matter; the mountain Himavat cannot be shaken; the Ganges cannot be dammed; the Brahmans cannot be conquered by any one on earth. The world cannot be ruled in opposition to the Brahmans; for the mighty Brahmans are the deities even of the gods. If thou desirest to rule the sea-girt earth, honour them continually with gifts and with service" (*Anuddsanap*, 2160ff). Priestcraft has done more to enslave mankind than the sword of the most merciless oppressor. For a tyrant may be expelled in a day; but the mind once darkened by superstition loses the power of vision and forgets its own blindness. Brahmans have reigned in India for more than twenty centuries, and no one can foresee the day when their kingdom will come to an end. Even practical Rome was at one time in danger of falling under the sway of a dominant priesthood,—the rock on which the less practical India struck. There, as in India, "the neglect or faulty performance of the worship of each god revenged itself in the corresponding occurrence; and as it was a laborious and difficult task to gain even a knowledge of one's religious obligations, the priests, who were skilled in the law of divine things and pointed out its requirements—the *pontifices*—could not fail to attain an extraordinary influence" (*Mommsen's History of Rome*, Vol 1). From that rock Rome was saved by the non-hereditary character of the priestly office, the indomitable enterprise of her people, their intense patriotism and attachment to political freedom—all which conditions were wanting to India. When we reflect that Brahmanism has absorbed and assimilated every other religious agency that has crossed its path, has attenuated every national or tribal hero into a saint of the Brahmanical pattern, abolished or brought into discredit every form of marriage rite except what was recommended by its own teaching, distorted every legend derived from the heroic age into conformity with Brahmanic precepts, supplanted almost every indigenous language with its own Sanskrit or Hindi, we cannot be surprised, but should rather regard it as an inevitable consequence, that it has impressed its own image upon industry also, and that every other class in the community possessing some hereditary function should have attempted to shape itself upon the same pattern as that furnished by the Brahman original.

174. In theory then, as we have seen, a caste is a trade-union, seeking to secure its own monopoly against all outsiders and denying the right of membership to any one not born within its own ranks from *both* parents. But theories affecting such a complex organism as that of human society are seldom or never completely carried out. The rule about marriage was very simple and could be easily enforced; for one caste could easily refuse to give its daughters in marriage to men of other castes, and this practice has been faithfully adhered to. But hunger is above all rules; and it was quite impossible for any one caste to prevent the members of any other from encroaching upon its own function, if sufficient inducement existed. Thus while the caste system has remained very complete and perfect so far as marriage is concerned, it has become, and was from the first, far less efficient in regard to function. Even the Brahman has not been able to secure the monopoly of his own function, the priesthood, against all outsiders; for the Goshayen as temple-priest of Shiva, and the Bairagi as temple-priest of Vishnu, have poached, and are still poaching, very largely in his preserves (see paras 146, 148). If the most powerful of castes could not maintain the monopoly of its own most specialized and jealously guarded function—the priesthood—it is not likely that the less powerful castes, exercising purely secular and less specialized functions, such as those of landlordism, agriculture, cattle-grazing, &c., would be able to shut their doors effectually against all encroachments from without. Thus in all the industries or castes "connected with the land" (as I have described them in my tables of classification), from the hunter and fisherman to the landlord, there is, and has long been, a constant intermixture of function which, owing to the inevitable spread of cultivation and other causes, goes on increasing every century. The castes whose functions have been least intermixed are the "artisan castes," upper and lower, and the "serving or professional," because in these a greater degree of skill is necessary and such skill cannot easily be acquired except under a father's guidance. In these, then, the industries have continued for the most part hereditary up to the present day, and would have remained so none the less, if no attempts had been made to secure them against outsiders by the rules of caste or trade-unionism. Commerce has always been open to all comers; and as no speciality of skill is required for buying and selling, the "trading" castes are perpetually receiving new accessions from without, and ruined traders are perpetually entering into occupations connected with the land.

175. Caste, then, though the primary object of its existence was to impose restrictions on trade, craft, or function, has interfered but little with the natural course of industrial activity, and it is not on this account that it deserves the reprobation which it has received. A people like that of India, which stopped short at the agricultural stage, and to which the scientific and commercial spirit of modern times was wholly unknown, could not have been expected to make greater progress than it has done in the arts and industries of civilized life; and caste, by insisting on the hereditary nature of functions, has aided, rather than retarded, the acquisition of artistic skill. Moreover, as several different castes or marriage unions have assumed the same function or calling, the element of competition, so necessary to industrial activity, has not been wanting. The evil which caste has inflicted upon the people of this country is physical and moral rather than industrial; physical, because the race has deteriorated through the restrictions placed on the natural freedom of marriage; moral, because the chief motive to union, confidence, and respect between the different classes of the community has been destroyed. Society, instead of being constituted as one organic whole, is divided against itself by inorganic sections like geological strata. The sense of insecurity thus engendered could not but lead to a loss of independence and courage in the characters of individuals. For a man soon ceases to rely on himself if he thinks that no reliance is to be placed on the good will and fair dealing of those around him, and that everything which he may say or do is liable to be suspected or misconstrued. Thus the two greatest defects in the Indian character—a want of reliance on one's self and a want of confidence in

others—have sprung from a common source—the terror-striking influence of caste. The caste arrogance of the Brahman, which first sent these evil spirits abroad, has corrupted the whole nation and descended to the very lowest strata of the population. A scavenger, the lowest of castes, is as proud of his birthright, and almost more punctilious about its rules, than a Chattri or a Kayasth. His arrogance has even led to a disruption within his own fraternity: for some Bhangis will no longer eat what comes from their master's table, and these men have formed themselves into a distinct sub-caste on that basis. Every Bhangi despises the Chamár because he eats carrion; while the Chamár despises the Bhangi because he earns his living by removing refuse. The lower castes, having no valuable monopoly to defend, have set up the most frivolous distinctions as grounds for despising their neighbours. Not only has caste demoralized society at large, but it is a constant source of oppression within its own particular ranks. If a man, in some incautious moment, happens to do something forbidden by caste rules, some spy at once swoops down upon him like a bird of prey and summons a *panchayat* or caste council, by whose decree he is compelled to perform penance, on pain of expulsion from the caste, by giving a banquet to the *biradari* or "brotherhood" falsely so called. Caste is therefore an instrument both of widespread disunion abroad and of the meanest tyranny at home; and the latter of these evils has intensified the want of courage and self-reliance, to which we have lately alluded as being one of the greatest defects in the Indian character.

It is of course quite foreign to the purposes of this paper to discuss either the merits or the failings of the natives of this country. The latter have been alluded to in this place, only because they appear to me to be the natural outcome of the institution of caste—an institution for which no individual is responsible, but for which the character of many individual men has been made to suffer. The existence of such defects does not at all detract from the fidelity and high sense of gratitude observable in the native character.

176. The other question to be examined was—In what relation does *caste* stand to the earlier organization of the *tribe* which it superseded?

The history of almost every country, if we look to the earliest stage of its career, takes us back to a period when the population was divided into tribes and tribes sub-divided into clans. The bond, which first brought the different clans together and formed them into a single tribe, has been different at different times and places. It may have been some particular deity whom the various clans agreed to venerate as their common protector, or some particular river or forest which they regarded as the common cradle of their race, or some fortress which they used as a rallying-point at times of attack from without. Or clans may have been drawn together by some peculiarities of custom, apparel, or totem. The most usual bond, however, has been that of attachment to some victorious chief, who welded the clans together into a compact brotherhood for purposes of war or defence against neighbouring tribes or confederacies. The man who thus founds a tribe comes in after years to be regarded as its ancestor, and the idea of kinship or a common ancestry thus formed is one of the strongest of ties. A tribe, then, is simply a collection of clans called by a common name, and bound together by the possession of a common deity, or a common domain, or a common totem, or a common ancestry, or common customs, traditions, pursuits, &c., or by two or more of these bonds combined.

177. What we are most interested in observing in this place is that the bond of union which first drew the clans together and formed them into a single tribe was *not* unity of craft or occupation. In fact, as each tribe aspired to be a self-sufficing body, independent of all other tribes for the tools, weapons, food, and other commodities necessary to its existence, diversity, rather than unity, of craft among the component clans was the thing desired, for the peaceful interchange of commodities among tribes, whose normal relation towards each other was one of war, was of course the

last thing to be expected. For example, it has been said of the Aht tribe in Vancouver's Island, "that, though living only a few miles apart, the tribes (clans) practise different arts. One is skilled in shaping canoes, another in painting boards for ornamental work, or making ornaments for the person, or instruments for hunting and fishing. Individuals as a rule keep to the arts for which their tribe (clan) has some repute, and do not care to acquire those arts in which other tribes (clans) excel. There seems to be among all the tribes (clans) a sort of recognized monopoly in certain articles produced or that have long been manufactured in their own district" (*Scenes and Studies of Savage Life*, by G. M. Sproat, page 19). Sometimes the clans most skilled in handicrafts fall into the position of serfs or inferiors to some dominant clan, which, being more skilled than the rest in fighting, undertakes the entire responsibility of defending or enlarging the tribal domain. This is true, for example, of the Kandhs or "mountaineers" inhabiting the steep and forest-covered ranges which rise from the Orissa coast. Here the Kandh proper "engages only in husbandry and war," while the inferior clans supply families of hereditary weavers, blacksmiths, potters, herdsmen, and distillers" (*Hunter's Indian Empire*, page 77). Almost all the indigenous tribes which once covered the plains of Hindustan have long been dispersed into castes; but such few remnants as have survived display a greater versatility of genius than the castes or functional unions which have succeeded to their places. The Kanjar tribe, for example, is skilled in skinning off hides, making drums, collecting drugs from forest herbs, trapping the jackal, shooting birds with the pellet bow, manufacturing mill-stones, plaiting osiers into mats and baskets, twisting cotton into thread, digging for *kaskas* roots, manufacturing the weaver's brush, &c. : such versatility will not be found among the lower castes of the Hindu community. Indeed, the industries practised by Kanjars are the very industries upon which several of the lower castes, such as Chamár, Behna, Dharkar, Bhuna, &c., have been formed.

178. In reply, then, to the question which has been asked concerning the relation of tribe to caste, I should say that caste acts as the solvent of tribes. The formation of a caste implies that clans or fragments of clans, possessing some craft or occupation in common, but belonging to different tribes, have been seceding from their respective tribes and forming themselves into a new group united by the common craft or industry. The new group thus formed is a caste or trade-union. There is no bond of sympathy in human society that draws and binds men more closely together than that of a common industry or (which comes to the same thing in the end) a common interest. It is customary in our own language to speak of men, who are of the same cloth or practice the same calling, as "brethren"; and *biradari* or brotherhood is one of the terms used by the natives of India to express the caste relationship. The process, by which tribes are broken up and trade-unions or castes formed out of the fragments, is much facilitated, and in fact almost invariably preceded, by conquest ending in the amalgamation of tribes into a nation under some central government. So long as tribes are at war with each other, and each tribe is thrown upon its own resources for the supply of all its wants, diversity of industries or crafts among its members is necessary to its existence. But when tribes hitherto at war have lost their independence and become joint subjects of some larger kingdom or empire, commodities can be freely interchanged, and industries are thrown together to an extent which was impossible in the previous state of things. The tribe, having thus served its end and become useless, begins now to crumble away and disappear, and groups of men associated in hereditary professions, trades, or crafts succeed to its place. The ceremony or contract which completes the detachment of clans or families of men from their ancestral tribe, and renders all return to it or admission into any other association impossible, is marriage. When two or more fragments, drawn from different tribes, have been thus cemented by marriage into a single group, and when marriage within the group has been made a condition of membership (*vide* para. 169), a caste has been completely formed. This crumbling away of tribes into their component elements, followed by the regrouping of men by some hereditary craft or

industry, whether secular or religious, is a process so simple and natural, and in its season so useful and beneficial, that there are few, if any, nations in the world in which it has been wholly unknown. What stereotyped the system in India, and prolonged it to a season far beyond its capacities for usefulness, was (as we have shown) the caste arrogance of the Brahman. It is this which by the contagion of its own example has infected not only the upper, but the middle and even the lowest classes of the community who have no craft or industry worth inheriting or defending, and has thus multiplied the number of castes on Indian soil to an extent unparalleled in human history.

179. In order to illustrate the process by which tribes become gradually dispersed into castes, after they (the tribes) have been first amalgamated into a nation as parts of a larger whole, we will select a few examples from the tribes and castes existing at this day in Upper India.

The Kols, with similar aboriginal tribes, such as Bhárs, Cherus, Sioris, Doms, &c., were once occupants of a large portion of the plain of Hindustan. Some sixty-three thousand Kols, according to the census of 1881, may still be found in the districts south of the Ganges, where their condition is but little, if at all, advanced above that in which their forefathers were living some three thousand or four thousand years ago. A large number more, living in a similar status, may be found in the hills and forests of Central India. Those who remained in Hindustan, north of the Ganges, have been dispersed, partly into a semi-savage tribe called Musarhas, who are only now beginning to settle on the outskirts of Hindu villages as watchmen and pig-rearers—partly into cattle-grazers, amongst whom they appear as a section called "Kor" of the large pastoral caste of Ahir—partly into agriculturists of the caste of Káchhi, which caste is in some places called Koeri, in others Murao, and in others Sani, each of these names having been derived from tribes which have helped to make it up. Here, then, we have the three successive stages of industry—hunting, nomadism, and agriculture, all represented by portions of the single tribe of Kol. Other portions of the tribe have gone into the various handicrafts. Some (there is reason to believe) took to iron work and have contributed to the caste of Lohar. Others took to weaving; and the weaver caste is better known to this day by the tribal name of Kori than by the functional names of Bunkar or Joria. Others took to hide-dressing and tanning, and appear as a section called Kori in the caste of Chamár.

180. Another example may be taken from the tribe of Dom. The sites of ruined forts and the names and traditions attaching to them show that Doms, Domkatars, Domras, or Donwars (for all these names occur) were once a powerful race in Hindustan, especially in the districts north of the river Gogra. The Chattri clan of Donwar, many of whom still reside in the Gorakhpur and neighbouring districts and who profess to belong to the venerable Bharadwaj *gotra* or order, bear living testimony to the power once held by this widely extended tribe. But while some few succeeded in acquiring territorial sway and raised themselves into the ranks of the Chattri caste by attaching bards and Brahmans to their persons and learning the ways and manners of orthodox Hindus, the rest can be traced only in castes standing much below them in rank and function. Some have gone into the Bhangi or sweeper caste; others into the Dharkar or basket-making caste; others have contributed to the Turha or fishing caste; others to the Dhobi or washerman caste; others to the Dhánuk or bow-making caste, from which the Muhammadan caste of Kamángar has sprung; others to the Muhammadan caste of musicians known by the name of Dom Mirasi. The remnant of the aborignal tribe, out of which so many castes or sections, from the warrior to the sweeper, have descended, is a coarse, repulsive savage, an eater of dogs, a burner of corpses, and executioner of the living. But in Kumaun, where some of the better portions of the original tribe have survived, Doms are the chief artisan class and are employed as carpenters, masons, and the like, which would lead one to infer that the same tribe contributed many of its families in ancient times to the corresponding castes in Hindustan.

181. Another and still more striking example may be taken from the tribe of *Gaund*, which is pronounced and spelt in English as *Gaur*, one of the most conspicuous names in the caste system of Upper India. The original tribe is no longer to be found, so far as I know, in its purely savage state, as in the case of the Kol and Dom. But we have a near approximation to the aborignal savage in the large fishing tribe (for we can scarcely call it a caste, though it has outwardly assumed the status of one), which under the name of Gaur or *Gaund* is still very numerous along the river tracts of Oudh and the eastern districts of the North-Western Provinces. Like most of the other aboriginal races, the Gaurs were once a widely dominant tribe, and have given their name or some variation of it, not only to many of the villages of Northern India, but to the large district, which is spelt and pronounced in English as "Gonda," but which the natives themselves pronounce (with a *nasal* accent) as "Gaura." When it is remembered that the highest and noblest pursuit of these aboriginal tribes, in times before they were denationalized by Brahmanical usages and broken up into castes after the Brahmanical model, was that of war, we ought to feel no surprise at the fact, that a large and powerful clan of Chattris or Rájputs, called by the name of Gaur, exists at the present day. Between the Gaur Chattri and the Gaur fisherman there are many other Gaurs scattered among the intermediate castes. For instance there is a Gaur sub-caste of Kayasths or writers; a Gaur sub-division of Tagás—a community of land-holders ranking a few degrees below Chattris proper; a Gaur sub-division in the caste of Darzi or tailor; another in that of Halwai or confectioner; and another in that of Barhai or carpenter. In paragraph 64 I had already given expression to the conjecture, that the caste of carpenter took its origin out of tribes to whom fishing was the chief occupation; and my reason for supposing this was that the first fishermen must have manufactured their own boats,—those single-logged canoes which are so commonly found among backward races in other parts of the world, and are still very common in India. This conjecture is now unexpectedly confirmed by finding the name "Gaur" occurring among the sub-castes of Barhai or carpenter, while the Gaur tribe as distinct from the carpenter caste is still addicted to boating and fishing.

We have thus shown how largely the aboriginal Gaur tribe is represented among the various castes or functional groups of Upper India at the present day. But there is one other caste more important than any yet named, in which the name of Gaur holds a conspicuous place, and that is the Brahman. To one who is accustomed to look upon Brahmans as being in the main pure-blooded descendants of the ancient Aryan invader, the appearance of such a name in such company is at first sight rather startling. But as the caste of Brahman is known to have been closely allied from the very first to that of Kshatriya or Chattri, and as the name of Gaur, together with those of many other aboriginal tribes or backward castes (of which a long list could be given if necessary), appears among the sub-divisions of the modern Chattri, no surprise need be felt. My own conjecture is that the Gaur sub-caste of Brahman is made up of three elements, which were eventually amalgamated into one by intermarriage: (1) those who were nearly related by blood and by social position to Chattris of the same name and tribe, but who assumed priestly functions in the place of kingly ones, after the example handed down from kings of the Vedic age; (2) Brahmans of other than Gaur origin, who were domiciled in the Gaur country under the protection of the Gaur kings and landlords, and who therefore received the name of Gaur; (3) priests of the aboriginal Gaur tribe itself, whom Brahmans of the two kinds just named admitted into their own caste by investing them with the sacred thread. The motive which drew these three elements together was that of a common function and common interest. The bond which cemented the union and consolidated them into a distinct social unit was marriage. Intermarriage once established, the Gaur sub-caste of Brahman was completely formed. The caste once formed retained its generic name of Gaur, but sub-divided itself into *gotras* or orders similar to those assumed by the other Brahmanical sub-castes. All this of course is only a conjecture; but the process described is in accordance with facts, which are known to have occurred in other instances, and with the principles on which castes in general are believed to have been established. This theory seems at least to be more probable than that which derives the Gaur Brahman of Upper India from the Gaur Brahman of Bengal. The truth probably is that the Bengali Gaur was a colony of Hindustani Gaurs who were planted in the Gangetic delta about a thousand years ago by King Adhishwara.

182. We have seen, then, that a caste is formed out of fragments drawn from various different tribes; that the motive which brings such fragments together is community of function and interests; and that the bond which finally consolidates them into a distinct social unit or caste is the establishment, by mutual consent, of the right of intermarriage. We may now exemplify this process once more by showing how new castes have been formed, not out of the fragments of tribes, but out of fragments of castes which were themselves previously formed out of the fragments of tribes. The process in this latter case would naturally be the same as that in the former.

183. It has been usual to speak of Indian castes as being "fissiparous," like those animals and plants in the natural world which are continually throwing off fragments or sections from the main body, each fragment acquiring after separation a complete individual life. If this metaphor is intended to express a scientific fact, I believe it to be entirely misleading. A plant or animal of the kind in question acquires its separate life from a *single* fragment detached from the parental stock. I question, however, whether any body of men in India can ever become so entirely detached from their hereditary caste as to form a new caste of their own, until they have become amalgamated by marriage with some other body of men drawn from some other caste. When two or more fragments have thus been united by marriage into a single group, a new caste has been formed, and return to the ancestral caste on either side is then impossible.

The Khattri or banking caste, for example, has in the main sprung (as its name implies) out of the great generic caste of Kshatriya or landlord; and it is easy to see how the possession of wealth, implied in the term landlord, should have led certain members of this community to devote their money to some purpose other than that of acquiring new land or living in idleness on the acquisition. But the mere change of function from landlordism to banking could not by itself have detached them from the caste of their forefathers, or prevented the possiblity of return to it; for any man, whatever his caste may be, can take to trading or banking, if he has the capital, and without forfeiting his caste by so doing. Moreover, the caste of Kshatriya is one to which any man would be proud to belong, and which no one would desire to leave without necessity. I hold, then, that the cause which detached the Khattri from the Chattri or Kshatriya and shut out all possibility of return to the ancestral caste was the establishment of a marriage union between fragments or clans drawn from several different sub-castes of Kshatriyas, between whom no connubial rights had hitherto existed, or from sub-castes of Kshatriyas mixed with those of Brahmans. There is much reason to believe that Brahmans as well as Kshatriyas have contributed to form the new caste of Khattri; for Brahmans of the Sarasvat sub-caste will to this day eat food cooked by Khattris, but no Brahman of any sub-caste will eat food cooked by a Kshatriya. Several other circumstances might be named which point to the same conclusion.

184. To take another example, the new caste of Bohra. This is a banking and money-lending caste, whose name is derived from *beohár*, which signifies "business." They are undoubtedly an offshoot from Brahmans; for the tradition of their origin is so recent that many persons still speak of them as Brahmans, though they have in fact become quite distinct. Now the word "Brahman," like the word Kshatriya, is the generic title for a large number of separate sub-castes; and what distinguishes one

sub-caste from another, and entitles it to be called a separate unit, is the fact that no one is permitted to marry outside this circle. If we suppose, then, that the Bohra caste was made up of fragments drawn from several sub-castes of Brahmans, between whom no right of inter-marriage had previously existed, the detachment of the Bohra from the parental stem of Brahman is explained. The establishment of connubial rights among fragments of sub-castes, between whom no such rights previously existed, creates (as the reader already knows) a new caste at once and renders all return to the abandoned communities impossible.

185. The Kayasth or writer caste might be quoted as another example. Originally the younger sons or near relatives of Chattri and occasionally of Brahman landlords, by whom they were employed as managers of estates and collectors of rent, they became gradually amalgamated by intermarriage, and formed a new group possessing separate marriage rights of their own and denying such rights to all outsiders. According to the Mánava Code (X, 6). the male progeny of Brahman husbands and Kshatriya wives, or of Kshatriya husbands and Vasiya wives, occupied a rank between the two and were called Kayasth. It was only natural that men so born (if Manu's account of their birth is correct), having no distinct status, either as Brahmans, Kshatriyas, or Vaisyas, among the ranks of the twice-born classes, should form a caste or trade-union of their own, the several constituents of which were cemented into a single group by the right of intermarriage.

186. It is the incapacity of fragments drawn from various different castes to become amalgamated by marriage into a single brotherhood, which prevents the partially developed castes from becoming completely formed. In illustration of this we will produce two examples—the Gadahla and the Sangtarásh. The Gadhala, if such a caste existed, would be a caste of ass-breeders; and as such it would take its place with the Rewari or camel-breeder, the Pàsi or pig-rearer, the Khatik or fowl-breeder, the Gadariya or sheep-grazer, and the Ahír or cattle-grazer. But the caste of Gadahla cannot come to the birth, because the fragments of the various castes by whom the industry of ass-rearing is practised (*viz.*, the Bhangi or sweeper, the Kumhár or potter, and the Dhobi or washerman) are as proud of their ignoble castes as if they were Brahmans, and are therefore too conceited to form a new marriage union. The Sangtarásh or stone-cutter has been described already in para. 62. At the bottom of the scale of stone-cutters stands the savage Kanjar, who makes and mends millstones. Next to him stands the Khatik, who practises the same craft. Next to the Khatik stands the Ahír, who cuts stones from the quarries and prepares them for the masons. Next to the Ahír, but very distinct from him in every respect, stands the Gokain, who, though properly an engraver in wood, is not less skilful in carving stone. Next to these stands the Goshain, a priestly caste, some of the members of which make idols and other symbols of stone. Above the Goshain stands the Brahman, who shares with the Goshain in the art of image-making. In all this list, it would be difficult to find any two fragments sufficiently akin to consent to becoming members of a new marriage union and thus forming a new caste; and so the caste cannot at present be said to exist.

187. Although caste has, as we have shown, acted as the solvent of tribes by dispersing the component clans or fragments of clans into different directions, and then gathering them up again into new groups, drawn together as by a loadstone into the brotherhood of a common industry, yet the organization of the tribe or primary group appears to have been the model, upon which that of the caste or secondary group was constituted. If castes were formed out of tribes, it was only natural that the child should bear some likeness to its parent. The resemblance has shown itself in two different ways: (1) in the rules for the regulation of marriage within the ranks of the caste itself; (2) in the prohibition of intercourse in the matter of eating and drinking with outside communities. A few words on each of these points will be necessary before closing the subject.

188. First, then, as to the rules in regard to marriage. Every caste or sub-caste is sub-divided into sections or smaller groups, which, so far as the upper castes are concerned, are called *gotras*. The number of *gotras* to any given caste may vary; but whatever the number may be, the caste as a marriage union is made up of the sum of these *gotras*. On the one hand, no member of the caste is allowed to marry outside the circle of this union. On the other hand, no one is allowed to take a wife from the same *gotra* as his own. Among all the upper castes this is a clear-cut rule, to which no exception exists. The explanation given by Brahmans as to the reasons why a man is thus prohibited from taking a wife of his own *gotra* is that every *gotra* is descended from some Rishi or sage of the Vedic age; and consequently all persons born within its ranks are in the relation of brother and sister. Marriage, therefore, within the same *gotra* would be incest. Now this gotra system of Indian castes appears to bear a close analogy to the clan system of tribes. A tribe of the ancient type, like the caste of modern India, was a marriage union, that is, a wider circle within which a man was compelled to marry, but containing within its circumference a number of clans or smaller circles within which marriage was disallowed. The analogy however, though close, is not quite exact. For in the case of the caste it is only the *gotra*, but not the caste or union of *gotras*, which claims descent from a common ancestor; whereas in the case of the tribe, not only does each clan sometimes set up an ancestor of its own, but the tribe or union of clans sets up a more ancient ancestor, who is himself supposed to have been the father or forefather of the several minor ancestors. The long and sanguinary dispute which the plebeians waged against the patricians of Rome, one of whom demanded and the other refused the right of *connubium* or inter-marriage, and the reluctance with which the right was at last conceded, show how very difficult it was, even under a republican Government, to break through the line of the outer or tribal circle. It is probable, in the absence of any evidence to the contrary, that every Aryan tribe which migrated into India some four thousand years ago had a clan system of its own, similar to that which has prevailed so widely elsewhere; and a considerable number of names which appear to be tribal occur incidentally in the Vedic hymns. From what we know, too, of the indigenous tribes of India at the present day.—those at least whose original character has not yet been defaced through conversion to Hinduism—it is probable that a similar system prevailed among the ancient aboriginal tribes, with whom the invading Aryans were brought into contact. If, then, the modern Hindu has sprung, as I hold that he has, out of the amalgamation of the two races, and if caste has sprung out of the dispersion of tribes, it is no wonder that the caste should have organized its own constitution upon the same model as that of the tribes out of which it arose.

A gotra in the strict Brahmanical sense is an exogamous group, the members of which are supposed to be descended from a common Vedic saint. As we have stated already, such groups are only to be found among the upper or "twice-born" castes, that is, among those which have become completely Brahmanized. Among Chattris, but not among Brahmans or Kayasths or other high castes, there are clans of the strictly tribal type as well as gotras of the Brahmanical type; and a Chattri in choosing a wife decides for himself what are the limitations to his choice as regards the clan, but leaves it to the Brahman to decide what limitations exist in regard to the gotra. Among the lower castes the rule of exogamy is worked in various different ways. Sometimes we find a caste made up of clans of the tribal type, that is, clans which have retained their identity as such after having detached themselves from the parent tribe in order to enter the caste or functional brotherhood. Sometimes we find a caste broken up into small exogamous groups, which are known in the caste itself as *gots*, but are not the same as Brahmanical *gotras* sprung from a Vedic saint. In castes where no clan or *got* or gotra can be traced the rule of exogamy is always applied to the *gharána* or circle of blood relationship, on the male side, traced back to the fourth or fifth generation. The *gharana* is of course a much smaller circle of prohibited degrees than the modern *gotra* or the ancient clan.

The rule of exogamy is found in full force at the present day among several of the aboriginal tribes of this country, such as the Santals and Kandhs of Central India, the Tharus, Nats, Kanjars, and Doms of Upper India, and the Bhils, Grassias, and Minas of Rajputana. The clan may not always be of the most perfect type—*viz.*, that which claims descent from a common ancestor; but the rule of exogamy is strictly enforced. Speaking of the Kandhs, Dr. Hunter remarks :—"The clan consists of a number of families sprung from a common father, and the tribe is made up in like manner from a number of clans who claim descent from the same ancestor" (*Indian Empire*, page 76). Here the smaller group, which he calls a clan, and the larger one, which he calls a tribe, alike coincide with the Brahmanical conception of *gotra*—a body of men related by blood on the male side through descent from a common father or forefather. Further on he says regarding the same people, "marriage between relations, or even within the same tribe, is forbidden" (page 77). The same writer, speaking of the Santals, says—"The Santals know not the cruel distinctions of Hindu castes, but trace their tribes, usually fixed at seven, to the seven sons of the first parent :" and of their marriages he adds :—"The Santal must take his wife not from his own tribe, but from one of the six others" (page 73). If we substitute "tribe or clan" for "gotra," the organization of the Santal and Kandh communities gives a very fair representation of that of an Indian caste formed on the Brahmanical model.

189. The other point, in which the discipline of the caste resembles that of the tribe, consists in the rule by which intercourse in the matter of eating and drinking with outside communities is forbidden on pain of expulsion from the fraternity. The range or circle of the convivial union, if I may so call it, is co-extensive with that of the marriage union ; for *convivium* is the necessary sequel to *connubium*.

Fire and water, food and drink, which (as every one's experience must tell him) constitute the life of the individual body, have been regarded in almost every tribe or state, with whose traditions and customs we are acquainted, as symbols of the collective life of the tribe, state, or nation. "So strong is the bond of race," says Dr. Hunter writing of the Santals, page 73, "that expulsion from the tribe was the only Santal punishment. A heinous criminal was cut off from fire and water in the village and sent forth into the jungle. Minor offences were forgiven upon a public reconciliation with the tribe, to effect which the guilty one had to provide a feast with much rice-beer for his clansmen." We have only to substitute "caste" for "tribe," and the above passage gives as faithful a picture as we could wish of the internal discipline of an Indian caste. The symbol of caste membership, or of re-admission into caste when membership has been suspended for some offence against caste rules, is a common meal cooked at the same fire. Expulsion from caste means expulsion "from fire and water." A man who eats food cooked in strange fire and strange water breaks the tie that binds him to his own fraternity and becomes an outcaste. In the Roman commonwealth and in all the Greek States, whose institutions have been recorded, the sentence of banishment pronounced against a guilty citizen was expulsion from fire and water, and thus between the status of the banished citizen and that of an Indian outcaste there was no practical difference. In ancient Lacedæmonia the Spartiatœ, or citizens of Sparta proper, constituted a distinct marriage union or caste ; and the symbolism of caste membership was preserved by the institution of public meals (Syssitia). In a large number of communities both of the old and the new worlds a public fire was kept constantly burning on a central hearth or altar to symbolize the collective life of the horde, confederacy, or state. Among those tribes of Upper India which are still outside the pale of caste, and therefore form no part of the Hindu community proper (such as Thárus, Kols, Kanjars, Nats, Doms, &c.), the rule against eating and drinking with outside tribes is strictly observed. The same may be said of those tribes "allied to the hunting or fishing states," who stand in the very lowest stratum of Indian castes. A Banjara once informed me that his tribe will not even speak, much less eat or drink, with Kanjars. The three great tribes who

founded the Roman commonwealth, the Ramnenses, Tities, and Luceres, were at perpetual war, till they agreed to mingle their respective fires in the common hearth or altar of Vesta and thus constitute a single state.

190. As life is made up of food and drink combined, and not of food only or of drink only, so in the rules of caste it is the use of fire and water combined, not the use of fire only or of water only, which renders food cooked by one caste unfit for consumption by another. Thus any man, whatever his caste may be, can eat parched grain (chabena), that is, grain fried *without* water. Had no such qualification existed, no such caste as that of the Bharbhunja, who sells parched grain to the general public, could have come into existence. Again, any man may eat flour or grain sweetmeats cooked in both fire and water, provided the *immediate* contact with fire is shut off with butter. If the butter qualification had not been thought of, the caste of Halwái (baker and confectioner) could never have seen the light. The Bráhman has asserted his superiority over all other castes by making his case exceptional in these culinary matters. On the one hand, whatever he cooks, in fire and water both, is privileged so that no one of any other caste can lose caste by eating it. On the other hand, his own purity so far exceeds that of other castes that he may not eat either the parched grain prepared by the Bhunja or the buttered bread or grain sweetmeat prepared by the Halwái. Considering the immense amount of fuss attached by all the castes to questions of eating and drinking, the exceptional position, which the Brahman has acquired in these matters, is alone sufficient proof of the arrogance of his pretensions and of the success with which he has asserted them.

191. The right of convivium or eating together follows, as we have shown, that of connubium or intermarriage as closely as an effect follows its cause. But woe to the man who inverts the order, that is, who takes food cooked at a strange fire, food cooked by some outsider, with whom he does not stand in the marriageable relation, and who therefore belongs to a different caste. Such an act, wilfully or knowingly committed, entails dismissal from the fraternity, which in the case of the lower castes can be redeemed by a banquet, but in the case of the upper ones is absolutely beyond remedy. The condition of an outcaste is almost indescirable. He is completely cut off from society; for not only is he scouted by his own brotherhood, but no other caste will take him in or make him one of themselves. There are but three sources open to a man in such a case. He can either go away with his family to some distant place where no one knows him, and give himself out to be of such or such a caste, and thus regain some kind of social footing. Or he can renounce the world, attach himself to some religious order, and become a Goshain or some other kind of celibate, leaving his wife and children to be cared for by their relations or by his own: (for his own loss of caste does not entail the same infliction on them, unless they too have committed the same offence). Or lastly, he can change his religion altogether and become a Musalman or a Christian. I know of one case of a Kayasth who lost caste by eating food which had been cooked at a strange fire. Every conceivable attempt was made by the offender to recover his lost status, but all his offers of penance were indignantly rejected. The offence was unpardonable. At last, in utter despair, he turned Muhammadan by undergoing the rite of circumcision and repeating the confession. But even then his wife and family were detained by their relations and not allowed to join him. One night, however, by a preconcerted plan, she fled secretly into a house where her husband had arranged to receive her and to have some dinner ready cooked for her at his own fire. She had scarcely had time to enter the house and place a morsel of his food between her lips, when her pursuers rushed in and claimed her. But when they saw that she was chewing something that he had cooked at his own fire, they at once gave her up as lost, knowing that that one morsel of food had, by the rules of caste, cut her off for ever from all her kith and kin. Such is the efficacy in India of food cooked in a strange fire.

192. Assuming, then, that " functional union bounded by a marriage union" is the minimum difinition of an Indian caste, it is necessary to point out in conclusion

that the number of castes or marriage unions actually existing in the North-West and Oudh is far in excess of the one hundred and twenty-one names shown in the annexed tables. To be more precise, we ought to exclude the nineteen names of group I, representing "casteless tribes," and the two names of group VII, representing the "religious orders," as neither of these belong to the list of castes proper. This will leave us a list of one hundred different castes. Now what we have to observe is that each of these names is merely a major head descriptive of the general function under which a large number of minor heads or separate marriage unions are included. For instance, under the major head "Barhai or carpenter" (see table, group IIIB.) the number of minor heads or marriage unions comes to at least seven, and therefore the real number of Barhai castes is not one, but seven. Again, under the major head "Kayasth" (see table, group X) there are ten clearly-defined marriage unions, and therefore the actual number of Kayasth castes is ten and not merely one. Under the head "Chattri" there must be at least thirty marriage unions; for in this "elastic fraternity" (as Sir H. Elliot has most justly called it) marriage unions are very changeable, varying according to the wealth and status of individual families. Under the head "Brahman" there must be at least forty different castes or endogamous groups. The disunion which the Brahman has sown broadcast among the people by his own arrogance has thus recoiled with more than double effect upon his own head; for there is no caste in India which is broken up into so many hostile and mutually despising sub-castes as that bearing the generic title of Brahman. If it were possible to ascertain the precise number of marriage unions existing at the present time, this would be an exact measure of the number of castes. I believe that I am well within the mark when I say that to every major head named in the annexed tables the average number of minor heads or marriage unions is not less than ten. According to this, then, the total number of castes at the present time in the North-West and Oudh is not one hundred, but one thousand.

193. The number of castes in India is constantly changing, because every marriage union may admit new constituents or expel old ones. The circle of marriage unionship is not, nor ever has been, immutable. It might rather be compared to a circle, whose centre can change its point, and whose radius is perpetually liable to being lengthened or contracted. This process of extension in one direction, followed as it usually is by contraction in another, has been at work for the last two thousand years at least: and thus, while some castes once prosperous, such as the Kathak and the Bhat, are surely but not slowly dying out, and while others, such as the Baidya, have died out altogether, other castes, such as the Khattri and Kayasth, have been rising into importance in their places. When, therefore, a caste is said to die out, this does not mean that the families which belonged to it have died or been exterminated, but either that the function peculiar to this caste has become useless to the outside community, in which case the families constituting the caste are gradually dispersed into other functional and marriage unions, or if the function is still useful to the outside world, that some new and more energetic centre of activity, giving rise to a new marriage circle and assuming a new title, has supplanted the old one. The Baidya, as Baidya, has disappeared, but his descendants are still alive under other names.

194. It was necessary to allude to the above facts in order to explain the bulk to which the Brahman and Chattri, "the first-born and second-born of castes," have grown in the course of the last twenty centuries. According to the figures shown in the annexed tables, the one contains 4,690,850, and the other 3,127,207 persons. Considering that the function of the Brahman is to act as priest, and that of the Chattri as landlord or ruler, such numbers are obviously far in excess of the capabilities of the outside community. At least three-fourths of the men who call themselves by such names can find no scope for exercising the functions peculiar to their respective orders. But rather than change their names and fall into the ranks of any of the outside castes, whose functions they have assumed as a means of livelihood, they have clung to

the ancestral brotherhoods. From the very first both of these castes found that their interest lay in extension rather than in contraction. There are or were three kinds of landlords, rulers, or warriors, whom the original Kshatriya castes have admitted at different times into the ranks of their own fraternity by giving them their sons or daughters in marriage :—(1) men bearing the names of aboriginal tribes, who founded petty kingdoms and established local dynasties ; (2) men bearing the names of some of the inferior castes, who rose into power during the ascendancy of Buddhism or from other causes ; and (3) a class of chiefs, whose origin cannot be traced to any particular time or place, but who called themselves after some animal supposed to resemble them in character, such as Kachaura (tortoise), Baghel (tiger), Hárá (wasp), Rikh-bansi (bear), Nag-bansi (serpent), Sarpakheria (snake), Singhel (lion), Bains (buffalo). It is no wonder, then, that among the Chattri sub-castes or marriage unions now existing we find (as was pointed out in paragraph 188) clans of the tribal type co-existing with gotras of the religious type ; for the word Kshatriya or Chattri is simply a general name which came to be applied, in virtue of its own signification, to men of any tribe, clan, or caste, who have at different times risen into power as local chiefs and compelled by force of arms the obedience of the peasants, herdsmen, and others living within reach of their forts. Again, there are or were five kinds of priests whom the original Brahman caste has found it necessary to co-opt at different times into the marriage union :—(1) Kshatriyas, of any origin whatever, who voluntarily exchanged the function of ruler for that of priest ; (2) priests of the aboriginal tribes, who were admitted into the ranks of Brahmanhood as fast as their own tribes become Hinduized ; (3) priests of Buddhism who were admitted into Brahmanhood as fast as Buddhism itself melted back into the older creed ; (4) priests manufactured by kings out of various inferior castes for the occasion of some immense banquet or religious festival, when a sufficient number of Brahmans could not be found ready made ; (5) the illegitimate sons of the various celibate orders, who assumed the status of river-priests or temple-priests at the sacred rivers or shrines, where the monasteries stood. It is probable too, for reasons given in paras. 48, 33, and 97, that men of the Bari, Máli, and Nápit castes have occasionally crept into the ranks of Brahmanhood. The castes of Brahman and Chattri have been expansive and elastic from the beginning. But while new members have been taken in at different times, whose admission seemed likely to extend the influence of the castes which adopted them, many of the older families and clans, whose retention was of no use for such a purpose, have clung to the ancestral brotherhood with a tenacity which pride only can attach to poverty.

195. If it were possible to compress into a single paragraph a theory so complex as that which would explain the origin and nature of Indian caste, I should attempt to sum it up in some such words as the following. A caste is a marriage union, the constituents of which were drawn from various different tribes (or from various other castes similiarly formed), in virtue of some industry, craft or function, either secular or religious, which they possessed in common. The internal discipline, by which the conditions of membership in regard to connubial and convivial rights are defined and enforced, has been borrowed from the tribal period which preceded the period of castes by many centuries, and which was brought to a close by the amalgamation of tribes into a nation under a common sceptre. The differentia of *caste* as a marriage union consists in some community of function ; while the differentia of *tribe* as a marriage union consisted in a common ancestry, or a common worship, or a common totem, or in fact in any kind of common property except that of a common function. Long before castes were formed on Indian soil, most of the industrial classes, to which they now correspond, had existed for centuries, and as a rule most of the industries which they practised were hereditary on the male side of the parentage. These hereditary classes were and are simply the concrete embodiments of these successive stages of culture which have marked the industrial development of mankind in every part of the world. Everywhere (except at least in those countries where he is still a savage), man has advanced from the stage of hunting and fishing to that of

nomadism and cattle-grazing, and from nomadism to agriculture proper. Everywhere has the age of metallurgy and of the arts and industries which are coeval with it been preceded by a ruder age, when only those arts were known or practised which sufficed for the hunting, fishing, and nomad states. Everywhere has the class of ritualistic priests and lettered theosophists been preceded by a class of less cultivated worshippers, who paid simple offerings of flesh and wine to the personified powers of the visible universe without the aid of an hereditary professional priesthood. Everywhere has the class of nobles and territorial chieftains been preceded by a humbler class of small peasant proprietors, who placed themselves under their protection and paid tribute or rent in return. Everywhere has this class of nobles and chieftains sought to ally itself with that of the priests or sacerdotal order; and everywhere has the priestly order sought to bring under its control those chiefs and rulers under whose protection it lives. All these classes, then, had been in existence for centuries before any such thing as caste was known on Indian soil; and the only thing that was needed to convert them into castes, such as they now are, was that the Brahman, who possessed the highest of all functions—the priestly—should set the example. This he did by establishing for the first time the rule that no child, either male or female, could inherit the name and status of Brahman, unless he or she was of Brahman parentage on *both* sides. By the establishment of this rule the principle of marriage unionship was superadded to that of functional unionship; and it was only by the combination of these two principles that a caste in the strict sense of the term could or can be formed. The Brahman therefore, as the Hindu books inform us, was "the first-born of castes." When the example had thus been set by an arrogant and overbearing priesthood, whose pretensions it was impossible to put down, the other hereditary classes followed in regular order downwards, partly in imitation and partly in self-defence. To a nation mesmerised by Brahmans and blinded with superstition and ignorance no other course was open. Immediately behind the Brahman came the Kshatriya, the military chieftain or landlord. He therefore was the "second-born of castes." Then followed the bankers or upper trading classes (the Agarwal, Khattri, &c.); the scientific musician and singer (Kathak); the writing or literary class (Kayasth); the bard or genealogist (Bhat); and the class of inferior nobles (Taga and Bhuinhar), who paid no rent to the landed aristocracy. These, then, were the third-born of castes. In all communities, such classes must stand rather high in the scale of social respectability, since the stages of industry or function which they represent are high in proportion; but in India their rank was more precisely defined than elsewhere by the fact that they made a nearer approach than the castes below them to the Brahmanical ideal of personal dignity and purity. Next in order came those artisan classes, who were coeval with the age and art of metallurgy; the metallurgic classes themselves; the middle trading classes; the middle agricultural classes, who placed themselves under the protection of the Kshatriya and paid him rent in return (Kurmi, Kachhi, Máli, Tamboli); and the middle serving classes, such as Nápit and Baidya, who attended to the bodily wants of their equals and superiors. These, then, were the fourth-born of castes; and their rank in the social scale has been determined by the fact that their manners and notions are further removed than those of the preceding castes from the Brahmanical ideal. Next came the inferior artisan classes, those which preceded the age and art of metallurgy (Teli, Kumhar, Kalwar, &c.); the partly nomad and partly agricultural classes (Ját, Gújar, Ahír, &c.); the inferior serving classes, such as Kahár; and the inferior trading classes, such as Bhunja. These, then, were the fifth-born of castes, and their mode of life is still further removed from the Brahmanical ideal than that of the preceding. The last born, and therefore the lowest, of all the classes are those semi-savage communities, partly tribes and partly castes, whose function consists in hunting or fishing, or in acting as butcher for the general community, or in rearing swine and fowls, or in discharging the meanest domestic services, such as sweeping and washing, or in practising the lowest of human arts, such as basket-making, hide-tanning, &c. Thus throughout the whole series of Indian castes a double test of social precedence has been in active force, the Industrial and the Brahmanical; and these two have kept pace together almost as evenly as a pair of horses harnessed to a single carriage. In proportion as the function practised by any given caste stands high or low in the scale of industrial development, in the same proportion does the caste itself, impelled by the general tone of society by which it is surrounded, approximate more nearly or more remotely to the Brahmanical ideal of life. It is these two criteria combined which have determined the relative ranks of the various castes in the Hindu social scale. Outside the caste system altogether stand the few and shattered remains of those aboriginal tribes, out of which the whole series of castes was fashioned by slow degrees, through the example and under the guidance of the Brahmanical priesthood. Had the Brahman never come into existence and had his arrogance proved to be less omnipotent than it did, the various industrial classes would never have become stereotyped into castes, and the nation would then have been spared a degree of social disunion to which no parallel can be found in human history. There seems to be no likelihood of caste being banished from Indian soil until Brahmanism itself—the *fons et origo mali*—has died a natural death by the rise of the scientific spirit, and the fallacy of its pretensions has become an object of general scorn. As soon as the Brahman begins to disappear, the rest will follow.

JAINS.

196. The census report gives us very little information concerning the Jains, and that little is given doubtfully. In section IX, on the "Religions of the People," it says nothing about their tenets, and in section XXIII it tells us nothing about their castes. In form III, which shows the statistics of population according to religion, the total number of Jains, as distinct from Hindus, is set down as 79,957. This is in fact the only thing that the report tells us about them, and even this, as the compiler explains in page 59 of the Preliminary Dissertation, is probably incorrect:—"The Jains or Saraogis in these provinces are generally regarded as a sect of Hindus. Under the orders issued to enumerators by the Government of India, the castes and *not the sects* of Hindus were to be recorded, and consequently many Jains were returned as Hindus simply. Much was done by subsequent inquiry to correct this; but I have no doubt the number of this sect is considerably understated." The italics here given are the compiler's own. But there are some castes which are exclusively Jain; and hence it would not have been opposed to the orders of the Government of India to have collected the statistics of population assignable to each of these.

197. Jainism, though a keen rival to Buddhism, which it has regarded all along with the most cordial hatred, has yet been always called a sister creed or satellite, and the very resemblances between them afford a natural explanation of their hostility. If current traditions are to be trusted, both creeds made their appearance in the north of India at about the same time (*viz.*, about 550 B.C.) Whatever the differences may have been among themselves, there was one sentiment at least which they shared in common—antagonism to the pretensions and teaching of Brahmans. The word "Jain" means a follower of Jina the Conqueror, just as "Baudha" means a follower of Buddha the Enlightened. The word for "follower" in both of these creeds was "Srávak," a listener or disciple, and this word appears to have given rise to the name "Saraogi," by which Jains are not unfrequently called to this day. In ancient times, the most famous centre of Buddhist and Jainist teaching in Upper India was the city of Srávasti (in the Gonda district, Oudh), the ruins of which are now at last being exhumed: and the name Srávasti is probably a contraction of Sravak-sthiti, "the abode of the disciples," and not, as Mr. Benett has suggested in the Oudh Gazetteer, a derivative from Savitri, a Vedic name for the Sun-god. The saints and founders of the Jainist creed were called Jinas or conquerors, in virtue of the fact that they had prevailed over the temptations of the world, and could point out the way, the truth, and the life to all who desired a similar emancipation from the coils of mortal existence. They are also called

Tirthankárs, which simply means "teacher, preceptor" (from *tirthám*, precept, and *kár*, maker or doer), in contradistinction to Srávak, disciple. There are said to have been twenty-four Jinas or Tirthankars, spiritual conquerors or spiritual preceptors, who appeared on the earth at wide intervals of time apart. The first of the series was Rishab, and the last two Párswa Náth and Mahávir: the names of the twenty-one intermediate ones are very seldom heard of. The last, Mahávir or the "Great Hero," is said to have died in 526 B.C., and the almost universal tradition recorded in the Jainist Scriptures points to this man as the founder of the creed. The original tenets of Jainism were decidedly opposed to those of the Brahmans. It taught that there was no caste and no deity, and that the slaughtering of animals in sacrifices was an impious encroachment on the rights of the sentient creation. It denied the inspiration of the Brahmanical Vedas and set up a new Veda or inspired book of its own. It dwelt very strongly on the sanctity of animal life of all kinds, but authorized the slaying of a Brahman as the arch-enemy and seducer of mankind.

198. For several centuries past, however, Jainism has been steadily drifting back into the older creed of Brahmanism, from which it at first seceded with so much acrimony: and hence, if we look to the present state of Jainism and ignore its beginnings, it is now correct to say that its followers are merely a sect of Hindus. Probably, too, the disappearance of the sister creed, Buddhism, from Indian soil was less due to open violence than to the silent imperceptible power which Brahmanism has everywhere possessed of absorbing or winning back every form of schism or independent thought that has sprung up among the people; and this is the opinion now generally held by scholars. Most, if not all, Jains of the Upper Provinces are not only content to call themselves Hindus, but would reject with scorn the imputation of being Buddhists or of having any affinity with them, though I am told that in Rajputana the assimilation of Jains to Hindus is much less complete than elsewhere. The denial of the existence of gods or supernatural beings, on which the first Jains so warmly insisted, has not prevented their descendants from reverting to a kind of theism or polytheism of the Hindu pattern. The twenty-four Jins or Tirthankars have been raised to the rank of deities, and colossal images are erected in their honour at the Jain temples, notably in those of the Dekkan. Side by side with these deified mortals are a class of goddesses named Shásanadevis, who execute their commands, and whose presence in such company appears to be merely an adaptation of the doctrine of the Saktis or female powers associated with the three great gods of Hinduism. In addition to these, many other deities are recognised, all of whom have been borrowed one by one from the Hindu pantheon. The Jains have even multiplied the gods of the Hindu firmament by recognising four Indras or sky gods instead of only one. But they do not profess to give any preference to the three great gods of the Hindu Triad—Brahma, Vishnu, and Shiva; and theoretically all gods borrowed from the Hindus are subordinate to their own saints—the Jinas or Tirthankars. Even this theory has, however, been virtually set aside of late by the modern doctrine now generally accepted by Jains, that Rishab or Rishab Náth, the first of all the Jinas, was an *avatar* or incarnation of Vishnu. There is a temple in the south-west of Mewár (as Mr. Ibbetson points out in his late Panjáb Census Report), where Rishab is worshipped as a form of Vishnu by Jains and Hindus alike: and thus, if we are to look upon the Jains as a sect of Hindus, they belong to the Vishnuite rather than to the Shivite school of believers. Though the first Jains discarded Brahma, the great being whom Hindus have from the earliest times regarded as the supreme power in the universe, yet their descendants have put another being in his place, whom they call Jinapati, which being interpreted means "the lord of the Jinas or conquerors." The name Varddhamán, which is sometimes applied to Mahávir, the traditional founder of Jainism, savours strongly of the Hindu doctrine of Brahma; for it is derived from the root *vridh*, to grow or expand, just as the word Brahma is derived from *brih*, which is only another form of the same verbal root. All this betokens a very wide departure from the original atheism with which the creed set out. Brahmanism has in fact been too

strong for this, as it has been for every other, form of dissent, which has attempted to found a church in India outside the range of Brahmanic caste and ritual.

199. The tendency thus displayed by Jains to revert to the ways and notions of Hinduism is equally, if not more, marked in social than in religious matters. Notwithstanding all the professions once made about the rejection of Brahmanic pretensions and the natural equality of all men, they have themselves become broken up into castes fashioned after the Brahmanic model. The names of these castes, so far as I can learn, are Oswál, Sri Mál, Sri Srí Mál, Srí Mál Pattan, Bauddhmati, and Parwár, six castes in all. These are castes in the strict sense of the term—that is, they are trade unions which deny all right of intermarriage or convivial intercourse with outsiders. I learn, too, that in the disposal of property they follow the Hindu law of inheritance and call in Brahmans to decide doubtful points of succession. The name "Banddhmati" is evidently of religious origin, and implies that the first members of the caste were followers of Buddha, though their descendants are now without exception Jains. The remaining five names appear to be all geographical, and to indicate that the castes now settled in Hindustan came originally from Central or Southern India. Thus the Oswáls, the most important and influential of all the Jain castes, say that they came from Osia, a town in Jodhpur. The name "Sri Mál" is derived from the country Mál or Malwa, and the prefix "Sri" has been added merely to denote the good luck or prosperity claimed by the caste. The reduplicated "Sri" in the caste name "Sri Sri Mál" merely indicates that this rival fraternity claims a higher degree of prosperity than the other. The "Pattan" attached to the name, Sri Mál Pattan, implies that a portion of the caste came from the south, where "Pattan" is a common name for town or city. This caste, then, represents a marriage union between some Jains of Mal or Malwa and certain other Jains who came from further south; and as such it exemplifies the method on which, as I have attempted to show in this paper, castes in general have been formed. Parwar is merely a contraction of Palli-war (the name by which the caste is sometimes called), Palli being a town in the Jhánsi Division. The etymologies here assigned, and the inference to be drawn from them as to the quarter from which the castes immigrated into Hindustan, are confirmed by the fact that almost all the distinguished shrines and holy places frequented by Jain pilgrims are in Central or Southern, and not in Northern India; as for example, Mount Abu to the north of Gujarat; the hill Párswa Náth (generally misspelt as Parasnath), on the top of which Párswa, the last but one of the Jinas, is said to have died—that is, to have obtained his *nirván* or liberation from earthly life; the rock-cut caves at Ellora, Nassik, and other places; and the huge rock-cut idol of a Jina near Chinrai Pattan, in Mysore. There are many remarkable temples, too, in the state of Datia, near Gwálior. The secluded and mountainous character of these places appears to imply that, though Buddhism had been banished from the plains of Hindustan, the Jains were able to hold out in these safe retreats until the period of Muhammadan domination had set in. This domination, while it checked the progress and arrogance of Brahmanism, was tolerant of small sects or religious associations, from whom no political danger was anticipated; and under the protection thus afforded, certain Jain communities moved northwards and settled in the cities of Hindustan, where we now find them. In physiognomy, so far as I have been able to see, the Jain castes of Upper India, especially the Oswal, are fairer and better-featured than the average Chattri or Brahman, and appear to have retained a stronger dash of Aryan blood.

200. The chief, and in Upper India the only, *hereditary* industry in which the Jain castes engage is that of commerce or banking. The six castes named in the previous paragraph are pre-eminently trading castes, and would have been grouped under that heading in my appended statement, if the census report had furnished the names and figures. In almost all the large towns from Lahore to Bombay or Calcutta they hold a conspicuous place as traders or bankers; and the particular aptitude which they evince for this kind of calling is well in keeping with the prominent part played

by merchants, bankers, goldsmiths, &c., in the legends and chronicles of Buddhism, the sister creed. This, however, does not prevent individuals from taking service as writers, clerks, pleaders, accountants, &c., in all which capacities they have become the rivals to Kayasths and Brahmans, to whom they are in no respect inferior in intellectual quickness. The wealth which they have accumulated in banking or service has enabled some of them to purchase landed estates and set up as landlords, but not as warriors, after the manner of Chattris. In Central India, as for example in the Jhánsi Division, I learn on the authority of an eye-witness that many of them work in the fields as tenant farmers or labourers; and one writer affirms that to the Jains of Southern India agriculture is the usual occupation. This proves as conclusively as any argument that could be adduced the extent to which all castes in India, whatever their hereditary function may be, are being gradually thrown upon agriculture as a means of livelihood. For the objection urged in the Mánava Code to Brahmans holding the plough, "that the iron-mouthed pieces of wood not only wound the earth, but the creatures dwelling therein" (X, 84), applies much more forcibly to Jains than to Brahmans. The cardinal maxim of the Jain code of morals (and this they have steadily adhered to, notwithstanding all changes in the creed itself), is summed up in a single *sutra* or aphorism, "*Ahinsá paramo dharma*—regard for animal life is the highest virtue." To such an extent is this maxim observed that the more rigid of the Yatis, or ascetics of the Jain persuasion, will not drink water till it has been filtered, nor inhale air except through a veil, nor set foot on the earth till they have swept the spot for fear of unconsciously crushing some unseen insect. Amongst all Jains, whether ascetics or men of the world, it is a rule (honoured sometimes in the breach as well as in the observance) not to light lamps or candles after dark for fear some insect may be drawn into the flame, and not to take food after sunset for fear some insect may slip between their teeth. The only kinds of occupation fit for a people holding such views is to handle rupees or hold a pen; for in every kind of industry but these the destruction of animal or insect life is unavoidable.

201. In addition to the Jain castes proper there are certain other castes (all of the Trading class) which are partly made up of Jains and partly of Hindus. This remark applies especially to the Agarwál, Khattri, Maheshwari, Vishnoi, Jaiswal, and Lohiya castes, and there may be others. As regards the Khattri and following castes, it would appear that at the outset they were purely Hindu, but that owing to the greater attention which all the trading castes pay to religious matters, and to frequent association with members of the Jain castes who follow the same occupation (trade), some of their own body have contracted Jain views of morality and religion. But as regards the Agarwál caste, it would appear that the process was reversed, and that all Agarwáls were originally Jains, as the Oswals still are. This seems to be implied in the fact, on which an Agarwál, with whom I was once in conversation, laid great stress, that all members of his caste, whether Hindu or Jain (and my informant himself was a Hindu), abstain altogether from flesh diet. On this ground he claimed that his caste was a higher one even than that of Brahman; and he assured me that Hindu Agarwáls were quite as strict on the point of abstaining from meat as their Jain caste-fellows. I have had no opportunity of examining the question any further. There is one fact in connection with all these semi-Hindu and semi-Jain fraternities which deserves to be specially noticed. Diversity of creed has not in any way impaired the unity of the castes, and this shows the groundlessness of the theory, by which caste in one of its aspects has been described as a "spiritual brotherhood," a body of men "to whom a common rite or a common doctrine is everything." Caste, as I have defined it, is a functional union bounded by a marriage union; and now, in verification of this, we find two doctrines and two sets of rites co-existing within the same caste, and yet no disturbance to the marriage union resulting from such diversity. If the bridegroom is a Hindu, the girl is married according to Hindu ceremonies and with the help of Brahmans; if he is a Jain, according to Jain ceremonies, in which no Brahmans are employed. One of the peculiarities in the Jain marriage rites consists in the ceremony of killing a Brahman in effigy, a survival from the time when Jains and

Brahmans were at actual and bitter warfare. A figure of a Brahman is made of kneaded flour, and with hollow trunk, so as to admit of being filled with syrup or sugared water. The figure so filled is placed under the bench on which the bride and bridegroom are seated. After the pair have been united in wedlock by the Jain rites, the male relatives of the bridegroom kill the Brahman, catching his blood *alias* the sugared water, as it comes trickling out of the cavity of his body, and mixing it with fresh flour, out of which sweatmeats are at once made for distribution to the company present. In making marriage contracts no account seems to be taken of scruples which the girl or woman might feel at being mated to a man of different persuasion from that in which she was herself born and bred. What the author of the Bombay Census Report has recorded concerning the Jains of his own province is not less true of the semi-Jain and semi-Hindu castes of Upper India:—"The partition between Hindu and Jain is of the very narrowest description, and cases are not uncommon in which intermarriage takes place between the two sections. The bride, when she is with her Jain husband, performs the household ceremonies according to the ritual of that form of religion, and on the frequent occasions when she makes a temporary sojourn at the paternal abode she reverts to the rites of her ancestors as performed before her marriage." Between the domestic ceremonies of Jains and Hindus one radical difference should be noticed. Jains do not perform the *sraddh* or annual funeral feast for the repose of the dead—a practice the omission of which in the eyes of Hindus would be regarded as impious; for the Jain believes that the soul of the dead either enters at once into *nirván*, a state of blissful unalterable repose far beyond the confines of the earth, or into some new form of earthly existence; while Hindus believe that the soul still wanders in space and suffers hunger and thirst, if it is not fed. The mode of worship, too, performed at Jain temples differs from that paid at Hindu ones and approximates more nearly to the cultus of the Buddhists. There is a frequent use of little bells and candles as at Buddhist shrines; and the idols of the Jinas or deified saints are not dressed, washed, and fed with offerings, as are the images of gods in Hindu temples. The offerings of fruit sometimes paid by Jains to their deified saints are not given as food, but as complimentary presents. Thus in the marriage ceremonies, the funeral rites, and the cultus of idols, there is a considerable basis of diversity between Jains and Hindus, if either section chose to accentuate the differences: and hence the writer just quoted is hardly right in saying "that the partition between them is of the narrowest possible description." The truth appears to be, not that the differences are inappreciable, but that the sentiment of caste, or of "marriage *plus* functional unionship," has been strong enough to hold the two religionists together within the same brotherhood, in spite of the diversities that exist.

202. Among Jains, as amongst Hindus, there are sects of celibate ascetic orders who have renounced the ties of family and kin and live on the charity of the faithful. These are called Yatis, the "restrained or self-masters;" while Hindu monks, as we have shown above, are known as Sannyásis, Atits, or Beshdháris. As the census report has lumped all kinds of devotees together under the vague name of faqir, which, properly speaking, applies to Muhammadans only, it is impossible to say how many Jain ascetics there are in the united provinces at the present time. The Jain ascetics are distinguished into two great schools—the Svetambar, or those clothed in white, and the Digambar, or "those clothed in the four quarters of the horizon," that is, in nothing but air. At the present day Digambars are not allowed to go about in a state of nature; but during their meals, and when two or more are dining in company, they revert to the old custom of the brotherhood by discarding their clothes or rags. These men were known to the Greeks, who visited India in about 300 B.C. and later, as the "naked sophists." While Hindu ascetics wear matted locks (*jata*) in imitation of their great model Shiva, the Jain ascetics used at one time to pluck out their hair, which leads to a mass of short frizzled locks springing up in their place. This explains why the figures of the Jain saints are represented with frizzled locks.

The practice of depilation, however, is not observed by the Yatis of the present day, who either shave their heads or allow the hair to grow long. The Digambars have carried the ascetic principle much further than the Svetambars, and are regarded in all respects as the older and more orthodox sect. These designations have passed from the priests or monks—Yati—to the hearers or laymen, Srávak: and thus all Jains are expected to enrol themselves under one or other of these two banners. Digambars approach more nearly to Buddhists, Svetambars to Hindus. The former look to Mahávir, the twenty-fourth of the Jins, as their patron saint and founder; the latter to Párswa Náth, the twenty-third, who is said to have worn clothes, while Mahávir wore none. The former maintain with Buddhists that women are not capable of attaining *nirvan* or final beatitude, while the latter maintain with Hindus that they are. The canonical scriptures of the two sects are not at all the same. It is a remarkable fact, as showing the growing convergence of the Jain and Hindu creeds, that the ranks of the Yatis are not unfrequently recruited from Hindus of the Brahman caste: and the account which Horace Wilson gives of them as "skilful magicians, pretending to skill in palmistry and necromancy, dealing in empirical therapeutics and dabbling in chemical or rather alchemical manipulations," implies that they combine the arts of the Joshi Brahman, the Ojha Brahman, and the aboriginal wizard or medicine-man. A Jain temple is generally managed by some influential layman of the neighbourhood, who places some Yati in charge; and besides these there is generally a Máli, that is, a Hindu of the flower-gardener caste, attached to the service of the shrine. All offerings in cash, and the most valuable of the offerings in kind, are appropriated by the manager, who keeps the temple in repair; and a portion of this goes to the maintenance of the Yati. The minor offerings are appropriated by the Máli, who furnishes the flower-wreaths and sweeps out the floor of the temple. The function thus assumed by the Máli is well in keeping with what we have alluded to before in connection with Shivite shrines and offerings (see para. 33).

203. There is one great ceremony in which Jains do not allow Hindus of any kind to participate, and which marks them off more than any other custom that has survived as followers of a distinct creed. This is called the Ratha Játrá, and consists in yoking a huge wooden chariot, built two or three storeys high, to a pair of elephants, and making them draw it seven times round a large earthen mound, on which idols of the Jinas or deified saints have been previously placed for worship. Two instances or more of this performance have occurred within recent years in the Lalitpur district, and the account which I have received of them was given me by an eye-witness. Some wealthy layman, wishing to add to his stock of merit and thereby to increase his chance of *nirván*, invites co-religionists from long distances around, even from as far as Gujarat, Bombay, or Mysore, and holds a great religious festival which lasts for about one month, during which time all the Jains present are fed and maintained at his expense. The guests invited bring such idols as they can with them, and these are placed on the circular earthen mound or platform prepared for the purpose. On the last day of the feast the chariot drawn by elephants is led seven times round the mound, and as it passes, cocoanuts, cloves, and various kinds of fruit offerings are thrown at it by the multitude seated round it in a ring. If the elephant crushes the cocoanuts with his foot as he passes, this is considered fortunate. On the lowest storey of the chariot are placed the idols of the man who gives the entertainment; and in an upper storey is seated the man himself with several members of his family, some of whom are dressed up as idols. After the ceremony is over, every man in the assembly takes a turban in turn (one single turban having been prepared for all) and waves it over the head of the host. The host from this day forth is called a Singhai, the "lion" or chief of Jains, and is looked up to with veneration by his co-religionists till the day of his death. The use of the elephant in this ceremony for such a purpose as drawing a chariot is unique, and the sanctity attached to it as the only animal fit to be used in such a ceremony is peculiarly Buddhist. No Hindu deities are allowed to be named on these occasions; and the only idols worshipped are those of the Jinas or Tirthankars, the conquerors

or preceptors, by the last of whom the religion is said to have been founded more than two thousand years ago.

MUHAMMADANS.

204. For the Muhammadan castes (if such a thing as caste can be said to exist among persons of this creed) few words will suffice. Caste as an institution is entirely alien to the spirit of Islám, which has never raised any scruples about the class of women who can be taken as wives, or the choice of occupation which its followers may adopt. The strength of Islám lies in its levelling and democratic character, just as that of Brahmanism lay in its conceit and arrogance. Conversion consists in the simple process of submitting to circumcision and repeating the *kalima* or confession : and any Hindu on joining the ranks of Islam, "not only acquires freedom, but finds a society in which he can marry and give in marriage and satisfy the gregarious instincts of mankind." Nevertheless it is generally admitted that caste does exist in a certain sense among the Muhammadans of India ; and it will be the object of the remaining remarks to endeavour to ascertain to what extent and in what sense, as compared with the case of the Hindu castes, this is true.

205. The Muhammadans of India may be roughly divided into two main classes :—(1) those of foreign origin, descended from the original invaders (Persians, Afghans, and Turks miscalled Moghals), who crossed the Indus at different times and founded provincial or imperial dynasties at the old seats of Hindu power ; (2) those of indigenous origin, descended, that is, from Hindus or natives of India itself, who were converted to Islám at different times either by conviction, or through losing their own castes as Hindus, or by compulsion on pain of forfeiting their estates, or, in the case of the lower castes, with a view to shaking off the oppression to which they have been hopelessly consigned by the dictates of the Brahmanical creed. The distinction between these two classes is not by any means perfect : for Muhammadans of the former class, like the Aryans whose invasions preceded their own by about three thousand years, have undoubtedly taken wives from the people of the land, and there are but few of them, as their physiognomy plainly testifies, who can claim to be the pure-blooded descendants of the original Muhammadan invaders. There can be scarcely any doubt that in the long run the miscegenation will become as complete as it has already become in the case of the Aryans and aboriginals. All races which become domiciled in India merge eventually into the type of the native.

206. Muhammadans of the former class are generally classified under four great headings or tribes, *viz.*, Sayyads, Mughals, Patháns, and Shekhs. Sayyads are chiefly of Perso-Arabic descent and claim to have inherited, on the male side, some portion of the blood of the Prophet through his daughter Fatima, who was married to Ali, the fourth and (as the Shiah sect maintains) the only true Caliph. Almost all Sayyads are Shiahs as distinct from the other great sect, Sunnis, who pay no special regard to Ali "as the Caliph of God," and observe only the tenth day of the Moharram festival. Mughals and Patháns are invariably, or with extremely rare exceptions, Sunnis. Shekhs, being themselves of mixed origin, may be either Shias or Sunnis, but are mostly the latter. The Mughals (really Turks) are descendants of those Musalmáns from Central Asia who invaded India under the standards of Timur and Babar. The Patháns are descendants of the Ghaznivites, Ghorians, and other more recent comers from Afghanistan. But the name "Pathán" is becoming ambiguous ; for it is not unfrequently assumed by Rajput or Chattri converts, who have a partiality for this name in consequence of the military reputation associated with it. The Shekhs are of no nationality in particular. The name "Shekh" means "venerable," and was applied originally to any Musalmáns who might be distinguished for learning and piety. Men from the Pathán and Mughal tribes have assumed the title of Shekh at different times, and, following the example of Hindus, have bequeathed the same as an hereditary decoration to their descendants. This, too, is the title which Muhammedans of Indian origin (other than Rajputs or Chattris) are in the habit of assuming when they seek to secure a higher status in society. Any successful

tradesman, artisan, or professional man of any kind, if he succeeds in becoming rich or acquiring social importance in any other way, seeks to dissever the traditional connection which binds him to his former Hindu caste by assuming the name of Shekh. Moreover, converts from creeds other than Hinduism, such as Christianity for example, take the name of Shekh, and are so termed by their co-religionists.

207. In no sense can any of these four tribes be called a caste, and nothing but confusion as to the meaning of the word "caste" can result from placing them in such a category. The three following facts are decisive on this point:—Firstly, they can intermarry with each other, whenever individual members happen to be so minded. Whatever the tribe of the woman may be, her children take the rank of the father. Thus, if a Pathán or Shekh girl becomes the wife of a Sayyad, her sons are as much Sayyads as if their mother had been a Sayyad's daughter on both sides of her parentage. On the other hand, if a Sayyad girl becomes the wife of a Pathán, her children are Pathán and not Sayyad. This is directly opposed to the Hindu principle of caste and to the rule laid down by Manu as to the purity of caste blood:—"In all classes they, and they only, who are born in a direct order of wives *of the same class* are to be considered as the same in class with their fathers" (X, 5). Secondly, in the event of a man's choosing a wife from his own tribe, no attention is paid to the Hindu rule of *gotra* or *gharáná* (agnatic relationship). Endogamy and not exogamy is the rule among Muhammadans of high rank, and this is in direct opposition to Hindu principles. Thirdly, there is not, nor ever has been, any pretence to distinctiveness of function or occupation among these four tribes. Any tribe may take up with any occupation that individual members may select, and there is no such thing as tribal or traditional preference in the selection. Any man from any of these tribes may act as Imám or conductor of prayers in the mosque, if his neighbours consider him to be competent in learning and piety. The Sayyad and the Shekh are, it is true, more usually found in this capacity than Patháns or Mughals; but neither have any monopoly or hereditary rights in the matter, similar to those enjoyed by Brahmans, Goshâyens, and Bairágis amongst Hindus. In short, the tribe in the Indo-Muhammadan sense is neither a functional union nor a marriage union; whereas a caste consists in these two unions combined. All that can be admitted is that the names by which the above tribes are called denote a certain degree of social precedence, and to this extent only can these tribes be said to bear any resemblance to Indian castes. For example, a Sayyad is respected by all classes of Muhammadans, whatever his personal character or pecuniary status may be, much in the same way as a Brahman is respected by Hindus independently of all questions of personal merit. Again, more indulgence is shown to the peccadilloes of a Sayyad than to those of other Muhammadans: and if a Sayyad is in want, he is much more likely to be relieved than any other Muhammadan would be in similar circumstances. A Moghal ranks somewhat above a Pathán, and a Pathán above a Shekh.

208. Although the above tribes cannot be called castes, it is none the less to be regretted (as I think) that no statistics have been given in the last census report of the number of persons belonging to each of them, as was done in the separate census reports of Oudh and the North-West Provinces published about ten years previously, and as has lately been done in the Panjab census report of 1881. We have therefore no data for comparing the changes which may have occurred in the numbers during the interval of ten years between the last census and the preceding one. There is a Persian proverb current in Upper India, *Peshazin qassáb budem, bádazán gashtem Shekh; Ghalla chún arzán shawad, imsál Sayyad Meshawem*—"Last year we were butchers, after that we became Shekh; if the price of food rises, we shall this year become Sayyads." This shows that even in the case of Sayyad, with whom heredity of descent from the Prophet is everything, the question of birth is much less keenly scanned than it would be amongst Hindus, and that the tribal names are marks of social status as much as of actual origin. As Mr. Denzil Ibbetson has remarked of the Muhammadans of the Panjáb, "the process of manufacture in these cases is too notorious for it to be necessary for me to insist on

it; and so long as the social position of the new claimant is worthy of the descent he claims, the true Mughals, Shekhs, and Sayyads, after waiting for a generation or so till the absurdity of the story is not too obvious, accept the fiction and admit the new brother into their fraternity" (*Panjab Ethnography*, para. 342). The process, in fact, is very analogous to that which I have described respecting the manufacturing of Brahmans and Chattris; and the Hindu process of manufacture differs from the Muhammadan one only in being more gradual and difficult.

209. Muhammadans of the other class, as distinct from those of the four tribes who profess to be of foreign blood, are those of Indian extraction, descended from men of Hindu castes who have been converted to Islám. These have preserved to a certain extent, as will be explained below, the customs and traditions of the castes from which they have sprung. But the information given in the last census report is very incomplete as compared with what was given in the previous Oudh report. Of these Muhammadan-Hindu castes there are only five whose numbers have been recorded; and the figures (extracted from form VIII. A.) are as follows:—

Muhammadan-Rajputs ...	122,055
" Gujars ...	39,858
" Játs ...	10,401
" Tagás ...	26,070
" Mewátis ...	26,666
Total ...	225,050

If we deduct this sum from the total Muhammadan population of the North-West and Oudh recorded in the census report, *viz.*, 5,922,886, there is a remainder of 4,677,836 persons of whom no account has been given. This remainder is of course made up partly of the four tribes already described and partly of Muhammadan converts from the various Hindu castes. The latter are much the most numerous body of the two. Even the total of 5,922,886 is obviously incorrect: for several Muhammadan castes have been included in form VIIIB., although the castes mentioned in this form profess to be exclusively Hindu (see remarks given above in para. 5.)

210. Muhammadan converts can be conveniently arranged under two main headings: (*a*) those converted from high-caste Hindus; (*b*) those converted from the lower castes. The very fact that such a distinction can still be traced after the lapse of so many centuries shows that caste has, in a certain sense, survived the change of creed, notwithstanding the utterly casteless character of the creed, to which they have declared allegiance.

211. Regarding Muhammadans descended from high-caste Hindu converts. Mr. Williams has written as follows in his Oudh Census Report of 1869, Vol. I., page 77:—"The only high Hindu caste among whom there have been occasionally large conversions to Muhammadanism is the Rajputs, and the consideration that brought it about has in almost all instances in Oudh been the same. Either new lands, were granted free of revenue or on favourable terms, or lands forfeited by rebellions were restored, or some similar privilege or favour was bestowed; and the Rajput tribe forthwith became Mussalmáns; that is, they submitted to the rite of circumcision and began to pray in a mosque instead of in a temple, but otherwise they retained almost all their Hindu customs and manners." There are a few other high castes from which converts have been occasionally made, *viz.*, the Kayasth, the Brahman, and some of the upper trading castes, such as the Khattri and Bohra. Probably, too, many members of the Baidya or physician caste, now extinct in Upper India, but not extinct elsewhere, have embraced Islám owing to the higher reputation of Muhammadan medicine, and taken the name of hakim or Muhammadan doctor.

212. As regards the Rajput converts, the main points on which they have preserved the tradition of their origin are the following:—(1) they have retained the habit of drinking wine, notwithstanding the prohibition of their adopted creed; (2) in selecting a wife (if they cannot get one from some Mughal, Pathán or Sayyad

family, which some prefer to do if they can), they choose one from some Muhammadan Rajput clan, and never from converts of a Hindu caste lower than their own; (3) they invariably adopt the Hindu rule of exogamy, notwithstanding the custom observed in high Muhammadan families of marrying those near of kin; (4) for negotiating such marriages they employ a Brahman, who settles all preliminaries as to dowry, &c., between the parents of the bride and the bridegroom; (5) in the celebration of the marriage ceremonies they employ a Brahman to fix upon the auspicious day for each part of the performance and to throw the first handful of straw on the ground under the *mandap* or canopy where the ceremonies are held; and they give him the customary fee, after the Qazi (or Muhammadan officer) has given the seal to the union according to Muhammadan rites; (6) in funeral ceremonies, though they have discontinued the Hindu custom of the *sraddha* or funeral feast, they still employ a Brahman and a Mahá-Brahman for certain services to be rendered to the dead immediately after burial. These customs are, it is true, less strictly observed than they used to be; but the same may be said of *all* Hindu customs at the present day, even amongst those Hindus who have not adopted Islám as their creed.

The same remarks apply to the Muhammadan Kayasth; but the conversion of Kayasths to Islám has of course arisen out of different motives.

213. The number of Muhammadan Brahmans is much smaller, and their descent from the Hindu priestly caste cannot be so easily traced. Mr. Denzil Ibbetson, in his outlines of *Panjab Ethnography* (which consists of extracts from his late census report), alludes to them in the following terms in para. 512:—"There are 3,500 Mussalmán Brahmans, chiefly in the Delhi district. These men are known as Huseni Brahmans, and are said to receive oblations in the name of the Hindu gods from Hindus and in the name of Allah from Mussalmáns." I have heard of the same kind of Brahmans in these provinces also. There is another kind of semi-Muhammadan and semi-Brahman priest; and this is to be found at the tombs of saints, at which Hindus and Muhammadans alike go to pay their offerings. For example, there is the shrine at Kachauchha, in the Fyzabad district, where Makhdum Sahib, a Muhammadan saint, was buried; but it is well known that this was once a Hindu temple presided over by Kamál Pandit, whose soul is still worshipped there in common with that of the Mussalmán Makhdum. Invalids of either sex go there to be cured of blindness, lameness, infecundity, and the various diseases ascribed, by Hindus and Muhammadans alike, to demoniacal possession. The priests who are in charge of this shrine and who receive the offerings on behalf of the saints are said to be descended from those Brahmans who were owners of the temple before it became the shrine of a Muhammadan saint. Other instances might be named. Such men constitute a kind of caste, for their office is hereditary and they take presents from Hindus as well as Muhammadans. Both of these peculiarities favour the supposition of their Brahmanical origin, for there is no such thing as an hereditary priesthood amongst Muhammadans; and the custom of feeding or feeing temple priests, in the hope of propitiating the god or saint who resides at the shrine, is peculiarly Hindu.*

214. Muhammadans descended from lower-caste Hindu converts are very numerous. In addition to the few castes named in the census report (see para. 209) we may enumerate the following. Wherever it is possible, I have given in a bracket the Muhammadan name against the corresponding Hindu one. In one case (that of Darzi), the Muhammadan name "Darzi" has already entirely superseded the Hindi name "Suji" for tailor; and in another instance (that of confectioner,) the Muhammadan name "Halwai" has superseded the Hindi name Mithiyá. In two cases, *viz.*, Rangrez and Dom Mirási, no Hindi name exists. Both of these have been marked with an asterisk:

I.	Bhangi (Mihtar, Lal Begi)	Sweeper.
II.	Dhobi (Gazur)	Washerman.
	Kunjra (Mewafarosh, Sabzifarosh) ...	Greengrocer.
	Gaddi (Ghosi)	Milkman.
	Khatik (Chik or Chikwa)	Butcher.
III.	Suji (Darzi)	Tailor.
	Nai (Hajjam)	Barber.
	Kabár (Bhisti)	Water-carrier.
	Bunkar or Kori (Juláhá)	Weaver.
	Rangrez*	Dyer.
	Bhatyárá	Innkeeper.
	Dhuniya (Naddáf)	Cotton-carder.
	Kumhár (Kasgár)	Potter.
	Chhipi	Cloth-printer.
	Lohar	Ironsmith.
	Barhai (Najjár)	Carpenter.
	Manihár	Bracelet-maker.
	Mithiya (Halwai)	Confectioner.
	Dom Mirasi*	Musician.

215. The industries of the above fraternities have been briefly described already in connection with their Hindu equivalents, and what we have now to do is to attempt to show to what extent these fraternities can be called castes. Caste, as we have seen, implies three things : (*a*) heredity of function, (*b*) prohibition against marrying with outsiders, (*c*) prohibition against eating and drinking with outsiders. The Muhammadan fraternities certainly possess the first ; for heredity of function is of the very essence of their being. As a general rule they possess the second also ; for though inter-marriage with other fraternities is not prohibited by rule, on pain of expulsion, as amongst Hindus, yet it is discouraged by public opinion and is seldom or never practised in fact. The third condition is not observed in the case of any of the above fraternities except the first, that of the Lal Begi or sweeper, which in *all* respects is as complete a caste as any Hindu caste could be. The headings I, II, III are intended to signify the order of social precedence in which the several fraternities stand to each other, and here again, something of the caste system of the Hindus comes out. Those under heading III are the classes or castes from whom the Shekh tribe is occasionally recruited, independently of its natural increase from within.

216. Roughly, then, it may be said of the above fraternities that they are castes of the Hindu pattern, so far as the two principles of trade-unionism and marriage unionism are concerned, but not (except in case of the sweeper) so far as convivial intercourse is concerned. That they consider themselves to be castes like their Hindu brethren is certain ; for Mr. Williams remarks in the Oudh Census Report, Vol. I, page 81, that "there were separate columns in the enumerator's return for caste and profession, and the instances were simply innumerable in which entries were made in both columns for persons with Muhammadan names ;" and this is confirmed by the experience of every one who has enquired into the subject. If a man tells you that he is a Hajjam by caste, and you find that he has been earning his livelihood from a boy as a gardener, it is evident that he looks upon caste from the same point of view that a Hindu does. The case here described is not an imaginary one, and similar ones are of constant occurrence. Most of the above fraternities, too, have retained the Hindu caste custom of settling disputes by a *panchayet* or council of arbitrators selected from among the brotherhood. If the subject brought before the panchàyet relates to some question of trade or business affecting the fraternity as a whole, Muhamadans will be found associating with Hindus and forming part of the same assembly. Moreover, all the Muhammadan castes or trade-unions observe the Hindu rule of not taking a wife from within the *gharána* or circle of agnatic relationship reaching back to the fourth generation. If we had space to discuss the customs

and traditions of each Muhammadan caste individually, it would be found that each of them retains some link connecting it with its Hindu ancestors. For example the Chik or Chikwa caste of butcher is the Muhammadan counterpart of the Hindu Khatik. But the Chikwa has so far retained the traditions of his descent that he will not slay the ox: so that a new class of Muhammadan butcher, called by the generic name of Qasáb, has come into existence, in order to supply Muhammadans with their favourite flesh diet, beef. The Chikwa will not intermarry with a Qasáb, but only with Chikwas; and thus the Muhammadan fraternities come within the description of "a functional union bounded by a marriage union," which I have given in para. 192 as the minimum definition of caste.

217. In further proof of the fact that the lower classes of Muhammadans are castes in the Hindu sense of the word, Mr. Williams adds that "they consider the marriage of widows unlawful" (page 79). This, however, is not merely irrelevant as an argument, but is incorrect in point of fact. Every one of the Muhammadan castes enumerated in para. 214 allows the practice of widow remarriage, and so does every corresponding Hindu caste. It is a popular error to suppose that Hindus do not allow their widows to re-marry. The prohibition is quite of modern date, and is even now confined to the few "twice-born" castes who stand at the top of the tree. Among all the middle and lower castes, Hindu and Muhammadan alike, widows can be and are remarried without reproach. High-class Muhammadans have in some instances imbibed a prejudice against the custom from high-caste Hindus: but this is entirely opposed to the teaching of the Qurán, which strictly disallows widows to remain single.

218. It is much to be regretted (as I think) that no details have been given in the last census report as to the number of Muhammadans represented in each of the several castes. A comparison of such figures with those given in the previous census of Oudh and the North-West Provinces would have shown what progress Muhammadanism is making against the indigenous creed of Brahmanism. Mr. Williams' remarks on this point are worth quoting :—"It appears to be an almost invariable rule that in those professions which Muhammadans have adopted they form the great majority, and probably they do in time succeed in monopolizing every trade they adopt. By this I do not mean that their competition drives out the Hindus (for Muhammadans are generally not so industrious as Hindus), but that all the Hindus of any caste, the principal occupation of which has been invaded by Mussalmáns, eventually become Mussalmáns. The conversion is rendered easier when it does not involve the abandonment of an hereditary trade; * * * and when this is not a necessary accompaniment of a change of religion, the attractions of comparative freedom from caste rules, greater laxity in the choice of food, less subjection to priestly influence, and a certain rise in the social scale, all of which Muhammadanism offers to the new convert, become too great to be resisted. The Saikalgars (cutlers, metal-polishers, or sharpeners) are an instance. They are now exclusively Muhammadan; in Rae Bareli alone, the district where Muhammadans are fewest, there are a few Hindus still following this professión. The name of the (Hindu) caste is Baria; elsewhere they all seem to have become Muhammadans and call themselves Saikalgars." Many other instances might be quoted of Hindu castes becoming almost, if not entirely, Muhammadan. To quote from the Panjab census report lately compiled by Mr. Denzil Ibbetson (and the same proportions are likely to apply without much difference to the North-West and Oudh, if we make due allowance for the fact that here the rate of Hindus to Muhammadans is about fifteen per cent. against about fifty per cent. in the Panjab), in the Mochi or cobbler caste there are only 1,366 Hindus, but 347,900 Muhammadans; in the Dhobi or washerman caste there are 23,317 Hindus, but 109,889 Muhammadans; in the Rangrez or dyer caste there are 103 Hindus, but 4,957 Muhammadans; in the Kunjra or green-grocer caste there are 72 Hindus, but 5,928 Muhammadans; in the Kamángar or bowmaker and painter caste there are 265 Hindus, but 2,893 Muhammadans; in the Manihár or

bracelet-maker caste there are 2,950 Hindus, but 57,739 Muhammadans ; in the Darzi or tailor caste there are 10,022 Hindus, but 22,441 Muhammadans. It is evident that the Hindu element in some of these castes must soon cease to exist ; for isolation and the difficulty of procuring wives will soon render their position untenable, and Hinduism has nothing to offer them in compensation for these inconveniences. The above examples are taken exclusively from the Artisan and serving castes, who dwell chiefly in towns. But there is reason to think that a similar revolt against Hinduism is commencing in villages also among the rural or agricultural population. But as the figures are wanting, this is only matter of conjecture.

219. As amongst Hindus and Jains, so also amongst Muhammadans, there are several sects of religious orders, which differ, however, from those of Hindus and Jains in the fact that marriage is an openly recognized practice. The place where a family of devotees resides is called a *takiah*, that is, a "pillow" or resting-place from the cares of the world ; and the dwelling-house may be either a hovel made of mud or straw like a hermit's hut, or a well-built masonry mansion. The paterfamilias in such establishments leads a perfectly idle life, beyond reading or repeating the Kurán and receving what is given to him by the pious. Some are quite illiterate, but are supposed to make up for their want of reading by thinking very earnestly and profoundly. As amongst Hindus, the number of these Muhammadan sects is very great and, like Hindus, they have two great stages of asceticism. The first and easier is called that of the Sálik, "one who treads in the appointed path," and this is the counterpart of the Hindu *banaprastha.* The second and most severe, being the final one, is called that of the "Majzúb," that is, "one who is absorbed in the divine nature": this is the counterpart of the Hindu *Sannyási* (see para. 138). This idea of absorption into the divine spirit is not at all in character with the personal beatitude promised in Muhammad's Paradise, and has evidently been borrowed from Brahmanical teaching. For reasons already stated in paras. 150 and 202 it is impossible to ascertain from the statistics shown in the census report how many of the devotees recorded under the name Faqir are Hindu, how many are Jain, and how many Muhammadan.

220. I would beg to offer one or two suggestions in conclusion as to the form in which the statistics of the next census might be compiled. Against each caste name there should be four columns, headed "Hindu, Jain, Muhammadan, and Others," so as to show the number of persons within each caste who belong to each of the three main creeds. This is the method which has been followed by Mr. Denzil Ibbetson in compiling the results of the last Panjab census. Something similar to this was done in the Oudh census report of 1869 compiled by Mr. Williams. But (as we have already remarked) in the last census report of the North-West and Oudh there is nothing to show to what extent the different religions are represented within the several castes.

221. I would also suggest that against each caste name there should be two more columns, one showing the *original* function of the caste— that from which its specific character and, in almost all cases too, its name have been derived—and the other showing the various other occupations besides the original one followed at the present time. If these suggestions are accepted the form of the statement would be as follows :—

Name of caste.	*Occupation.*		*Numbers by religion.*				*Numbers by sex.*		
	Original function.	Present occupations.	Hindus.	Jains.	Muhammadans.	Others.	Male.	Female.	Total.

222. I have already said something about the synonyms of caste names in the places where I have described each group of castes. But in page xxxv, Appendix No. 12, of the census report, a list is given of the "local names of certain castes and of the caste in which they have been included in form VIII." Some of these identifications, which have not yet been alluded to, appear to be incorrect. Thus Gangáputra, Gangábási, and Ghátwál are set down as synonyms or local names of Bhát; whereas they undoubtedly belong to the general head of Brahman and are never applied to the caste of Bhát. Again, Bhagat is set down as a local synonym of Chamár; whereas Bhagats exist in *every* caste and not merely in that of Chamár; for the name is applied to those individuals of any caste who make a merit of abstaining from flesh and wine. Again, Kathak is set down as a synonym of Kanchan, Rádhá, and Ramjani: but the caste is as distinct as possible; for the Kathak is a high and much respected caste of musicians who wear the Brahmanical thread; while the others are hereditary prostitutes, who combine this vile function with that of singing and dancing. Again the Beldár is set down as a synonym of Roniá; but the former is a general name for navvy and is not even a caste, while the latter is one of the trading castes.

223. As it is presumed that these identifications have been used in compiling the figures in form VIII, the number of persons entered against the castes corresponding cannot be correct. And there are certain other entries, not previously alluded to which appear to be inaccurate also. For example, against the Hindu caste of Manihar there is an entry of only 6,612 persons of both sexes. But if we assume that there is an equal number of Muhammadans belonging to the same caste, even then a total of 13,000 persons seems a very small number for a caste whose function of making glass bangles is almost universally employed by the female half of a population of about 44,000,000 souls (see para. 60). Again, there is an entry of only 1,385 persons of both sexes against the Brahmanical sub-caste of Mahá-Brahman or "funeral-priest." Considering that his functions as such are indispensable to a population of over 38,000,000 Hindus, and that individual families of this caste are widely scattered among the towns and villages of the united provinces, the number of 1,385 must be a great deal smaller than the fact. Again, against "Bengáli" (one of the foreign races not returned by caste") there is an entry of only 2,521 persons of both sexes. But it is well known that in Benares alone there are more than three times as many as this number, and that in all the chief stations of those provinces the number of Bengalis has been steadily increasing for several years past.

J. C. NESFIELD,

Inspector of Schools, Oudh.

28th February, 1885.

GROUP I.—*Casteless Tribes.*

Serial No.	Name of tribe.	Census of 1881.	Remarks.
1	Tharu	27,172	
2	Bogsha	5 664	
3	Kanjar	19,524	
4	Habura	2,170	
5	Gandila	667	
6	Dom	176,615	
7	Barwar	5,711	
8	Dalera	2,039	
9	Aheri	...	Mixed up in census with Baheliya.
10	Banmánush	33,253	
11	Musarha	...	Mixed up in census with Banmánush.
12	Cheru	4,367	
13	Siori	2,099	
14	Nat	45 402	
15	Kanchan	25,488	
16	Bhil	552	
17	Gond	463	
18	Saharia	12,452	
19	Kol	63,991	
	Total ...	427,629	

Group IIA.—*Castes allied to Hunting State.*

Serial No.	Name of caste.	Census of 1881.	Remarks.
1	Bauriya	22,096	
2	Babeliya	67,860	
3	Bhar	360,270	
4	Arakh	64,713	
5	Dhanuk	119,341	
6	Khangár	32,304	
7	Pási	1,089,961	
8	Khairwár	573	
9	Dhingar	4,914	
10	Dusádh	...	Omitted in census.
11	Khatik	152,030	
	Total ...	1,863,562	
	Occupations not returned by caste ...	6,448	Tarikash, &c.
	Grand Total ...	1,870,010	

Group IIB.—*Castes allied to Fishing State.*

Serial No.	Name of caste.	Census of 1881.	Remarks.
1	Meo	13,246	
2	Bind	72,581	
3	Chain	49,410	
4	Mallah	616,909	
5	Dhuriya	4,026	
6	Kewat	...	Nos. 6, 7, 8, and 9 are not named in census, but are included under the general name of Kahár with 1,222,672 persons.
7	Gaud	...	
8	Gaundia	...	
9	Dhimar	...	
		1,222,672	
	Total ...	1,977,837	
	Occupation not returned by caste ...	299	Sanghár.
	Grand Total ...	1,978,136	

Group IIC.—*Castes allied to the Pastoral State.*

Serial No.	Name of caste.	Census of 1881.	Remarks.
1	Goshi or Gaddi	12,626	
2	Ahar	257,670	
3	Gújar	269,036	
4	Gadariya	860,220	
5	Rewari	1,382	
6	Ahir	3,584,185	
7	Ját	672,068	
	Total ...	5,657,187	

Group IID.—*Agricultural Castes.*

Serial No.	Name of caste.	Census of 1881.	Remarks.
1	Lodha	1,000,599	
2	Bayár	17,362	
3	Kamboh	6,134	
4	Bhot	12,396	
5	Kándu	78,552	
6	Káchhi	1,943,540	
7	Kurmi	2,205,892	
8	Tamboli	209,777	
9	Máli	239,573	
10	Tagá	101,615	
11	Bhuinhár	188,080	
	Total ...	6,003,520	
	Pattiar	547	Perhaps intended for pattidar.
	Grand Total ...	6,004,067	

Group IIE.—*Landlord and Warrior Caste.*

Serial No.	Name of caste.	Census of 1881.	Remarks.
1	Chattri or Rajput	3,127,207	

Group IIIA.—*Artisan Castes preceding the stage of Metallurgy.*

Serial No.	Name of caste.	Description of arts.	Census of 1881.	Remarks.
1	Bansphor or Dharkar ...	Basket-maker ...	73,310	
2	Bári ...	Leafplate-maker ...	74,530	
3	Chamár ...	Tanner ...	5,360,896	
4	Mochi ...	Cobbler ...	2,396	Name of Mochi not given in census,
5	Dhúna ...	Thread-twister ...	37,717	
6	Kori and Juláha ...	Weaver ...	899,779	
7	Teli ...	Oil-maker ...	685,552	
8	Kalwár ...	Spirit distiller ...	345,365	
9	Kumbár ...	Potter ...	644,088	
10	Lunia ...	Salt-extracter ...	387,292	
		Total ...	8,510,925	

Group IIIB.—*Artisan Castes coeval with Metallurgy.*

Serial No.	Name of caste.	Description of handicraft.	Census of 1881.	Remarks.
1	Sangtárash ...	Stone-cutter ...	3,286	
2	Kamángar and Tirgar ...	Bow-maker and painter ...	1,674	
3	Barhai ...	Carpenter ...	497,207	
4	Gokai ...	Wood-carver ...	290	
5	Lohar ...	Ironsmith ...	501,241	
6	Kasera ...	Brass moulder ...	5,979	
7	Thathera ...	Brass engraver ...	27,312	
8	Sonar ...	Goldsmith ...	248,761	
9	Manihar ...	Bracelet-maker ...	6,612	
10	Turkihar ...	Earring-maker ...	2,513	
11	Darzi ...	Tailor ...	88,980	
12	Patwa ...	Braid-maker ...	29,860	
13	Chhipi ...	Cloth-stamper ...	24,306	
14	Rangrez ...	Dyer ...	2,936	
15	Halwai ...	Confectioner ...	65,907	
		Total ...	1,506,864	

Group IV.—*Trading Castes.*

Serial No.	Name of caste.	Description of trade.	Census of 1881.	Remarks.
1	Banjára ...	Forest-trader ...	41,846	
2	Kunjra ...	Green grocer ...	2,101	
3	Bhunja ...	Grain-parcher ...	301,086	
4	Rauniya ...	Pedlars and small retail dealers who seldom keep regular shops.	41,507	
5	Kuta ...		3,439	
6	Bilwár ...		4,839	
7	Bhurtia ...		1,229	
8	Lohiya ...		...	Not named in census.
9	Kasondhan ...	Traders who keep regular shops and deal in larger quantities of grain, spices, perfumes, cloth, &c.	565	
10	Kasarwáni ...		1,169	
11	Vishnoi ...		...	Ditto.
12	Rastogi ...		1,561	
13	Unáya ...		...	Ditto.
14	Orh ...		18,983	
15	Maheshwari ...		...	Ditto.
16	Dhusar ...	Bankers, money-lenders, wholesale dealers, &c.	...	Ditto.
17	Agrahri ...		...	Ditto.
18	Agarwál ...		...	Ditto.
19	Bohrá ...		1,292	
20	Khatri ...		47,577	
		Total ...	467,194	
		Traders not returned by caste.	1,204,196	Called in census Baniya and Gandhi.
		Grand Total ...	1,671,390	

GROUP V.—*Serving Castes.*

Serial No.	Name of caste.	Description of service or profession.	Census of 1881.	Remarks.
1	Bhangi ...	Scavenger ...	426,252	
2	Dhobi ...	Washerman ...	518,872	
3	Kahár ...	Water-carrier and general servant.	...	Not separately named in census.
4	Nápit or Nái ...	Barber and surgeon ...	639,957	
5	Páwariya ...	Singers and mussicians ...	559	
6	Dhári ...		5,858	
7	Dom Mirási ...		...	Ditto.
8	Kathak ...		...	Ditto.
9	Bhát ...	Bard and genealogist ...	131,157	
10	Kayasth ...	Estate manager and writer...	513,495	
		Total ...	2,236,150	

GROUP VI.—*Priestly Castes.*

Serial No.	Name of caste.	Description of function.	Census of 1881.	Remarks.
1	Brahmans in general ...	Miscellaneous functions ...	4,655,204	
	Special Brahmans—			
2	(*a*) Ojha ...	Sorcerer ...	...	Not named in census.
3	(*b*) Pandá ...	Temple-priest ...	...	Ditto.
4	(*c*) Gangáputra ...	River-priest ...	...	Ditto.
5	(*d*) Joshi ...	Fortune-teller ...	33,303	
6	(*e*) Mahá-Brahman ...	Funeral-priest ...	2,343	Including Ácháraj
		Total ...	4,690,850	

GROUP VII.—*Religious Orders.*

Serial No.	Name of order.	Census of 1881.	Remarks.
1	Goshayen	118,308	
2	Others	226,122	
	Total	344,430	

Foreign Races not returned by Caste and "Unspecified."

Serial No.	Name of race.	Census of 1881.	Remarks.
1	Gorkha	532	
2	Bengali	2.521	
3	Gujrati	1,442	
4	Kashmiri	1,794	
5	Madrasi	520	
6	Mahratta	761	
7	Marwari	1,854	
8	Panjabi	848	
9	Pahari	2,156	
10	Unspecified	16.121	
	Total ...	28,549	